Jonah's Story, Our Challenge

Jonah's Story,
Our Challenge

*Reading a Biblical Narrative in Today's
Church and World*

Karl Möller

scm press

© Karl Möller 2023

Published in 2023 by SCM Press
Editorial office
3rd Floor, Invicta House,
108–114 Golden Lane,
London EC1Y 0TG, UK

www.scmpress.co.uk

SCM Press is an imprint of Hymns Ancient & Modern Ltd
(a registered charity)

Hymns Ancient & Modern® is a registered trademark of
Hymns Ancient & Modern Ltd
13A Hellesdon Park Road, Norwich,
Norfolk NR6 5DR, UK

British Library Cataloguing in Publication data

A catalogue record for this book is available
from the British Library

ISBN 978-0-334-06135-9

Typeset by Regent Typesetting
Printed and bound in Great Britain by
CPI Group (UK) Ltd

Contents

Preface

This book grew out of a module on biblical interpretation, which I taught at the now closed All Saints Centre for Mission and Ministry, sadly cut short before it could implement its new, exciting and now regrettably untried vision for ministerial education. The module provided an opportunity to explore a range of approaches to biblical interpretation in connection with reading the book of Jonah from different perspectives. The material has since been significantly expanded, and some new chapters had to be written as the original module covered texts from both the Old and the New Testaments. Here we focus only on the book of Jonah, allowing for even more angles to be explored in this rich and fascinating text.

As with so many things in recent years, the origins of the book have been affected by the Covid-19 pandemic, which prevented classroom teaching, thus making it necessary for the entire module to be delivered online. The notes that ultimately grew into the book were originally written as a basis for discussion. Students would read them in advance of our sessions, which were devoted entirely to further reflection and conversation, thus allowing for many voices to be heard. The questions that are interspersed throughout the book were designed to facilitate deeper reflection and discussion of the issues raised in the material, and I hope that they may still fulfil that purpose in the form in which they are presented here.

Teaching a whole module online was a new experience for me, and I owe a great debt of gratitude to the students who made the sessions so fascinating and enjoyable. It was not least the quality of their engagement with these materials that sparked my enthusiasm to make them available to others. Further votes of thanks are due to my daughter-in-law Holly Möller and my friend and former colleague John Applegate, who read drafts of the book and provided highly insightful feedback and many helpful suggestions for improving it. Finally, I would like to say a big thank you to my wife Maja who, during a very challenging year, was a massive encouragement with her visionary approach to the continuance of my vocation to teaching and writing.

I

Jonah's Readers:
Perspectives on Interpretation

Jonah and the 'whale' are among the Bible's best-known figures. It has even been suggested that 'Jonah is not a story you merely read or hear, but one into which you are born, as into a family ... Jonah ... is the story known in the bones, the story you can't remember ever not knowing' (Hampl, p. 291). But what are we to make of the book of Jonah and its 'accumulation of hair-raising and eye-popping phenomena' (Allen, p. 176), including a man-swallowing fish, a city of 120,000 people and their animals fasting and crying mightily to God, a tiny worm with alarmingly destructive powers, and some other curiosities thrown in for good measure? What are we to make of this book whose protagonist flees from God because of God's grace and mercy, who ends up becoming the most successful prophet in the history of ancient Israel and yet is so frustrated that he repeatedly wishes to die? What kind of book is this, and how might we read it in today's church and world?

The book of Jonah, a mere 48 verses long, has raised countless interpretive questions and occasioned an astonishing array of readings. Adele Berlin reckons (1976, p. 230) there are 'almost as many interpretations as there are commentators', while Andreas Kunz-Lübcke (p. 63), not unfittingly considering the role played by the sea, speaks of an 'ocean of possible interpretations'. Yvonne Sherwood (2000, p. 195) explains this with what she calls the 'infinite plasticity of this little text' and the book's 'capacity to reinvent itself'. But that capacity has, as we shall see, been stimulated or even demanded by the countless questions and perspectives brought to it by a multifarious readership that has read the book in different locations and over the course of more than two millennia.

This is not a commentary on Jonah. No attempt will be made to look at every verse, nor am I going to offer a linear explanation that proceeds from section to section until everything has been covered. My main conversation partners accordingly are not the commentaries.[1] Given the above questions – what kind of book is Jonah, and how are we to read it? – we are instead going to consider a range of approaches that have been adopted in the reading of this rich but also challenging text. These include historical and social-science approaches, narrative criticism or poetics, contextual, liberationist and postcolonial perspectives, psychological interpretations and ecological readings. They fall into different categories, depending on whether they focus on the book's author(s) and their context, on the text and its features or on the readers and their interests and meaning-generating powers. I have made no attempt to be exhaustive in my coverage of reading strategies, which, given the plethora of approaches – the 2004 volume *Methods of Biblical Interpretation*, edited by John Hayes, features well over 50 entries – would scarcely have been possible anyway. My main aims instead are:

1 To cover author-, text- and reader-centred approaches, with the emphasis being on the latter.
2 To introduce readers to the most inspiring readings of the book of Jonah I have encountered.
3 To give much space to contextual, liberationist and postcolonial readings that afford us fresh and often challenging perspectives from around the world that are important for us to hear.
4 To include psychological readings, which are often ignored but have contributed some intriguing observations to the study of Jonah.
5 To embrace ecological interpretation and its insights into the reading of Jonah and encourage an ecological reading of the Bible more generally.
6 To let different – and at times entirely contradictory – readings stand next to one another and thus allow for multiple voices to be heard.
7 To encourage reflection on the range of interpretations showcased here by the inclusion of questions designed for deliberation and discussion.

Having said that no attempt has been made to be exhaustive in the coverage of interpretive approaches, I should flag up two further limitations. First, my focus is entirely on current readings. As Sherwood has shown in her masterful study *A Biblical Text and Its Afterlives*, the interpretation of Jonah has varied greatly over the course of the book's reception history. This is shown, for instance, in early Christological readings that saw Jonah as prefiguring Christ having been almost completely abandoned and replaced by readings of Jonah as a nationalistic, religiously ethnocentric, bigoted Jew (more about that later). Readers interested in premodern and early Enlightenment readings will have to consult Sherwood's work, as these cannot be covered here. Second, the same is true for current Jewish and Muslim readings, as my focus here is on Christian interpretation. Jewish approaches are, again, well covered by

Sherwood, while Lena-Sofia Tiemeyer's recent work, *Jonah through the Centuries*, features Jewish, Christian, Muslim and secular readings.

Jonah probed and tickled

There are many books on biblical interpretation, which provide more or less detailed introductions to the various approaches on offer. Here, the focus is firmly on the book of Jonah being read from various perspectives and with a range of interests or agendas rather than on abstract technical discussion of interpretive methodologies. Some introductions to the various perspectives and approaches are necessary, but I would like to show you those readings in action as I want to show Jonah being probed and tickled by different readers, in different contexts, from different angles, for different reasons and to an astonishing array of effects. The reference to Jonah being tickled picks up on a comment by Tongan Methodist pastor Jione Havea (2021a, pp. 264, 265), who once said that interpretation is about 'tickling' the text 'to laugh, dance and play', adding that 'to interpret is to grab and excite the text, and it helps to realize that the text can slip through one's fingers'. Indeed, he invites those of us 'driven by the urge to find answers and resolutions to … let some of the questions and challenges stand … and come to terms with the illusions of control' (p. 242). Havea prefers tickling or exciting the text, asking good, left-field questions rather than seeking quick answers, and dancing and laughing with the text rather than being intent on controlling it and beating it into submission, making it say what we would *like* or *need* it to say. If all that sounds rather too playful for some, it might be worth adding that this playfulness might be helpful and even healing for some of us, given the stifling earnestness of some Christian biblical interpretation. This is in contrast to some Jewish midrashic[2] engagement with scripture with its more relaxed and quizzical approach (again, Sherwood has much to say on this). This playfulness, which is explored especially in our discussion of Jonah as a carnivalesque cartoon, is not to detract us from looking to the text for fresh, current, existential meaning and deep spiritual and theological significance – far from it, in fact!

Havea elsewhere maintains (2018b, p. 40) that we need to silence ourselves to hear the story as well as other tellings or interpretations of it. That is what this book is about, to encourage listening to a range of tellings or interpretations of the story of Jonah, to allow ourselves to be grabbed and tickled by the biblical text and the multiple ways in which it has been understood, to ask new questions rather than rush to find or rehearse all the supposedly 'right' answers. After all, the meaning discovered in the text will not be the same for everyone, but neither need it always be the same even for us. As Barbara Green says (p. 79), 'we cannot insist that our readings are adequate for all times or all people'. Of course, our ability to listen to other tellings depends on the company we keep for, to quote Havea again (2021a, p. 4), 'where and with whom one reads influence who and what one sees and hears in the text, as well as who and what one misses'. One of the delights of studying biblical texts in the twenty-first century is that we now have access to some of the fruits of global biblical interpretation; and I aim to showcase some of that interpretation and enable readers to enjoy, at least for the duration of travelling with me, some other company that extends our horizons, sparks our imaginations, and widens our hearts.

John Barton (1996, p. 5) once voiced his frustration that different approaches, in their search for the 'correct' reading, have so often tended to excommunicate each other. My aim is the exact opposite; it is to bring different readings and readers into dialogue with one another and thus foster an attitude of 'communality'. The importance of this has been emphasized by Louis Jonker (2010, p. 54), who urges us to develop a communal approach to reading the biblical text, to 'come to the liminal space of community in order to share, to contradict, to influence, to change one another's interests' and thus transcend our enculturation into set and certain ways of reading, thinking and believing. But the very liminality of the encounter with the 'other' is what makes the call to meet a diverse community of readers, to listen to different tellings, to join the wild dance with this tempestuous text, to forgo the illusionary safety net of preconceived or permissible answers such a challenging prospect. To do so involves transition, ambiguity, disorientation and the challenge to transcend our own limited understanding of the text. But in this encounter with the other lie the seeds of transformation, as the Ninevite king realized when, confronted with a different God, he said, 'Who knows?' (Jonah 3.9). Who knows indeed? We might even discover a different God – or a different side to God – for, as John Dominic Crossan once pointed out (p. 25), if God or 'the referent of transcendental experience' is trapped 'inside my story', then 'at least in the Judeo-Christian tradition … [that] God is merely an idol I have created'. Perhaps, therefore, we need the disorientation brought by the 'other' – reader and reading – to rid us of that idol, to help us to know again, in Crossan's words (pp. 29–30), 'the excitement of transcendental experience [that] is found only at the edge of language and the limit of story' and hence in the meeting with the other.

Now, at the outset of our journey – before we think some more about reading and interpretation and eventually encounter that colourful smorgasbord of different interests, perspectives, intimations and interpretations – I would like to invite you to reflect on your own understanding of the book of Jonah, before pondering some of the key points of this section.

For further reflection

1 What kind of book is Jonah? How do you (and/or your church) read it? How would you (and/or your church) describe its meaning and purpose?

2 Are you aware of any other ways of reading the book? What for you (and/or your church) characterizes a good reading of the book of Jonah?

3 What do you make of the notion of the book of Jonah being probed, tickled and excited, of us laughing, dancing and playing with the text, of us giving up all illusions of control over the text? How should we read the text if we are looking for fresh, current, existential meaning and deep spiritual and theological significance? Are the two – the dancing and the search for deep significance – compatible?

4 And what about us silencing ourselves so we can hear the text and other tellings of it? What do you make of the notion of communality in relation to reading the biblical text and the disorientation, liminality and potential transformation that the encounter with the 'other' reader and reading might entail?

The author, the text and the reader

Following the period of the Enlightenment, which sparked a strong interest in historical study, biblical studies have long been dominated by historical-critical approaches, such as source, form and redaction criticism. In more recent times, the application of social-science approaches has provided better tools for the study of the social world of the Bible but, beginning in earnest in the late 1960s and gathering pace in the 1970s and 1980s, first text-centred approaches and then increasingly also reader-centred ones have made important contributions to the study of the biblical literature. While historical critics were interested in how the texts came into being, or saw them as resources for the study of the history of Israel or the 'historical Jesus', literary critics read biblical stories as stories, attending to their plot, characters, settings and so on.

Reader-centred approaches or reader-response criticism focused on the contribution made by readers to the construction of meaning. One model for the interpretation of literature understands it as a form of communication involving the elements shown in Figure 1 (see Powell, 1990, p. 9; Ben Zvi, 2003a, p. 130).

Sender ➡ Message ➡ Receiver

Figure 1 The sender-message-receiver model of communication.

In the case of a literary work, the sender may be identified with the author, the message with the text, and the receiver with the reader, as shown in Figure 2.

Author ➡ Text ➡ Reader

Figure 2 Literature as communication.

Of course, if these are the main elements in the process of interpretation, then readers ideally should pay attention to all three. However, in practice, we often focus on one aspect to the (partial) neglect of the others. The three types of approaches identified above – historical criticism, literary criticism, and reader-response criticism – have accordingly concentrated on what has been called the worlds 'behind the text', 'in the text' or 'in front of the text', respectively, as shown in Figure 3.

'Behind the text' ➡ 'In the text' ➡ 'In front of the text'

Figure 3 The 'worlds' of the text.

It should be noted that, in contrast to the two communication diagrams (Figures 1 and 2), where communication is envisaged as proceeding somewhat unilaterally from the author via the text to the reader, the arrows in this case and in Figure 4 below indicate merely the sequential development of the three orientations. These might be further characterized as follows:

- *'Behind the text'*: this typifies the historical-critical interest in the historical context in which the text originated and to which it points. It has been said that this approach effectively treats the text as a *window* on to that historical context. The historical approach emphasizes the importance of reading texts while being alert to their historical dimension. By way of (partial) illustration, we might note, for instance, how

William Wordsworth's (1770–1850) famous line, 'a poet cannot but be gay' (in his poem 'Daffodils'), could very easily be misunderstood if it was read without any historical awareness.

- *'In the text'*: this characterizes the literary-critical approach, which focuses on the text as text, treating it, we might say, like a *painting* that we look at closely and intently. Narrative criticism, with its close analyses of a text's structure, plot, characters, settings, stylistic devices and so on, exemplifies this approach. Bruce Birch and his co-authors have stressed the importance of this type of focus, pointing out that 'the search for a historical reality behind the text sometimes did violence to the imaginative and rhetorical integrity of the text itself' (Birch et al., p. 22).

- *'In front of the text'*: this sums up the reader-centred perspective adopted by ideological approaches, such as feminist, liberationist or postcolonial readings. The stress here is on the reader, who actualizes the text or even creates the literary work, which is understood as a *mirror* that reflects readerly interests. Reader-centred approaches tend to be critical of historical criticism's claim to neutrality, stressing instead the historical rootedness of every interpreter and the fact that readerly presuppositions need to be acknowledged rather than denied or ignored.

The text may therefore be perceived as shown in Figure 4.

Window ➡ Painting ➡ Mirror

Figure 4 Metaphors for the role of the text.

Having said that, psychological (psychoanalytical) approaches offer yet another angle with their interest in the subconscious, which has given rise to and is reflected in the text in the form of symbols or archetypes. The focus here is on what is 'underneath the text', thus effectively offering a fourth perspective. In Figure 5, the direction of one arrow has been changed to indicate that everything influences and converges in the text.

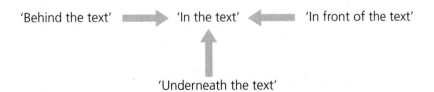

Figure 5 An expanded version of the 'worlds' of the text.

7

This, then, leaves us with just a few final comments before we set out on our journey on that turbulent sea of readings. I wish to begin by saying that I have avoided using the masculine pronoun for God, speaking instead of God, Yahweh, the Lord or the divine. As for the divine name, in quotations from other scholars, this is sometimes rendered YHWH or Yhwh, which reflects the Jewish convention of not pronouncing it. I have also avoided gendered language, using the plural 'they' where appropriate. However, when gendered language does occur, as in some quotations from older sources, I have simply let it stand without further comment. Despite the problematic nature of the term 'Old Testament', I have decided to keep it as it is such an integral part of the tradition of most readers of this book. I would, though, want to repudiate any supersessionism that can so easily accompany the use of the term and has marred too many readings of the book of Jonah. Contemporary forms of Judaism and Christianity trace their earliest roots to the Old Testament, Torah, Tanakh or Hebrew Bible, and have all grown out of those roots in their own distinctive ways. The New Testament, just as the Talmud, has added further layers of scripture/interpretation without rendering those ancient roots in any way inferior to subsequent developments. Lastly, it is worth noting that in Jonah there is a discrepancy between the English and Hebrew verse numbering in that Jonah 1.17 in our English Bibles is 2.1 in the Hebrew text. This means that every verse number in chapter 2 is higher by 1 in the Hebrew, so that 2.1 in English is 2.2 in Hebrew and so forth. With the beginning of chapter 3, the two traditions are in sync again. Here I have adopted the English verse numbering, but some quotations from other scholars might reflect the Hebrew system. Biblical quotations are taken from the NRSV, or are my own or those of the scholars cited.

2

Jonah's World:
Historical and Social-Science Perspectives

From historical to social-scientific criticism

We begin with historical-critical readings, which have not only been the dominant approach to biblical interpretation from the mid-nineteenth century until at least the 1970s, but are still of importance today. As the name 'historical criticism' indicates, there is a focus here on issues such as the historical background of the biblical books and how they came into being. To be sure, this attention to the development of the biblical texts combines historical and literary interests. Indeed, as John Barton (1998, p. 14) claims, 'it is in the sophistication of their literary analysis that most so-called "historical" critics excelled', an analysis that led to the development of approaches such as source criticism, form criticism, tradition history, or redaction criticism.[1]

Alongside all that, historical critics are interested in the text's 'original' meaning, in 'what it had meant to its first readers, and not what it might mean to a modern reader' (p. 10). Barton adds: 'The concern was always to place texts in their historical context, and to argue that we misunderstand them if we take them to mean something they could not have meant for their first readers.' Another concern is to read the biblical texts with an eye to what they reveal about ancient Israel and thus to what is 'behind the text', as we said earlier. As Ehud Ben Zvi confirms in his study *Signs of Jonah* (2003a, p. 3), 'I am mainly interested in the book of Jonah as a historical source for the study of ancient Israel.' A similar approach has been employed in most standard scholarly commentaries on the book, including those by Jack Sasson (1990), James Limburg (1993) and Uriel Simon (1999). A further characteristic of the historical-critical approach – that is, the belief or aim to proceed in a value-neutral, objective or disinterested fashion – has been strongly criticized by contextual, liberationist and postcolonial readers, as we shall see in Chapter 4.

Historical-critical approaches were eventually supplemented by literary and reader-centred ones, which are presented in Steven McKenzie and Stephen Haynes's book *To Each Its Own Meaning* under the heading

9

'Overturning the tradition'. However, closer to the interests of historical criticism, and hence discussed in a section entitled 'Expanding the tradition', we find social-scientific criticism,[2] an early expression of which was practised by Norman Gottwald (1979), who at the time spoke of a 'sociological method'. There was a perceived need for such expansion in that previous historical studies increasingly came to be seen as deficient (Whitelam, p. 38). For instance, it was pointed out that far from giving us access to the past 'as it actually was' (a cherished aim of the historical approach (Barton, 1998, p. 12)), the biblical traditions offer us insights only into 'perceptions of [historical] reality from particular points of view' – namely, those by a privileged 'literate stratum of society revealing little or nothing of the "sub-literate culture"' (Whitelam, pp. 40, 41). In other words, what we get are the views of the literary elite of the time, who demonstrate little interest in the lives and concerns of the illiterate majority. Social-scientific criticism, therefore, as Louis Jonker and Roger Arendse (p. 50) note, helps us to see that the biblical texts are 'social and cultural productions' that reflect specific social realities and need to be understood as such.

To understand the nuances of a biblical text, what is required therefore is an approach that reads it as the product of a range of factors and processes, including economic, social, political and religious ones, and as reflecting the specific interests of the group that produced it. The text thus understood is that group's contribution to the debate of the time. Social-scientific criticism therefore stresses the importance of understanding the text in the context of its interaction with the socio-cultural world in which it originated. While the practice of historical criticism may have included some sociological awareness – though restricting itself to more traditional historical tools – social-scientific criticism, which encompasses a wide range of disciplines, moves beyond historical criticism in self-consciously adopting models from the social sciences, sociology and anthropology (Martin, 1999, p. 125; Gooder, p. 20).

As with virtually all modern approaches to biblical interpretation, it has sometimes been suggested that social-scientific criticism imposes anachronistic models on ancient texts. However, this has been countered by pointing out that the self-conscious use of such models is designed precisely to avoid unconscious anachronism and ethnocentrism (Martin, 1999, pp. 130–1), which denotes our tendency to understand other cultures in terms of our own norms and customs. Keith Whitelam (pp. 45, 46) agrees, noting that the appeal to social-scientific theories makes models and assumptions explicit, thus enabling criticism and debate. All this also comes with an enhanced awareness of how the social location of contemporary scholars, their traditional embeddedness in modern

Western cultures, has impacted their perception of both the biblical texts and the social realities behind them. To provide an example, the application of sociolinguistics, for instance, rests on the understanding that 'all language is ineluctably social' and hence needs to be understood in the context of the 'complex fabric of social structures and symbolic matrices' (Martin, 1999, p. 132); in other words, it needs to be understood in connection with the discourse of the time. After all, 'all meanings expressed in language derive from the speaker's or writer's social system' (Malina, p. 14) and cannot be properly understood without reference to that social and cultural context.

Considering the contributions made by social-scientific approaches, Bruce Malina (p. 13) distinguishes between a historical dimension and an anthropological one, noting that 'the historical dimension is intended to filter out the anachronistic features that contemporary readers bring to their reading, while the anthropological component attempts a comparative understanding of those ancient foreigners to overcome a reader's ethnocentrism.' The overall aim is 'to understand the biblical writers on their own terms with modern historical and cultural features removed' (Malina, p. 14), to see 'how the people of the ancient world could have thought, felt, acted, and communicated', as Jonker and Arendse put it (p. 57). However, as Dale Martin (1999, p. 131) cautions, it would be an illusion to believe that we can completely escape any ethnocentric bias. No model, however sophisticated, 'will enable [us] to see things the way ancient Mediterraneans saw them'. Another danger, highlighted by Whitelam (pp. 44–5), is that of circular reasoning. After all, we are by and large seeking to understand 'the social world of the Bible from the biblical texts themselves'. But let us now consider two interpretations of the book of Jonah, one by Ben Zvi, whose stated interest in the book as a historical source we already noted, and one by Lowell Handy, who reads it from a social-science perspective.

For further reflection

1 Is it important to place the text in its historical context and ask, as historical critics do, what it would have meant to its first readers? Why?
2 What do you make of (a) the general notion that the texts reflect certain social realities, and (b) the more specific point that they represent the perspective and interests of the literate elite who wrote them? What does such sociological awareness mean for how we read them today?

3 What can we do to avoid (or at least weaken) anachronistic and ethnocentric tendencies in our reading of the biblical texts?

The book of Jonah as read by Jerusalemite literati in Persian Yehud

In contrast to traditional historical-critical readings, Ben Zvi (2003a, pp. 3–8) is not so much interested in the book's original author(s) or editor(s) and their intentions, as in its reception by the ancient communities of readers for whom (and within whom) it was written. He defines this group as Jerusalemite literati, people with a high degree of literacy, who were an integral part of the governing elite of their society and whose 'social-literary activities' included the writing, reading and re-reading of the book of Jonah. This, Ben Zvi suggests, happened at some time in post-exilic Judah or Persian Yehud,[3] and he describes the literati as a mixed community – consisting of former Babylonian exiles and those who had stayed behind in Palestine – that was profoundly shaped by the trauma of the exile (see also Ben Zvi, 2003b). Ben Zvi is thus interested in the original, intended readers of the Jonah story, in how they read and re-read it, in their assumptions and strategies.

Throughout his study, Ben Zvi is alert to the fact that the book can be read from two perspectives. The first is the one suggested by the text itself, according to which Nineveh is not destroyed by a merciful YHWH, while the second reflects the historical awareness that it was not only destroyed but also never again rebuilt. Ben Zvi suggests (2003a, pp. 27–8) that the interaction of those two readings within the ancient community of readers led to a 'sophisticated theological discourse', with YHWH being understood as both saving Nineveh from judgement and executing judgement against it. After all, according to Exodus 34.6–7, the text cited only partially by Jonah in 4.2, YHWH is indeed 'merciful and gracious', but as the text goes on to say, YHWH is 'by no means clearing the guilty, but visiting the iniquity of the parents upon the children and the children's children, to the third and the fourth generation'. YHWH's mercy, therefore, as Ben Zvi notes (p. 118), was 'of much relevance to the people who lived at the time', but it did not save the city in the long run. The book of Jonah ridicules its protagonist for opposing YHWH's mercy, but given Nineveh's ultimate fate Jonah is doubly ridiculed because he also did not realize that mercy and compassion are not the only characteristics of YHWH. Both readings furthermore ridicule an upset prophet who takes himself too seriously (p. 30). But although Jonah's theology may be criticized, the issues he raises, according to Ben Zvi (p. 79), resonate with the literati and 'point to some of the central [theological] issues … of the time'.

Ben Zvi thinks it possible (pp. 47–8) that the literati identified Jonah with the prophet of the same name mentioned in 2 Kings 14.25. They thus construed him as a northern Israelite who lived during the reign of Jeroboam II and understood Israel's psalms 'as a normative standard of piety, theological thought and literary expression', as the many borrowings from the psalms in Jonah's prayer in chapter 2 indicate. In line with that historical context, there is no awareness of Nineveh's future violent actions against Israel, nor is Jonah portrayed as expressing hostility against the Assyrians. That said, however, Ben Zvi notes (p. 52) that the reading of the literati would have been aware of Nineveh's (Assyria's) subsequent violence against Israel, so that 'ancient rereaders strongly informed by the image of Nineveh as a terrifying oppressing city were likely to view Jonah as strongly hostile to Nineveh' (p. 57). Another interesting feature of the book highlighted by Ben Zvi (p. 75) is what he describes as the 'partial Israelitization' of its non-Israelite characters, the sailors and the Ninevites. The book thus effectively communicates that even Nineveh is Israelitizable (p. 97). What Ben Zvi has in mind is that the non-Israelite characters not only fear or respond positively to God but even use language that any good Israelite might have used in doing so, language that, Ben Zvi believes, was also characteristic of the discourse of the literati community. He comments (pp. 89–90) that:

> The characterization of the secondary characters, such as the sailors and the Ninevite king, serves to convey a construction of the 'foreign' as Israelitizable – as having the potential to behave as an Israelite, to talk and act as a good Israelite. Thus, it reflects a tendency to use 'the other' to confirm the in-group's perspective for an ideal, 'Israelitized' world.

The book of Jonah, in other words, allows us a glimpse into the way these literati thought about the wider, non-Jewish world in which they lived. Ben Zvi further points to several abnormalities in the book:

- Whereas normally a prophet is either worthy or unworthy of the divine mission, this is reversed in that Jonah deems YHWH to be unworthy to be served by him (Jonah 4.2b; pp. 87–8).
- Typically, a prophet's words are rejected by those hearing them, but here all characters, whether humans, animals, plants or natural forces – apart from Jonah – immediately act in accordance with YHWH's will.

- The Ninevite king hopes for YHWH's mercy as afforded to the Israelites long ago (Exod. 32.14), thus effectively taking up the role of Moses, while Israel's current prophet is scandalized by such mercy (p. 88).
- The book's atypical ending, which highlights issues such as 'the role of the prophet and the character of YHWH' (p. 95).

For Ben Zvi (p. 89), it is precisely in these atypical features that one of the keys to understanding the book lies, for they serve as a commentary not only on the character of Jonah, who is fulfilling the role of a prophet, but also more generally 'on the "office" of prophet, on prophecy and on prophetic books'. He concludes that 'the authorial voice in the book rejects Jonah's positions' and that the book is what he calls a 'meta-prophetic' book. As such, it addresses more generally 'issues that are of relevance for the understanding of the messages of ... prophetic books' (p. 85).

Jonah has frequently been read as a satirical attack on other groups' beliefs or practices. One interpretation sees it as criticizing the 'exclusivism' of Ezra-minded groups that sought to exclude foreign elements (see, for example, Ezra 10). However, Ben Zvi maintains (pp. 102–3) that there is no support for this reading in the text itself. Another view sees the prophet Jonah as representing a nationalist, xenophobic group in Israel opposed to the concept of salvation for the nations which, it is claimed, is ridiculed by the book. According to Ben Zvi, however, nationalism or xenophobia are never specifically addressed. Second, the description of texts from the Persian period as 'xenophobic', 'nationalistic' or 'self-righteous' has recently come under increased criticism as displaying Christian anti-Semitic prejudice (see, for example, Blower, ch. 2; and our discussion in the next chapter). And third, as Ben Zvi himself points out (2003a, p. 149), not only did the Jewish author of Jonah identify with God's opposition to the prophet but so did the Jewish communities that accepted the book as part of their scriptural canon. Ben Zvi (pp. 99–100), by contrast, reads it as inner-communal reflections by the literati, as a form of critical self-appraisal, which demonstrates 'an awareness of the problematic character of the knowledge they possessed'. The book's burlesque tone, its humorous and satirical features, in that context serve the literati's critical engagement with themselves and their own claims of theological knowledge. Any mockery of Jonah's behaviour, therefore, is nothing other than self-mockery (pp. 11, 114).

There are two key points here: the critical meta-commentary on prophets and prophecy on the one hand, and the literati's critical self-appraisal on the other. The former expresses the literati's rejection of the authority of any other contemporary prophets claiming to communicate messages from YHWH. What is very clear in the book of Jonah is the stress on YHWH's sovereignty vis-à-vis a prophet who does not fully comprehend the deity's behaviour. It is now the literati themselves whose role it is to broker the 'divine instruction contained in the texts that they alone could directly approach' (p. 106), as access to them was limited to the literary elite of the time. New prophets are no longer required and are, as the story of Jonah shows, not to be trusted. As for the literati's critical self-appraisal, it is important that Jonah is portrayed as being well-acquainted with Israel's religious texts, which – like the Jerusalemite literati themselves – he interprets (pp. 108–9). And yet he struggles to make sense of YHWH's behaviour. This portrayal of Jonah, according to Ben Zvi, 'hints at a self-recognition among the literati that to be one of [them] and to be well acquainted with the correct texts does not necessarily guarantee correct theological knowledge or attitude'. In fact, this 'knowledge' was further undermined or made problematic by the fact that seemingly opposite claims about YHWH were advanced not only in different texts, but also by opposite readings of even a single book such as Jonah.

For further reflection

1 What do you think of Ben Zvi's double reading of the book of Jonah – that is, of YHWH being seen as saving Nineveh from judgement and then subsequently executing its punishment? What does this contribute to our interpretation of Jonah?

2 What do you make of the book's partial Israelitization of its non-human characters, its use of '"the other" to confirm the in-group's perspective for an ideal, "Israelitized" world', as Ben Zvi puts it?

3 And what about Ben Zvi's conception of Jonah as a meta-prophetic book that serves the purpose of the Jerusalemite literati's critical self-appraisal, of them mocking their own claims to biblical understanding and theological knowledge? What might that mean for how we engage with the biblical texts and with theology?

Social science and the reading of prophetic story

Handy's 2007 study *Jonah's World* carries the subtitle 'Social science and the reading of prophetic story', which highlights his social-science approach. Handy notes (pp. 3–4) that the book of Jonah was once regarded as a historical text, but from the end of the nineteenth century onwards came to be more commonly understood as a parable or fable; this was a shift connected to Assyriological publications that demonstrated that in the eighth century BC 'Nineveh was nobody's capital'. Handy's focus is on 'the social world inhabited by the book of Jonah', as he seeks to explore its social context, author and original readers. His social-scientific approach employs 'sociology, anthropology, economics, political science, and archaeology to determine the influence of the social context on a text and, in turn, the text's influence (or intended influence) on that context' (p. 5).

While Jonah's identification as the 'son of Amittai' (1.1) situates the events of the story in the eighth century BC during the time of King Jeroboam II (2 Kings 14.22–29), Handy dates the book's composition to the Persian period and more specifically the fifth or early fourth century (p. 6). He observes Jonah's affinities with other biblical 'short stories' from the Persian period, noting (p. 10) that, as in the case of Jonah, 'major parts of the stories of Ruth and Judith take place outside Israelite territory and all the activity of Esther, Daniel ... and Tobit[4] takes place outside of the "promised land"'. Turning to the author of the book of Jonah, Handy (pp. 11, 14) regards him as a scribe, 'someone with an education, training in writing ... a sense of literary cleverness' and a vast range of 'biblical knowledge'. Like Ben Zvi, Handy suggests (p. 12) that the text was composed by 'a member of a specialized segment of the upper echelons of ancient Judean society', as scribal training would have been 'almost exclusively the realm of the elite families' (p. 15). Proposing that the story's piety is that of 'the religious circles of the Temple cult in Jerusalem' (p. 118), he portrays the scribes as connected to both the Jerusalem temple and the Persian administration and concludes (p. 15) that 'Jonah reflects both a Judean theology and an imperial polity'. Handy believes (pp. 18, 74) that the story portrays Jonah from a scribe's perspective as a person of some position who commands the wealth required to make long-distance sea and land journeys to Tarshish and Nineveh. Such wealth 'would have been available to a scribe sent off on a task by a governor or priest'. Jonah's stylish prayer in chapter 2 also suggests a scribal background (p. 19). Another observation relates to Jonah's world view for, like the scribes, he 'is presented as having a definite sense of order, complete with notions of correctness, righteousness, and conformity'.

According to Handy (p. 23), the author 'creates a world that never existed out of locations that had existed'. Tarshish, imagined by Jonah as a place where even Yahweh was not to be found, is an exotic, imaginary place unlike anything the audience would have known (p. 25). Joppa's 'sea-driven culture', too, would have been foreign, strange and distant (pp. 26–7), while beyond Joppa lay a foreign, imaginary, 'totally different "other world"'. In turn, Nineveh, for Handy (pp. 33–4), was the 'capital of their worst nightmare'. However, as Nineveh, 'the embodiment of political power in empire', had never actually subjected *Judah*, a scribe writing in Yehud could treat it in a benign manner.

The story's portrayal of the 'divine realm' once again tells us something about the author's and audience's shared socio-religious world. Given the polytheistic background of most cultures at the time, it comes as no surprise that the sailors each pray to their own deity (p. 43). Intriguingly and in stark contrast to other Old Testament texts, however, the story of Jonah neither ridicules nor criticizes the sailors' appeal to these deities (p. 46). This leads Handy (p. 47) to regard 'the Persian religious climate' as the most likely background for the story, which is further confirmed by Jonah's reference to God as the 'God of heaven' (1.9), a reflection of the Persian designation for their leading deity Ahura Mazda (p. 48). As Douglas Stuart explains (p. 461; see also Olley), 'the epithet "God of Heaven" … was a convenient way for the Israelites to describe Yahweh's identity to syncretistic, polytheistic foreigners'. When it comes to the Ninevites and their response to God (Elohim), Handy concludes (p. 53) that they are not portrayed as real Assyrians but as fictional characters 'in the mode and model of the author's making' who act exactly like good Jerusalemites. As for the book's understanding and portrayal of Yahweh, Handy sees this as being in line with how God is generally understood in the Old Testament historical and prophetic books – that is, as a male warrior god,[5] who is powerful, knowledgeable, holy, trustworthy, a covenant God, and a strict judge (Handy, pp. 56–8). For Handy, the unresolved differences between Jonah and Yahweh echo the differences between the book of Proverbs' beliefs in an ordered, understandable, reliable world on the one hand, and those of Job and Ecclesiastes in a hidden and mysterious God and a cosmos that makes no sense on the other.

Turning to the story's human characters, Handy (pp. 61–5) notes that Jonah, a 'literary construct', is presented as an intermediary between the divine and human realms, as someone who, from the audience's perspective, operated 'a long time ago, when prophecy was a more common phenomenon'. Jonah's message would have evoked other 'oracles against the nations' (for example, Isa. 13—23; Jer. 46—51; Ezek. 25—32; Amos 1.3—2.15; Obad.; Nahum), a tradition that is, however, self-critically inverted in that the Ninevites do not believe in its traditional 'nationalistic ideology', but repent and are saved (p. 66). Handy emphasizes (pp. 67–9) that a Judean scribe would have had little first-hand knowledge of the sea trade, which he sees borne out by the story. Joppa, a minor harbour, was not a place from which long-distance merchant ships sailed; there were no dedicated passenger ships, so prospective passengers would have had to wait a while for a ship going to their destination and would normally take one headed in the general direction before changing ships along the way. Ships had no fixed schedules; provisions for a lengthy journey would need to be acquired and stored aboard; sleeping arrangements would have had to be made – all of which would have made a quick getaway highly unlikely, if not impossible. The story as told, therefore, 'reflects a literary notion by one not really familiar with booking passage on ships or one unconcerned with the minutiae of the story's details' (p. 69).

According to Handy (pp. 71–4), ancient sailors were understood to have been religious but 'of the lowest social standing in the ancient Mediterranean world', greedy and even quick to commit crimes, while in Jonah they are presented as 'ideal types'. Noting that ancient stories about sea travel were adventure stories about foreign lands and experiences that ignored the everyday tedium of life on board ship, Handy concludes that the story of Jonah clearly fits into that tradition. Nineveh and the Ninevites, who 'stand for the activities of the entire empire', are known in biblical tradition as 'a city of blood, corruption, loot, and plunder', as a place of 'idolatry, prostitution, [and] sorcery' (pp. 74–6). None of this is mentioned in Jonah, but Handy suggests that 'by leaving the "wicked-ness" of the Ninevites not described, the author has allowed the readers to imagine whatever evil they wish to impose on the literary Ninevites'. That in the book of Jonah the wicked Ninevites never do anything evil from Handy's perspective, 'may well be an intended irony in a book filled with exaggeration and irony'. While the epithet 'King of Nineveh' does not correspond to any known title used by the Assyrians (though Greek writers did apply it to Sardanapalus, the Assyrians' legendary last ruler), the literary character, identified as the 'Great Ruler of the World', 'represents the greatest extent of human power on earth' (pp. 74, 78, 81). Intriguingly, and in contrast to other great rulers, who are frequently portrayed as grandiose, power-obsessed potentates driven to arbitrary, unwise, self-defeating rulings, the King of Nineveh's decree is a rather better move, even if, as Handy notes (pp. 81–2), 'it upsets Jonah'.

Playing a key part in the story is also what Handy calls the 'unnatural nature' (ch. 5). Two examples may suffice here. The first is the 'big fish' (דָּג גָּדוֹל, *dag gadol*), 'most likely a creative literary construct by a land-living author' (p. 85). Based on David Gilmore's study on monsters (Gilmore, 2003), Handy suggests (pp. 86–8) that the big fish ticks all the boxes for being considered one. Examples include it being huge, swallowing a human being rather than being eaten by humans in a reversal of social constructs, being androgynous (the fish is דָּג, *dag*, masculine, in 1.17; 2.10 and דָּגָה, *dagah*, feminine, in 2.1),[6] living in the depths of the sea at the edges of the known world, and being a (potential) deliverer of death (according to Handy, Jonah in his prayer thinks of the fish as Sheol, the underworld). In the reception history of the book, there certainly are plenty of examples that depict the fish as some type of sea monster – for example: Maarten van Heemskerk, 'Jonah is Cast Ashore by the Fish' (1566), and Pieter Lastman, 'Jonah and the Whale' (1621).[7]

Handy concludes (pp. 88–9) that this creature is 'an imaginative caricature of a fish invented by the author ... to further the plot, save Jonah, demonstrate the power of God, show the obedience of the natural world, and provide some entertaining horror'. At the other end of the scale, there is the tiny worm (pp. 89–90) with its voracious appetite for vegetation. This would have resonated with an agricultural community – the devastation of crops being a recurring theme in the Old Testament (for example, Joel 1.4; Amos 7.1–2). The designation of the worm as תּוֹלֵעָה (tole'ah) – known not only as a crop-destroying curse (Deut. 28.39; although the demise of the plant being caused by a single worm is, of course, another unnatural, fictitious element), but also for consuming corpses and existing in Sheol (Isa. 14.11) – would have once again evoked an element of horror. A similarly horrific aspect pertains to the sea weeds or reeds (סוּף, suf) wrapped around Jonah's head like tentacles in 2.5 (p. 93).

As is already apparent, Handy's conclusion regarding the book of Jonah is that it is 'demonstrably fictitious, exaggerated and ironic' (p. 110). That, however, should not be seen as detrimental, given that 'outside the sphere of modern western civilization ... truth is conveyed by fiction', and the story of Jonah 'clearly has something to say about God and about prophets that the author thought needed recording'. As has been frequently noted (see, for example, Van Seters, 1983; Garbini, 1988; Halpern, 1988; and Brettler, 1995), our modern concept of historiography and the reduction of truth to facticity should not be anachronistically applied to Old Testament writers. Handy maintains (p. 113) that the portrayal of the prophet suggests that 'the book of Jonah is intentionally a spoof of the far more serious historical (and prophetic) narratives. This is a short humorous story, not a lengthy historical reconstruction.' Reflecting on its purpose, Handy suggests (p. 123) that this text, written by a member of the literary elite *for* the literary elite, has something to say about political authority, acknowledging such authority on the part of a foreign empire, while insisting that there is above it 'a much higher hierarchy under the control and moral jurisdiction of Yahweh'. The reference to the temple in Jonah's prayer (2.7) identifies Jerusalem as the religious centre of the world, thereby maintaining that 'the norms, political and ethical, for the entire world are posited to be those of the author's ethnic and social circle'. There is, therefore, as Handy notes (p. 106), an assumption that:

what is good as defined by Judean tradition is what is good for the wider world. Both the power and the word of Yahweh are presented as the defining authority for not only the Israelite Jonah but also the seafaring mariners and the city-dwelling Ninevites. This places gentiles to the west and to the east of Yehud under obligation to Judah's deity ... The moral norm for all peoples is that of Yehud's elite.

That said, Handy is also acutely aware (pp. 101–3) of the story's concern with the question of the ethical behaviour of God. It is interesting that Yahweh, the literary character, behaves in ways that would seem to be rather problematic at times, such as apparently toying with some of the human characters. The storm at sea, for instance, raises serious questions in that Yahweh appears to have no qualms about killing off the sailors even though they have been behaving righteously throughout. However, while this makes for quite a 'chaotic fictional world', Handy perceptively comments that it is the kind of world 'that is recognizable as the one which humans actually inhabit'.

For further reflection

1 What do you make of Handy's point about the story being set in imaginary, foreign, strange, distant, exotic places? What does that say about what kind of story this is?

2 What about Jonah being a humorous, fictitious story, a spoof of more serious historical and prophetic narratives? If, as Handy suggests, truth can be conveyed by fiction, what truths does the story of Jonah communicate?

3 Where in Handy's reading of Jonah might the interests of the scribal elite be most apparent?

3

Jonah's Art and Reception:
The Poetics of a Biblical Narrative

Narrative criticism and biblical poetics

Biblical narrative criticism was developed in the late 1970s and 1980s. Some key texts include Jacob Licht's *Storytelling in the Bible* (1978, 2nd edn, 1986), Robert Alter's *The Art of Biblical Narrative* (1981), Shimon Bar-Efrat's *Narrative Art in the Bible* (1989), Jean Louis Ska's *'Our Fathers Have Told Us'* (1990), David Gunn and Danna Fewell's *Narrative in the Hebrew Bible* (1993) and Jan Fokkelman's *Reading Biblical Narrative* (1999). Others prefer to speak of poetics, a term that goes back to Aristotle's work of the same title, the first systematic study of literature. Kenneth Craig, in *A Poetics of Jonah*, describes poetics as the 'systematic and scientific study of literature', with scientific being understood as 'the rigorous application of various analytical tools' (1993, p. 4). Phyllis Trible (1994, p. 64) sees its aim as 'articulating the structures, rules, and conventions of discourse', with the goal being 'a grammar of literature'. According to Bulgarian-French structuralist literary critic Tzvetan Todorov (1939–2017), poetics seeks 'to propose a theory of the structure and functioning of literary discourse' (Todorov, p. 7). Influential examples in biblical scholarship include Meir Sternberg's *The Poetics of Biblical Narrative* (1987), Adele Berlin's *Poetics and Interpretation of Biblical Narrative* (1994), Robert Funk's *The Poetics of Biblical Narrative* (1988) and Jonathan Culler's *Structuralist Poetics* (2002).

I am not going to distinguish between narrative criticism and poetics but will mainly use the former term.[1] Both approaches seek to facilitate close readings, helping us to ask questions of texts that enable a deeper level of understanding as well as an appreciation of the *art* of the biblical storytellers. Commenting on Jonah, Craig (p. 144) speaks of the author as an artist, while James Ackerman (1989, p. 234) describes the book as 'a literary masterpiece that has captivated its readers and stirred artistic imaginations'. Narrative criticism seeks to determine the effects that texts are expected to have on their audiences and how textual signals guide readers in making meaning. As again Craig points out (p. 5), 'instead of discovering or assigning meaning, poetics strives to elucidate the *conditions* of meaning'. Applied to the book of Jonah, 'the goal is to see how the Jonah text *made* and *makes* sense based on various interpretive operations'. Narrative criticism focuses on the text itself as its object of study rather than on the realities behind the text (such as the author and their time); it emphasizes the text's final form rather than the process through which it has come into being (Powell, 1990, pp. 6–9). It assumes its unity, being interested in how the whole text 'works' as a piece of art, rather than seeking to identify the sources out of which it may have been composed. The goal is to understand the narrative, and the text is understood as part of an act of communication, in which a message is passed from the author to the reader.

The building blocks of narrative

Plot or story line

For any text to qualify as a narrative, it must have a story line or plot. Aristotle, in his *Poetics*, defined plot as the ordered succession of events in a narrative. Put simply, plot is a sequence of actions that lead from an initial situation or exposition, through some complication, to a sense of resolution and the results of that resolution, also known as the denouement (see Figure 1).

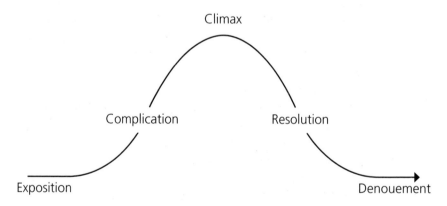

Figure 1 The elements of a plot.

A story may, of course, have more than one climax or, as Philip Jenson says (p. 11), there may be a false climax preceding the real one. The analysis of a narrative's plot or story line helps us to understand how the story unfolds. We become aware, for instance, of the rising tension, of turning points, and of the resolution of tension – or the lack of it. Parts of the plot of Jonah develop along the following lines:

- *Exposition*: God commands Jonah to go to Nineveh.
- *Complication*: Jonah flees and tension develops.
- *Further complication*: in the episode involving Jonah, the sailors and the storm, the tension increases.
- *(False) climax*: Jonah is thrown into the sea.
- *Turning point*: Jonah prays to God from inside the big fish.
- *New exposition*: God repeats the command.
- *Descending action/resolution*: Jonah delivers God's message at Nineveh.
- *New complication*: Jonah is displeased at the Ninevites' repentance and tension rises again.

Having outlined the plot along these lines, it should be noted that Gunn and Fewell (p. 129) see the story as breaking 'the rules right from the start' in that there is hardly any exposition. Neither Jonah nor God are introduced, which leaves us wondering about them, especially about the oddly behaved prophet. Jenson, commenting on the tensions noted above, offers one interpretation when he points out (p. 11):

> The initial tensions point to the major concerns of the story which will be played out in various ways as the story proceeds. In Jonah the question of whether God or Jonah will get their way is largely resolved by the end of chapter 2. The question of the consequences of Nineveh's wickedness is resolved by the end of chapter 3. But in chapter 4 the deepest question of all, that of the attitude of Jonah to God and Nineveh, is left unresolved.

According to this reading, the book of Jonah ends with an open question that is effectively addressed to its implied readers: should God not spare the Ninevites and be concerned about them?

Authors, narrators and readers

Having mentioned the book's *implied* readers, we must now look at narrative criticism's notions of authors and readers. As we shall see, one of its key concepts is precisely that of implied authors and implied readers.[2] More generally, narrative critics distinguish between the empirical or real author, the implied author, the narrator, the audience (or narratee), the implied reader and the empirical or real reader, all of which are part of a spectrum as shown in Figure 2.

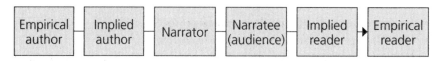

Figure 2 *Authors, narrators, readers.*

The *empirical or real author*, while being responsible for the text's production, sits outside the text and thus is of no real interest to narrative critics. In the case of anonymous ancient texts like the book of Jonah, we do not know anything about the real author anyway. The *implied author* is a literary construct; it is the author we imagine or construe based on our reading of the story, although that is putting it from a reader's perspective (more on that later). American literary critic Wayne Booth (1921–2005) describes it from the author's perspective as the author creating 'an image of himself' (Booth, p. 138). Narrative criticism interprets texts with reference to their implied authors – that is, the perspective from which the work appears to have been written (Powell, 2004, p. 169). Observing, for instance, that our story of a mere 48 verses features quite a few prayers, which sets it apart from other Old Testament stories, Craig proposes that this tells us something about the implied author's perspective on prayer. As he puts it (p. 123), 'recourse to prayer in Jonah testifies to an [implied] author's perspective of God's saving power and to the efficacy of human speech in the form of prayer'.

The *narrator*, then, is the voice that controls the narrative, the eye of the camera that determines what we see, or the '"center of consciousness" through whom authors have filtered their narratives' (Booth, p. 153). One of the story's main characters may assume the role of the narrator, as happens frequently in modern fiction but only rarely in the Old Testament. There are different types of narrators; some are essentially omniscient while others have more limited knowledge. Craig points out (p. 45) that 'in Jonah, the narrator ... describes action, introduces speakers, summarizes conversation, provides explanatory glosses, and tells us what various characters, including even the Lord, think and feel'. Having access to privileged information, the narrator knows everything that is going on, including in the belly of the fish, what God perceives and thinks (3.10) and how Jonah feels (4.1, 6). Jenson (p. 9) describes Jonah's narrator as quietly authoritative, while Craig (p. 46) sees the narrator as 'omniscient'. Commenting on this, Sternberg notes (p. 183): 'If a narrator shows himself qualified to penetrate the mind of one of the characters and report his secret activities – a feat impossible in everyday life – he has established his competence to do so in regard to all other inaccessibles as well.'

In traditional narrative-critical understanding, biblical narrators are seen as reliable (Craig, p. 127), but this is now questioned by ideological approaches. However, perhaps one of Jonah's narrator's most striking characteristics is that they never explicitly tell us what we are to make of the prophet's behaviour but simply report his words and actions. As Craig says (p. 54), 'the narrator never gives any moral evaluation in the entire story'. This reticence with respect to evaluation has been shown to be a common feature of Hebrew storytelling, although there are some notable exceptions. For us as readers, the narrator's lack of evaluation means that that task falls to us. Importantly, however, an absence of criticism does not indicate that the narrator condones the characters' words or actions. Another important point to note is that, in biblical narrative, 'the implied author and the narrator to whom he delegates the task of communication practically merge into each other' (Sternberg, p. 75). The biblical narrator therefore 'is a plenipotentiary of the author, holding the same views, enjoying the same authority, addressing the same audience, pursuing the same strategy'.

Let us consider some of the Jonah narrator's key moves. In the opening scene (1.1–5) there is a strong focus on action (Craig, p. 47) without any explanation of significant aspects, such as Jonah's attempted flight. That said, in 1.4 'the ship is granted the faculty of thinking' (p. 49) – the NRSV's 'the ship threatened to break up' does not quite capture the sense of the Hebrew text, which employs the verb חשב (khashav), 'to think, devise'. According to Jack Sasson (p. 3), 'the ship expected itself to crack up', while Yvonne Sherwood comments (1998, p. 50) that 'the author brilliantly pushes the idea of physical disintegration, or immanent wrecking, into psychological disintegration. The ship, fearing her wrecking, becomes literally a nervous wreck.' All this leads Craig to conclude (p. 49) that 'even at this early stage it appears the narrator wishes to draw us into the world of the fabulous'.

Throughout chapter 1, narration of the story is fast paced, which leads to nuances of thought and feeling being consistently de-emphasized. Alan Hauser furthermore observes (p. 24) that Jonah, after his initial flight, is presented as quite passive in contrast to the sailors' intense activity (note also Jonah's curiously uninvolved five-word 'sermon' in 3.4) and comments (p. 31) that readers are here being skilfully misdirected, being led to expect Jonah's passive compliance throughout. Commenting on Jonah's death wish (1.12), Craig suggests that in this 'ambiguous psychological portrayal' (p. 133), the narrator has strategically withheld any clues that would give the reader any satisfactory explanation for the prophet's surprising reaction; while Hauser suspects (pp. 26–7) that Jonah's apparent offering of his life to save the gentile sailors might lead readers to expect him to act similarly towards the Ninevites. As for God's initial activity of hurling a storm onto the sea, this suggests to Hauser (p. 27) that we are dealing with a wrathful deity, especially since God 'seems to exact vengeance that substantially exceeds the offense'. Nor does God's vengeance abate until the guilty person has at last been punished (1.15), all of which might lead readers to conclude that the fate of Nineveh whose wickedness had come up before God (1.2) is sealed. With God being insistent that Jonah go to Nineveh to deliver God's message, Hauser (p. 32) argues that 'the image of God projected continues to be that of the aggressor'.

Three times in the first three chapters the two main characters speak to each other. God speaks to Jonah in 1.2 and 3.2, while Jonah addresses God in 2.2–9. However, in none of these cases does the addressee respond verbally. That only finally happens in 4.2–4. Craig comments (pp. 80–1) that 'the direct speech between Jonah and God in chapter 4 serves as a contrast to the silence, ambiguity, and indirection of the initial three chapters', which were, of course, deliberate and are characterized by Craig as 'informational suppression', something he regards as one of the narrative's distinguishing features (p. 82). And so, it is only in chapter 4 that we suddenly find Jonah 'angrily [taking] on God over the issue of whether the sinful but repentant city should be spared' (Hauser, p. 23). The seemingly passive, non-aggressive prophet, who had shied away from proclaiming doom, is now burning with wrath, while God, who previously had come across as a God of wrath, is in fact forgiving and merciful (pp. 32, 35). The narrator's earlier misdirection thus allows for some surprises to be sprung on the reader at the end of the story. But, says Hauser (p. 35), upon reflection, 'readers would realize that, while there has been a great deal of blustering on God's part, no ships have been sunk, no cities have been destroyed, and no lives have been lost, even though Jonah and the people of Nineveh have done more than enough to deserve God's punishment.'

According to Craig, the narrator's informational suppression also allows for the story's main point to be masked. Hence it is only in the final chapter that we are shown that the story ultimately is not about the Ninevites' repentance. Craig comments (p. 155): 'Toward the end of the story we realize that the storyteller has misdirected us: judgment is not ... primarily for the Ninevites ... but for Jonah as well, a prophet of God who fulminates against an act of mercy.' And the silence with which the book concludes is an invitation for readers to reflect. As Craig suggests (p. 161): 'maybe Jonah is not the only one who needs to catch a glimpse of the world as God sees it.' The subtitle of Craig's book is *Art in the Service of Ideology*. The story of Jonah, he wants us to see, makes an ideological or, we might say, theological point. And the nature of its narration, the way it is told, is designed to drive home that point.

Sometimes, a narrative includes references to an audience, the people to whom the story is told. In analogy to the narrator, Seymour Chatman (pp. 147–51) here prefers to speak of a 'narratee'. Biblical examples include Jesus speaking to crowds of people in the Gospels, but nothing of this sort happens in Jonah. The *implied reader*, then, another textual construct, is distinct from any real, historical reader in the same way that the implied author is distinct from the real author. In fact, as Robert Fowler notes (1991, p. 33), 'the implied author and implied reader ... are mirror images of each other'. In the book of Jonah, we are not told much about places such as Nineveh or Tarshish, as the implied author clearly expects the implied reader to have the requisite knowledge. Crucially, while Nineveh was approximately 600 miles east of Israel, Tarshish lay in exactly the opposite direction – that is, about 2,400 miles west of Israel. It may even have been the westernmost point known to the ancient Hebrews. The implied reader, therefore, realizes not only that the prophet sets off in the opposite direction but that he is trying to get as far away as humanly possible from where he was supposed to go. Similarly, when the text refers to Nineveh's wickedness, the implied reader is expected to know what that implied. But the concept of the implied reader is about more than a reader's knowledge. As Trible points out (1994, p. 68; see also Fowler, 1991, p. 33):

> For reading to work successfully, the actual reader must agree to become the implied reader, to subordinate his or her ideas to textual values and commitments. The desired identification of implied author and ideal reader ought to happen through the rhetoric of the text. ... In the process author, text, and reader converge.

The *empirical* or *real reader* is you and me and all the past, present and future readers of the book of Jonah. A model taking all the above into account, together with the roles played by characters, settings and style (which will be discussed below), looks like Figure 3 (see Jonker, 2005, p. 98).[3]

As Figure 3 shows, both the empirical author and the empirical reader lie outside the boundaries of the text and so are of no real interest to narrative critics. Everything else, the text's message (carried within the settings, plot, style and characters), and its implied author and reader,

The text

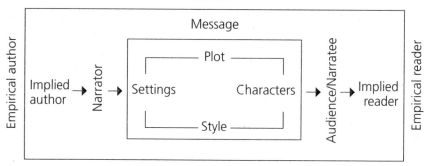

Figure 3 The elements of a narrative.

narrator and audience (or 'narratee'), is inscribed within the text. The goal of narrative criticism is to read the text as the implied reader, to assume that reader's knowledge and adopt their attitude, a practice that is intended to limit the subjectivity of our reading, although this has been contested by reader-response criticism, as we shall see below.

Characters, round, flat and otherwise

There would be no plot without characters – the actors in the story, who carry out the activities that comprise the plot.[4] Characters can be people, animals, robots or other non-human entities. In the book of Jonah, a big fish has an interesting role to play, as has a little worm. Characters need not be individuals either; an entire group can function as a single character. In Jonah, this is true of the sailors in chapter 1 and the Ninevites in chapter 3. Characters are constructs of the implied author. Even in a biography, a genre intended to provide insight into a real person's life, the character that emerges in the telling is the construct of the implied author. After all, by informing us about certain events and character traits, while withholding information about others, the implied author is constructing the character in a specific way. Narrative critics distinguish between different kinds of characters. The best-known such distinction is that of English novelist and essayist E. M. Forster (1879–1970) between *round characters*, which possess a variety of potentially conflicting character traits, and *flat characters*, whose traits are consistent and predictable. In addition to these, there are so-called *stock characters*, which embody no more than a single character trait (Forster, pp. 103–18; see also Abrams, p. 185). Sometimes, the terms *fully fledged characters*, *types* and *agents* are used to describe these three categories.

Examples of stock characters in Jonah include the big fish and the worm, neither of which are interesting as characters in themselves, even though both play important roles in the story. The anonymous, ignorant but exemplary sailors and the repentant Ninevites are flat characters, who 'serve largely to illuminate the prophet and the Lord' (Craig, p. 64). However, this is by no means to say that they are unimportant. In chapter 1, for instance, the cumulative effect of the repeated references to the sailors' fear is to highlight their increasing anxiety as the storm builds. The image that emerges is thus one of 'innocent, desperate sailors seeking to save their lives' (p. 131), which stands in marked contrast to an apathetic prophet whose behaviour we struggle to comprehend. That we, the readers, empathize with the sailors while adopting a more critical attitude towards Jonah is, of course, a calculated effect of the author's characterization. A similar effect is achieved in chapter 3 where, as Ackerman notes (1989, pp. 238–9), 'the response of the Ninevites is unprecedented in the prophetic tradition: Jonah barely enters the city and speaks five Hebrew words ... and thereby instigates the most frantic reform ever heard of.' As readers, we are not all that interested in the Ninevites, nor does the implied author want us to be. The point again is the contrast between two characters: the Ninevites and the prophet Jonah, both of whom act in surprising ways, but with Jonah coming out the worse in comparison. According to Judson Mather (p. 284), however:

> the idealized sailors and Ninevites are not actors; they are (like the big fish) props that through their exemplary behavior furnish a foil to the bumbling and all-too-human prophet. In the operative world of the story, it is as if the whole of nature and society – storms and crew, fish and urban sprawl, ritualized abjection and the life-cycle of plants – have been arranged by God for the manipulation and potential edification of Jonah.

Finally, Jonah and God, the only characters 'who have a name and thus an identity' (Craig, p. 63), are rounded or fully fledged characters. They possess a variety of potentially conflicting character traits, and therefore may behave in unexpected ways or perhaps even contradictory ones. They also have the potential to develop and are the ones around whom the story unfolds. Much of the debate about the book of Jonah centres on what we are to make of the actions of these two characters. Craig notes (p. 63) that they enter the stage without any preliminaries: 'Who is the Lord and who is Jonah, the son of Amittai? Without any overt exposition, the reader can only piece it together based on the action and conversation itself.'[5] The last chapter is particularly interesting as far as Jonah's development is concerned. Some have maintained that in the dialogue with God he comes across as quite a pathetic figure, thus appearing in stark contrast to the more positively portrayed pagan sailors and Ninevites, although that view is not shared by all. God, as we saw, initially appears as someone to be feared, while, as the story develops, God's grace and mercy increasingly come into sharper focus. Lastly, we might just note that, for John Miles (p. 205), our story features only stock characters – and that includes even Jonah and God.

Booth (pp. 3–20) once observed that implied authors have two options when it comes to characterization: they can reveal characters either by telling readers about them or by showing readers what characters are like. The technique of *telling* employs the voice of a reliable narrator to speak directly to the reader. A well-known example of this occurs in Genesis 6.9 where Noah, God's chosen leader in a time of massive crisis, is characterized as 'a righteous man, blameless in his generation'. However, as Craig points out (p. 2), Jonah's narrator 'refrains from providing explicit praise or condemnation for a single character' quite in line with the preferred method of characterization, which is *showing*. In this case, characters are made to reveal who they are through their words and actions, which we as readers must analyse. In the book of Jonah, the narrator's report, the characters' direct speech, dialogue and some prayers, which contribute to 'the characters' psychological portrayal' (Craig, p. 99), all play an important part in the storyteller's approach to characterization. As we eventually discover, this is a story 'that devotes more attention to the prophet than to his message', a story whose 'focus on the inner life', though not always noticed, is one of its key features (pp. 124–5). Jonah's behaviour is unique. In contrast to other prophets, who might voice their concerns about God's call (Exod. 3.1–4.17; Isa. 6; Jer. 1.4–10), Jonah protests 'with actions rather than with words' (p. 78). And while the likes of Moses or Isaiah are only momentarily hesitant in responding to their commission, Jonah maintains his defiant stance towards God and God's concerns all the way through to the end of the story (p. 60).

As Craig notes (p. 84), 'Jonah's speech in the initial chapter is surprisingly and significantly meager.' When the sailors in their panic want to know what to do, his answer 'is not "allow me, God's prophet, to intercede on your behalf" or "I will call to God so that the storm will not destroy you," but instead, "lift me up and hurl me into the sea and the sea will quiet down for you" (1.12)'. He is then quickly 'swallowed' (בלע, *bala'*) by the big fish (1.17), which, as Ackerman (1981, p. 220) observes, normally carries negative connotations. In Exodus 15, for instance, Moses and the Israelites are jubilant because the earth had swallowed Pharaoh's army (v. 12), while in Numbers 16.28–34 that same fate befalls those involved in Korah's revolt. Craig suggests (p. 87) that the narrator's use of 'swallow' in Jonah 1.17, combined with the prophet's thanksgiving psalm, is intended 'to highlight Jonah's *mis*understanding of the swallowing', portrayed by the narrator as ominous rather than salvific.

Finding himself in the belly of the fish, Jonah begins his psalm with the words 'I called to the LORD out of my distress, and he answered me' (2.2). When the prophet here 'calls' or 'cries out' (קרא, *qara'*) he is doing exactly what both God (1.2: 'cry out' against Nineveh) and the captain (1.6: 'call on your god') had asked him to do, only to no avail. Ackerman comments (1989, p. 237) that, 'having refused to cry out to save the others, [Jonah] changes his tune when he himself faces the prospect of violent death'. But Jonah's prayer, modelled on ancient Israel's psalms, deserves further comment. James Muilenburg (p. 680) once noted that 'the most striking characteristic of biblical poetry ... are the images and figures which the poet employs to embody his feelings and thoughts.' In Jonah 2, the narrator appropriates these images to portray Jonah's feelings and thoughts, using a pastiche in which almost every phrase comes from the Psalter,[6] to highlight 'the prophet's frenzied mental state', as Craig puts it (p. 93).

In verses 8–9, Jonah compares himself favourably to 'those who worship vain idols' and thereby 'forsake their true *loyalty*'. Idolaters, he suggests, are deserters of חֶסֶד (*khesed*). However, apart from the fact that the sailors, who had been crying out to their gods (idols), came out rather well in comparison with the prophet, Jonah himself will subsequently tell us (4.2) that he tried to flee from God precisely because of God's חֶסֶד (*khesed*). This is translated here as 'steadfast love', which is being offered to the Ninevites. Ackerman suggests (1989, p. 242) that this accusation against idolaters, combined with Jonah's pious proclamation to bring sacrifices and honour his vows to God, may have led to his sudden ejection from the fish's interior: 'When the song's piety becomes sickeningly sweet ... the prophet is vomited onto dry land just as he is about to hit the sea bottom.' Brent Strawn (p. 453) similarly concludes that the prophet's ill-fitting thanksgiving psalm makes the fish ill, thereby adding 'further question marks to the issue of Jonah's character'. But we must then wait until the end of the story to learn more about Jonah as a character. At the beginning of chapter 4, we find him praying to God again. Craig (p. 100) elucidates the surprising nature of what is happening here by comparing it with a typical plot pattern (Figure 4).

Crisis ➡ Prayer ➡ Deliverance

Figure 4 A typical plot pattern.

Afflicted by the storm (crisis), the sailors cry out to God (prayer) and are saved (deliverance; 1.14–15). Jonah, in his thanksgiving psalm, similarly says, 'I called to the LORD out of my distress, and he answered me' (2.2). The Ninevites, having been instructed by their king to 'cry mightily to God' (3.8), are also spared destruction. Yet in the book's final prayer we find a curiously reversed pattern (Figure 5).

Deliverance ➡ Crisis ➡ Prayer for death

Figure 5 A reversed, ironic plot pattern.

Struggling with the Ninevites' deliverance, which Jonah experiences as a major crisis, this sparks his final prayer (4.2–3). Craig points out (p. 135) that it shows Jonah for what he really is. Frequent references to 'I', 'my' and 'me' show the prophet to be preoccupied with himself:

> O LORD! Is not this what *I* said while *I* was still in my own country? That is why *I* fled to Tarshish at the beginning; for *I* knew that you are a gracious God and merciful, slow to anger, and abounding in steadfast love, and ready to relent from punishing. And now, O LORD, please take *my* life from *me*, for it is better for *me* to die than to live.

When the narrator informs us about Jonah's anger, they cleverly connect this with the repentance of both the Ninevites and God. As the Ninevites turn from their evil (רָעָה, *ra'ah*) ways, only for God to relent from the evil (רָעָה, *ra'ah*) God had planned for them (3.10), 'this "evils" [וַיֵּרַע, *wayyera'*] Jonah "a great evil"' [רָעָה גְדוֹלָה, *ra'ah gedolah*] (4.1), as Ackerman puts it (1989, p. 240), offering a literal translation of the Hebrew. The NRSV rather lamely translates what Alexander Abasili (p. 248) describes as 'one of the strongest ways of depicting annoyance in the Hebrew Bible' as 'this was very displeasing to Jonah'. Repentance from evil is a great evil to Jonah – what a brilliant way of characterizing the prophet's attitude. In contrast to the action-driven storytelling of chapter 1, there is a strong emphasis on Jonah's emotions at this point. Having experienced great anger, the prophet is mollified by the divinely appointed plant – קִיקָיוֹן (*qiqayon*) in Hebrew[7] – which gives him 'great joy' (4.6). Craig comments (p. 140) that 'Jonah's happiness – emphasized in the Hebrew as extraordinary happiness – follows his expression of anger (4.2) and request for death (4.3) and highlights his self-centredness.' However, the prophet's emotional rollercoaster is not over yet. When the shade-giving plant succumbs to the worm's deadly bite and, on top of all that, Jonah is troubled by a hot desert wind and the sun's relentless assault, he wishes to die. Craig notes that (p. 140): 'Jonah was angry because Nineveh had *not been* destroyed. [Now] the prophet is so angry that he prefers death because the tree *has been* destroyed. The shift is vividly brought out as the narrator allows Jonah to reveal his feelings thus condemning himself with his own words.' Craig's comment highlights the implied author's means of characterization, which is to let Jonah condemn himself by what he says. God, whose initial command got the story underway, also has the final word, for we now discover how God feels and that 'Jonah … is not the only one subject to disappointment and distress' (Blank, p. 30). Or, as Craig puts it (p. 67):

> The story about a prophet's apprehension, struggles, and fear turns out to be about God's own hurt as well … The intimidating, thundering God of the opening chapters turns out at the end … to be not only commanding and compassionate but also a God subject to distress, disappointment, and suffering at the thought of losing 120,000 Ninevites and much cattle.

Settings: navigating space

Settings, too, often play an important part in storytelling. Two examples to consider here are time and space. There are two kinds of story time: the time that elapses as events unfold in the story, also known as *narrative time*, and *narration time*, which is the time it takes to tell the story. Narration time tells us a lot about what is important to the implied author. Some events, such as the sailors' struggle with the storm, which would naturally have taken a significant amount of time, are dealt with rather swiftly. Far more significant to our storyteller are the dialogues that reveal the story's significance for God, Jonah and the sailors. For those moments, good narrators make time stand still (Jenson, p. 11), thereby prompting readers to pay special attention to them.

But let us focus on space, which is of particular significance especially in the early parts of the story. In 1.2, the prophet is told to go to Nineveh. What the text literally says is, 'Arise/get up [קוּם, *qum*] and go to Nineveh', although the directional aspect of getting up is sometimes lost in translation (the NRSV, for instance, has 'Go at once'). The reason for God's demand that Jonah go to Nineveh was that the city's wickedness had 'come up' (עלה, *'alah*) before God or literally into God's 'face' (לְפָנָי, *lefanay*). So what does Jonah do? He gets up (קוּם, *qum*) – again this is missed in the NRSV, which translates 'Jonah set out' – thus giving the impression that he is about to obey the divine command, but decides to flee instead (1.3). In horizontal terms, as we saw, Jonah is heading in the opposite direction to where he was supposed to go; he is attempting to travel to Tarshish, the westernmost corner of the world, as it was probably known to the writer of the book,[8] rather than eastwards in the direction of Nineveh. Jenson (p. 22) calls Tarshish 'the ancient equivalent of Timbuktu'. According to Mishnah tractate Baba Batra 3.2,[9] it took a whole year of sea travel to reach Tarshish, a place where Yahweh was not known (Isa. 66.19). Cyrus Gordon (pp. 517–18) notes that 'in literature and popular imagination it became a distant paradise', while Ackerman (1989, p. 235) comments that, 'for Jonah … Tarshish may paradoxically represent a pleasant place of security that borders on nonexistence'.

Rather significantly, Jonah's flight west also quickly turns into a sustained downward motion, as he *goes down* (ירד, *yarad*) to Joppa to *go down* (ירד, *yarad*) to board the ship where he *goes down* (again ירד, *yarad*) into its hold to *lie down* to sleep (וַיִּשְׁכַּב וַיֵּרָדַם, *wayyishkav wayyeradam*). As Anthony Rees (p. 41) notes, the repeated Hebrew term ירד (*yarad*), 'to go down', in our story always has Jonah as its subject. The second 'going down' is passed over by the NRSV, which reads 'went on board'. But the storyteller's choice of 'go down' seems deliberate, as has been observed by Rees (p. 44), who points out that this is the only case where this verb is used to describe the boarding of a vessel (normally, one would expect אֶל + בּוֹא, *bo'* + *'el*, literally 'go into'). The lying down is expressed using another verb (שָׁכַב, *shakhav*), but the word designating Jonah's sleep (יֵרָדַם, *yeradam*) is phonetically similar to ירד (*yarad*). Rees comments that 'given that there are other words for "sleep," it seems that the narrator has chosen this word to further highlight the downward aspect of Jonah's response' (see also Kunz-Lübcke, p. 65).

When the sailors realize that the prophet is indeed the cause of their trouble, they reluctantly – and only in response to Jonah's own request – hurl him into the sea (1.15). The sea is clearly of symbolic significance due to its association in Hebrew thinking with primeval chaos, the presence of sea monsters, and the realm of death.[10] Jonah stresses this in his prayer: 'I called to the LORD out of my distress, and he answered me; out of the belly of Sheol I cried, and you heard my voice' (2.2). Sheol is the underworld, the realm of the dead, where Jonah found himself until God rescued him by sending the big fish in whose belly he would spend 'three days and three nights' (1.17), the time it took to reach the underworld (Landes, 1967). Jonah's prayer (2.1–9) shows that he, just like the narrator, is keenly aware of his *downward journey*. As he says, having been cast into the deep, into the heart of the seas, the flood surrounded him. In a bit of a rhetorical flourish, he talks about seaweeds being wrapped around his head, but again the spatial, directional emphasis is worthy of note. He went down so far that he ended up at the roots of the mountains, as far down as it was possible to go, in the pit, the land whose bars closed upon him for ever, which is yet another reference to death. In stressing that Jonah keeps going down, the implied author draws attention also to the spiritual dimension of the prophet's journey (Magonet, 1983, p. 17). Rees (p. 47) sums it up well when he says: 'This is a geographical, physical, mental and spiritual descent of shocking proportion.'

But Jonah's prayer was the turning point, for God has brought *up* (עלה, *'alah*) his life from the pit (2.6). God has put a stop to that downward spiral. There may be a heavy dose of irony here, however, as God's rescue mission leads to one last upward movement when the fish throws up, vomiting the prophet up on to dry land.

Style: repetition

Stylistic features can play a crucial role in literature and storytelling. Lucy Ellmann, for example, uses the constantly repeated phrase 'the fact that' to great effect in her stream-of-consciousness novel *Ducks, Newburyport*; and repetition has also been very effectively applied in the book of Jonah where it draws attention to important developments within the story. Jonathan Magonet's study of literary techniques in Jonah has shown that the book features what he calls a 'system of repetition' of words, phrases and complete sentences, which culminates in structural patterns covering whole chapters (Magonet, 1983, p. 11). In Jonah 1, we read initially that when confronted with the mighty storm, the sailors 'feared' (וַיִּירְאוּ, *wayyir'u*; NRSV: 'were afraid', v. 5). As the situation got more and more desperate, 'the men *feared with a great fear*' (וַיִּירְאוּ הָאֲנָשִׁים יִרְאָה גְדוֹלָה, *wayyir'u ha'anashim yir'ah gedolah*; NRSV: 'were even more afraid', v. 10); but at the end, having been spared a catastrophic outcome, 'the men *feared with a great fear the* LORD' (וַיִּירְאוּ הָאֲנָשִׁים יִרְאָה גְדוֹלָה אֶת־יְהוָה, *wayyir'u ha'anashim yir'ah gedolah 'et-yhwh*; NRSV: 'the men feared the LORD even more', v. 16). Repeating the key terms 'to fear' (ירא, *yare'*) three times and 'with a great fear' (יִרְאָה גְדוֹלָה, *yir'ah gedolah*) twice, the narrator shows us how the sailors' fear not only grew but, by the end of their encounter with God, had turned into what the Old Testament calls 'the fear of the LORD'.

The example above also features the word 'great' (גְדוֹלָה, *gedolah*), arguably one of the most important terms in the book of Jonah. Repeatedly, Nineveh is called the *great* city (1.2; 3.2, 3; 4.11); God hurls a *great* wind (1.4) or a *great* tempest (1.4, 12) upon the sea; the sailors, as we saw, fear with a *great* fear, first the storm (1.10) and then the Lord (1.16); and God sends a *great* fish (1.17). Nineveh, having been spared by God, was a *great* evil to Jonah (4.1), while the divinely appointed bush gave the prophet *great* joy (4.6). Strikingly, the storyteller employs the term not only with reference to external realities – such as great cities, storms and fish – but also to draw attention to characters experiencing great emotions (fear, anger or joy). It is evident that the story features many great things, but what might be the significance of this?

'Evil' (רָעָה, *ra'ah*) is another important term throughout Jonah. Nineveh's great *evil* has come to God's attention (1.2). In the storm an *evil* has come upon the sailors (1.7), who want to know from Jonah why that *evil* is afflicting them (1.8). The Ninevites turning away from their *evil* ways makes God reconsider the *evil* God was about to bring upon them (3.10). This, as we saw earlier, *evils* Jonah a great *evil* (4.1), having known all along that God was always ready to relent from the *evil*, in this case the Ninevites' punishment (4.2). Lastly, in response to Jonah's distress, God appoints a bush to save the prophet from his *evil* or discomfort (4.6). The storyteller is clearly playing with the different nuances of the term 'evil' for ironic effect, as is suggested especially in God relenting from the evil (the punishment of the Ninevites) 'eviling' Jonah a great evil.

For further reflection

1 What do you make of narrative criticism's concepts of the implied author and reader? What is the point of distinguishing between real and implied authors and readers?

2 And what about the way the narrator tells the story? What do you think of the narrator's lack of evaluation? If the task of evaluation falls to us, on what basis are we supposed to assess the characters' words and actions?

3 How, according to (mostly) Craig, does the book of Jonah portray Jonah, God, the sailors and the Ninevites? Which observations do you find striking, insightful, surprising, or perhaps objectionable?

4 What do you make of the use of vertical space, of Jonah being portrayed as being on a spiritual downward journey?

5 What, finally, about the repetition of key terms, such as 'to fear', 'great' or 'evil'? What contribution do these repetitions make to the telling of the story?

Narrative criticism and the biblical story as art

Narrative criticism essentially prompts us to slow down when reading a story, to pay attention and reflect on what is going on in the text. It encourages us to ask questions such as: How is the story told? From whose perspective? How does the plot develop? How are the characters portrayed? What contribution do settings and stylistic devices make to the storytelling? Narrative criticism thus can be a useful tool as we engage with biblical stories. However, some brief reflections on what Alter calls 'the *art* of biblical narrative' may add some further food for thought. Alter highlights two interfused features of biblical stories, the 'pleasure of imaginative play', which makes them such a well-loved feature of the biblical literature, and 'a sense of great spiritual urgency', which Craig sought to get at by talking about art serving ideology. The combination of these two features leads Alter to conclude (p. 189) that 'by learning to enjoy the biblical stories more fully as stories, we shall also come to see more clearly what they mean to tell us about God, man, and the perilously momentous realm of history.' He adds that (p. 176):

> Fiction fundamentally serves the biblical writers as an instrument of fine insight into [the] abiding perplexities of man's creaturely condition. That may help explain why these ancient Hebrew stories still seem so intensely alive today, and why it is worth the effort of learning to read them attentively as artful stories.

Trappist monk, writer, poet and social activist Thomas Merton (1915–68), in an essay on 'Conscience, freedom, and prayer', offers some illuminating reflections on the value of art that help us to flesh out Alter's comment about biblical stories developing our understanding of God and humanity. Merton suggests (1955, p. 34):

> In an aesthetic experience ... the psychological conscience is able to attain some of its highest and most perfect fulfillments. Art enables us to find ourselves and lose ourselves at the same time. The mind that responds to the intellectual and spiritual values that lie hidden in a [piece of art] ... discovers a spiritual vitality that lifts it above itself, takes it out of itself, and makes it present to itself on a level of being that it did not know it could ever achieve.

Indeed, Merton adds (pp. 34–5):

the spirit that finds itself above itself in the intensity and cleanness of its reaction to a work of art is 'self-conscious' in a way that is productive as well as sublime. Such a one finds in himself totally new capacities for thought and vision and moral action ... His very response makes him better and different. He is conscious of a new life and new powers ... It is important, in the life of prayer, to be able to respond to such flashes of aesthetic intuition.

All this leads Merton to conclude (p. 36) that 'art ... introduces the soul into a higher spiritual order ... [It attunes] the soul to God'.

For further reflection

1 What do you make of Alter's notions of the 'pleasure of imaginative play' and the 'sense of great spiritual urgency' in connection with our reading of the story of Jonah?

2 And what about Merton's thoughts on art? In what ways might the book of Jonah enable us to find or lose ourselves, discover a spiritual vitality that lifts our mind above itself, or make us present to ourselves in a way not experienced before?

3 What new capacities for thought, vision and moral action might the book facilitate? Does our response to the book of Jonah make us better and different, give us new life and new powers? Do we expect our reading of the story to have any such effects?

The politics of genre

What kind of story is the book of Jonah? Scholars have come up with a veritable cornucopia of labels, ranging from allegory, biography, burlesque, cartoon, comedy, fable, fairy tale, folktale, history, legend, midrash, myth, novel, novella, parable, parody, prophetic tale, saga, satire, sermon, short story, tragedy and tragicomedy to wisdom literature (Trible, 1994, p. 108; and Gaines, p. 13). It would take up far too much space to review them all, but my interest here is specifically in the humorous, parodic or satirical elements observed by an increasing number of recent readers, which raise important questions for our reading of the story of Jonah.

Humorous elements in the book of Jonah

Once again, there is a smorgasbord of terms used to characterize the humorous elements of Jonah, including absurdities, burlesque, caricature, cartoon, comedy, distortions, fantastic situations, farce, grotesqueries, incongruities,[11] irony, joke, mockery, parody, ridicule, sarcasm, satire, slapstick, travesty, whimsicality and wit. However, before we explore the book from the perspective of its potentially humorous elements, some general comments on humour in the Bible are pertinent, with the key observation being that for a long period of the Bible's history humour used to go completely undetected. As Sherwood observes (1998, p. 50), 'the critical tradition has, until recently, maintained an incredibly straight face about the book of Jonah'. William Whedbee (locs 75–6) suggests that biblical humour had been obscured by 'centuries of liturgical and theological use of the Bible'. Francis Landy (p. 99) thought it was specifically the reverence accorded the Bible, often amounting to nothing less than idolatry, that prevented people from observing or admitting the presence of its humorous aspects. Indeed, Yehuda Radday (p. 22) and Whedbee (locs 78–9) note that the very detection of humorous elements in the biblical writings was deemed to be blasphemous. Humour was not seen 'as a valid way of worshipping God' (Landy, p. 99), the Bible was perceived as a 'stiff and serious document that never relaxes into a smile', and Christian theology has tended to 'make Christian theologians and exegetes blind to the humour of the Bible' (Radday, p. 35).

However, rabbinic and subsequent Jewish exegesis, as David Marcus (p. 3) points out, 'could tolerate light-hearted and often humorous interpretations for the narrative parts of the Bible'. Robert Carroll (1990, p. 170) in this context emphasizes the presence of irony, which he regards as deep-seated and prevalent in the Old Testament to the point that 'little of its narrative can be read without becoming aware of the ironizing distance between the narration and the narrated characters'. Humour, it has been noted, can be highly subversive, and Radday (p. 32) quotes American writer and humourist Mark Twain (1835–1910), according to whom 'only humour can blow to rags and nothing can stand against it'. Of course, if it now transpires that the Bible and especially the book of Jonah do contain humorous touches, then the question arises as to what kind of humour we might be dealing with, and what purpose the book's humorous elements might be serving. It is to this that we now turn but not without noting Radday's caution (p. 38) that not only is it generally difficult 'to tell the genres of humour apart', but also that 'it is twice as difficult to do so in the Bible', given that it comes from a different time and culture and is written in a different language.

Suggesting that 'Jonah ... presents itself as something very close to joke', Steven Walker (2013, pp. 26, 31) begins with the claim that by missing the humour of the Bible, we miss much of its essence, joy and meaning. And nowhere is this more self-defeating than in the book of Jonah, whose hero, Walker claims (pp. 28, 31), is the 'funniest biblical character', being comparable to Charlie Chaplin, while the book 'may be the funniest book of the Bible'. Conrad Hyers (pp. 96, 108) goes so far as to claim that it is not only a 'comic masterpiece' but 'one of the world's greatest ... comedies'. Carroll, for his part, maintains (1990, p. 171) that while 'Jonah has no sense of humour ... for the reader (or hearer) the story is hilarious'. As a starting point, it might be helpful to re-read Jonah with a focus on the book's funny and incongruous side, although it should be noted that the language used by readers to characterize the humour – the cartoonish, ironic, parodic or satirical elements they deem to have detected – is never neutral but always betrays their specific readerly perspectives. Those perspectives find expression especially in the rich stock of adjectives used to describe Jonah and his actions, compared to the noticeable dearth of such adjectives in the telling of the story by a far more reticent biblical narrator.

Chapter 1 opens with Jonah's burlesque, uniquely taciturn and uncooperative flight from God by which he completely belies his name – Jonah son of Amittai translates as 'dove, son of faithfulness' – proving himself to be unfaithful at the very first opportunity (1.1–3). The impact of Jonah's phlegmatic silence has been compared to silence after the question: 'Do you take this woman to be your lawfully wedded wife?' We then get what seems like a bit of a divine overreaction in the form of God's hurled wind, which causes a massive tempest – with the wind and sea obeying God (1.4), as do all forces of nature, plants, animals and human characters throughout the story – except for Jonah. This is quickly followed by the grotesque and fantastic notion of the ship thinking (worrying?) that it may be in trouble – that is, that it may be broken up. Further drama happens on board ship where the sailors' feverish but futile activity contrasts sharply with Jonah's utter passivity (1.5). The sailors even hold an ecumenical prayer service while the prophet's Chaplinesque act of falling asleep makes him doze during the life-threatening emergency. The captain's exhortation, 'Get up [קוּם, qum], call on [קְרָא, qera'] your god' (1.6), ironically echoes God's earlier commission, 'Get up [קוּם, qum] ... and cry out [קְרָא, qera'] against' Nineveh. When Jonah claims to be worshipping 'the LORD, the God of heaven, who made the sea and the dry land' (1.9), his entirely unexceptional theology unfortunately makes little practical difference, as he futilely seeks to flee from God by means of the sea that had been created by and was obeying that very God. On top of which, Jonah's proposed solution to the crisis (1.11–12), none other than human sacrifice, is totally alien to Israel's values. All the while, the sea was literally 'walking and raging' (the NRSV reads 'was growing more and more tempestuous'). Its waves, one after another, were smashing into the side of ship. The gentile sailors, worrying about shedding innocent blood (1.14), nonetheless ultimately accede to Jonah's request (1.15), thus setting in motion the timely and fantastic intervention of the great fish (1.17) who, like the wind and sea, conspires with God to disabuse the prophet of his escapism. Jonah, for his part, ignominiously disappears down the fish's gullet, thus triggering the sea's instantaneous calming. Meanwhile, the whole episode had been causing the willy-nilly conversion of all the sailors (1.16).

In chapter 2, we meet Jonah piously and eloquently at prayer, a scene that sits somewhat uneasily in its gastric setting between his having been swallowed by the ginormous fish and his eventual unceremonious expulsion from said fish (more about that in a moment). In his prayer, Jonah is oddly yearning for the presence of the God he has just fled (2.2, 4, 7). Somewhat absurdly, too, he blames God for his predicament – 'You cast me into the deep' (2.3) – when it was he who had asked to be thrown into the sea. Showing him to be well read in the scriptures, Jonah's prayer is full of quotations from the Psalms. But his troubles are not *like* waves washing over his head, as Israel's ancient psalmists were wont to say in one of their many vivid metaphors; his troubles *are* waves washing over his head (2.3) – and seaweed wrapped around it (2.5). When he remonstrates against 'those who worship vain idols' (2.8), presumably the non-Israelite sailors who had 'each cried to his god' (1.5), charging them with forsaking 'their true loyalty', he is ironically unaware of them having come to fear Yahweh, bring sacrifices, and make vows, just as he was being swallowed by that mammoth fish. And so the jury is out as to who it is that has been disloyal. To wrap things up, Jonah promises the very sacrifices and vows that the mariners had beaten him to (2.9). All this leads to salvation by spewing (2.10), to the pointed indignity of whale puke or the slapstick touch of fishy regurgitation, to Jonah being vomited head over heels across the dunes, possibly, according to an early tradition that adds insult to injury, now both naked and bald (see Summerfield, Ryken and Eldredge, p. 410). It is the fish's unceremonious response to Jonah's long-winded – certainly compared to his soon-to-come sermon at Nineveh – and exorbitantly pious prayer. Perhaps the fish is expressing its good taste with visceral disgust just when Jonah had been wrongly condemning those exemplary foreign sailors and triumphantly trumpeting that 'deliverance belongs to the LORD'. It did – in what must, however, be the most humiliating and undignified example of salvation in the Bible.

In chapter 3, the hilarities continue with Jonah stalking sulky and smelly into the hostile environs of Nineveh, venturing only a day's walk into a city that took three days to cross (3.1–3). In stupefying contrast to the prophets' lengthy speeches, which were generally ignored or rejected, the tiny stimulus of Jonah's five-word sermon (3.4) – literally, 'yet forty days, Nineveh overturned' – occasions a truly convulsive response (3.5–9), making him the most stupendously successful prophet of all time. The Ninevites' immediate conversion stretches beyond the unlikely to the absurd, with everyone fasting, donning sackcloth and crying out to God – including all their animals. It also stands in sharp contrast to Jonah's earlier instantaneous rejection of God's command and the sorriest sermon recorded in Scripture, perfunctorily delivered by a prophet who is content for his message to be heard by no more than some random passers-by. The Ninevites' repentance also disregards all established hierarchies. The normal folk repent well before their king gets the chance to issue his edict. When he does, the bizarre decree – rather implausibly and against all health advice – expects everyone (cows, sheep and goats included) to not even consume water (not standard fasting practice) and instead, from cow to king, take part in a prayer meeting. St Francis may have preached to the birds, but only Jonah brought about the prayer and repentance of cattle. But God was well pleased and, as the Ninevite king had hoped, did some repenting himself (3.9–10). Just as the Ninevites had turned each from their evil ways (מִדַּרְכָּם הָרָעָה, *middarkam hara'ah*), so now God changes his mind about the evil (הָרָעָה, *hara'ah*; the NRSV reads 'calamity') that he had devised against them.

The final chapter features the childish tantrums of Jonah who, in contrast to a prophet like Elijah, who had been upset because of the perceived failure of his mission (1 Kings 19.9–10), is petulantly bickering with God because of the mind-boggling success of his (4.1–3). Indeed, so angered is Jonah that he prays for his death. God's deliverance, something that Jonah had celebrated in his pious psalm, has now infuriated him so much that he can no longer face life. It is God's merciful qualities, celebrated repeatedly throughout the Old Testament (for example, Exod. 34.6–7; Num. 14.18; Joel 2.13; Pss 86.15; 103.8; 145.8; Neh. 9.17), that pique Jonah and had occasioned his disobedience in the first place, as he points out. Having accused the sailors of forsaking their loyalty (חֶסֶד, *khesed*; 2.8), Jonah is now ironically enraged by God's mercy (חֶסֶד, *khesed*; 4.2) – חֶסֶד (*khesed*) can mean 'faithfulness, loyalty' as well as the expression of that faithfulness in the form of 'graciousness, mercy'. There is also that ironic repetition of the key term 'evil' here, for, as we saw earlier, God relenting from the evil (רָעָה, *ra'ah*) that God had planned for the Ninevites (3.10) '"evils" [וַיֵּרַע, *wayyera'*] Jonah "a great evil"' [רָעָה גְדוֹלָה, *ra'ah gedolah*]

(4.1). Jonah, in any case, has decided that if God will not sit in judgement over the city he will (4.5). And so while the king of Nineveh had been sitting in the discomfort of ashes inside the city hoping it would be spared, Jonah sits in comfortable shade outside it, hoping it will go up in smoke, like Sodom and Gomorrah – the term 'overthrown' (הפך, *hafakh*) used by Jonah in his sermon famously occurs also in the Sodom and Gomorrah story in Genesis 19.12–29. Being impressively insensitive to the possibility of the Ninevites' suffering, Jonah does, however, leap for joy when a mild annoyance is removed from him (4.6). But the sudden appearance and whimsical withering of that fast-growing plant, destroyed by the attack of a plant-smiting warrior worm – נכה (*nakhah*) means 'to smite' (the NRSV reads 'attack') – followed by the sudden onset of a fierce east wind (4.6–8) leads to Jonah's renewed anger and death wish. All these dizzyingly rapid and exaggerated mood swings – when he is unhappy, he wants to die; when he is happy, he is overjoyed – cause a concerned God to enquire whether Jonah really thinks he is right to be that angry (4.9). 'Sure,' says Jonah, 'angry enough do die.' And all that takes us to the book's inconclusive ending (4.10–11). A prophet upset about a short-lived plant that he had done nothing to grow or sustain is asked by God whether God shouldn't be concerned for 120,000 Ninevites – or should that be one million[12] – and all their animals. Reverting to his initial taciturnity, however, Jonah, it would appear, is the only figure in the book (including the cows) who remains unrepentant to the end.

According to this reading, which fuses the descriptions and comments of several scholars,[13] everything in the book is either laughably big or laughably small, either over- or understated. As Marcus notes (pp. 101, 103–4), 'to achieve his purposes, God uses the greatest of creatures, a large fish, and the smallest of creatures, a worm', while Jonah's brief oracle, 'the briefest denunciation on record ... produced the greatest response ... a massive repentance'. The term 'great' (גָּדוֹל, *gadol*) features no fewer than 14 times in this book of just 48 verses,[14] leading to readers being deluged with 'successive waves of hyperbole' (Hyers, p. 104), and for Timothy McNinch to comment (p. 12) that 'everything in Jonah is supersized: the storm, the fish, the god-huge city, the קִיקָיוֹן [*qiqayon*] plant, and even emotional reactions – both great fear and great joy'. In Walker's perception (p. 32), the book also 'hurls scene after high-tempo comic scene, compressed skits volleyed at the pace of one-liners'. 'Every action', he suggests (p. 34), 'is deliberately overdrawn'; and 'the humor of Jonah ... is climactic; it gets funnier as it goes along', with the closing words – 'and also many animals' – functioning as the concluding punch line. But our earlier questions still stand: How is the book's humour best characterized? And what might be its purpose?

Jonah, satire and anti-Semitism

As we saw earlier, scholars have used a range of terms to characterize the nature of (parts of) the book of Jonah. One especially influential interpretation in recent decades has been to read it as satire, which Arnold Band (p. 180) defines as a direct attack on '"wickedness and folly" in human society'. To be sure, parody might be a more accurate characterization, as the book interacts with other texts, parodying them and/or the world they represent, but scholars reading Jonah along these lines have not always clearly defined and distinguished between parody and satire. It is precisely 'the intertextual density' of the book of Jonah, the fact that it features numerous allusions to a range of other biblical texts, that leads Band to describe it as a parody (p. 179; see also Miles). Intertextuality, according to Gail O'Day (p. 155), refers to the understanding of 'literature as a system of interrelated texts', which is highly apposite in the case of the biblical literature, which features numerous intertextual crosslinks. And while Michael Riffaterre and Gérard Genette see intertextuality as a feature of all literature, some writers, including the author of Jonah, deliberately 'play' with (allusions to) other texts. Among the intertextual echoes identified in the book of Jonah are:[15]

- Prophetic call stories: for example, Elijah (1 Kings 17.8–10) or Jeremiah (Jer. 13.4–5), compared to that of Jonah (1.1–3).
- The Psalms, several of which are quoted in Jonah's prayer in chapter 2.
- The destruction of Sodom and Gomorrah (Gen. 19.12–29), invoked by Jonah talking about Nineveh about to be 'overturned' (3.4), using the Hebrew verb הפך (hafakh) as in Genesis 19.21, 25, 29.
- God's self-characterization in Exodus 34.6 (note Jonah's quotation of this in 4.2).
- Elijah complaining to God about the perceived failure of his mission (1 Kings 19.9–10), compared to Jonah complaining about the success of his (4.1–3).
- The Garden of Eden story (Gen. 3), in which a tree and a serpent play a key role compared to the qiqayon and the worm in Jonah (4.6–7).

And yet it has been more common for interpreters to characterize Jonah as satire (for example, Good, Burrows, Holbert, Ackerman, Hyers, Marcus, Ingram, and Cook). Indeed, Marcus (pp. 145–7) presents a long list of scholars, beginning with Thomas Paine in 1794 and ending with Athalya Brenner in 1993, who have recognized satirical elements in the book; and there have been further satirical readings of Jonah since 1995 when Marcus' book was published.

But what characterizes these satirical readings? John Holbert (p. 61) quite unabashedly notes that 'the object of satire must be reduced to laughable proportions ... engendering laughter from the reader who is thereby offered "*the pleasures of superiority and a safe release of aggression*" [my italics]'. The final phrase of Holbert's statement is a quote from Leonard Feinberg's *Introduction to Satire* (p. 5), which helpfully pinpoints one of the defining features of satire and especially its essential attitude to its object. In this reading, the book of Jonah, as Edwin Good notes (p. 41), 'portrays the prophet in order to ridicule him'. Marcus (pp. viii, 94, 95) suggests its purpose is 'to satirize the prophet for behavior thought to be unbecoming to a prophet' and that 'Jonah is portrayed as a very negative model of prophetic behavior', which he regards as 'the principal message of the book'. Holbert elaborates (p. 70) that Jonah 'is shown to be self-centred, lazy, hypocritical and altogether inferior to the wonderful pagans who surround him' and that the book is 'an attack on Hebrew prophetic hypocrisy' (p. 75). Paul Murray (p. 58) ups the heat even more when he concludes that it is 'the harsh tribalism and religious prejudice of stiff-necked people like Jonah [that] are directly challenged'. According to Mark Biddle meanwhile (loc. 1304), 'we have gotten to know Jonah rather well as a petulant, prejudiced, prideful preacher of pitiful prophecy. Among the prophets of ancient Israel, Jonah has no equal.' Indeed, Jonah, he adds (loc. 1347), 'was a bigot of the worst kind'.

While the book of Jonah has frequently been read along humorous or satirical lines, some have expressed their unease with this type of interpretation. Craig, for example (p. 143), suggests that 'as we experience Jonah's thoughts and feelings first hand, we discover that the story is too earnest for laughter'. A similar conclusion had already been reached by Shelomo Goitein (pp. 73–4), who maintained that 'the whole tenor of the story is much too earnest for a satire', adding that 'Jonah is not painted with the brush of mockery or disdain, but drawn with the pencil of deep and sympathetic insight into human weakness'. According to Janet Gaines (p. 23), it is especially as we move to the end of the book that 'the mocking disdain found in satire and the lampooning irony found in parody ultimately disappear as an understanding narrator and a sympathetic deity deal gently with human weakness'. André LaCocque and Pierre-Emmanuel Lacocque, for their part, conclude (pp. xxii, xxiii) that 'the singer of the Jonah tale ... had too great a respect for his audience to waste their time with a shallow polemical satire' and that 'Jonah has nothing to do with a petty insubstantial Jew conceived by the deranged mind of an anti-Semite'. Responding to Miles's interpretation of Jonah as parody, Berlin (1976, p. 227) professes that she cannot see 'how a parody of prophetic writings, which were looked upon with utmost seriousness throughout the rest of the Bible, came to gain enough acceptance to be included in the Prophets'. She goes on to maintain that 'Jewish tradition regards the Book of Jonah with such reverence that it is read at the afternoon service of the Day of Atonement, hardly the appropriate occasion for a parody of the Bible'. Serge Frolov, in turn, reading the book as a former Soviet national and a Jew born after the Second World War, sees Jonah's death wish and his behaviour in chapter 4, which are frequently lampooned, as far more sincere, sensical and dignified than God's unreasonable, capricious, erratic and absurd treatment of Jonah, the Ninevites and (by implication) Israel. Other interpreters, notably among those who have pursued liberationist and postcolonial readings (see the next chapter), would agree.

In satirical readings, the target tends to be the prophet Jonah who, as we have seen, is invariably understood as acting out of turn, with his protest against an all-merciful God being dismissed as a 'lame excuse' for disobedience (Trudinger, p. 143) or 'an attempt to limit the scope and intention of God's word' (Holbert, p. 75). As Sherwood observes (1998, p. 54), the guiding assumption is that 'God and the author share the same attitude': that the author or narrator effectively speaks for God; and it is this equation of the narrator's viewpoint with God's that marginalizes Jonah's perspective and banishes 'his potentially explosive challenge to the deity from the text' (p. 56). Sherwood does not see this as an innocent move but states (p. 55) that 'watching critics read Jonah "as a satire" highlights the political issues at stake in reading biblical texts'. Jonah's opposition to an all-merciful God is frequently depicted as a vendetta against the gentiles or as nationalist hatred of foreigners, while the author of the book becomes a 'universalist', a 'pre-Christian Christian' or a 'twentieth-century liberal academic' who reflects the critic's own ideology (p. 58).

What worries Sherwood most in this form of engagement with the text is how 'commentary on the book of Jonah has been used as a forum for anti-Judaism', for painting Jonah and his fellow Jews in a bad light. Maintaining that the text is far more ambiguous than these satirical readings allow, she criticizes Hans Walter Wolff's contention that there is 'a right answer ... to which "our author" is leading us'. Instead, Sherwood sees this as an example of how *commentators* guide readers 'through treacherous ambiguities in the text towards the right answer' (p. 57). The interpretation is thus prescribed not by the author but by the reader. After all, as Sherwood emphasizes, '*there is no author here except the one constructed by the critics* [my italics], and Wolff almost implies this when he uses the phrase, "our writer"'. And she goes on to point out that in this kind of reading, the author functions as an ambassador for the values of the critics. The author is '"our man" ... in the recalcitrant and foreign world of the text'.

Quoting first British literary critic and moralist Arthur Pollard (1922–2001) and then Canadian literary critic and theorist Northrop Frye (1912–91), Sherwood (p. 60) suggests (a) that 'satire deals in "should" and moral imperatives, and is "always acutely conscious of the difference between what things are and what they should be"' (Pollard, p. 3) and (b) that '"satire is militant irony" [Frye, p. 223] or the conservative end of comedy, in which the potential anarchy of humour is restrained by didacticism, and the errant prophet is re-educated to conform to the status quo' – hence her claim that there are political issues at stake. In satirical readings of Jonah, it is always the prophet who is condemned in what to Sherwood (p. 55) is an 'increasing exploitation of the comic potential of the book'. What is taken for granted in these interpretations is that the laughter cannot be 'at the expense of the deity and the sacred texts'. So if the fish vomits in disgust, 'it cannot be in response to the language of the psalm, but rather to the hypocritical spirit in which it is uttered'. After all, as Good has suggested (p. 55), 'the alternative to Jonah's absurdity is the absurdity of God'. But perhaps that is precisely what we would have to entertain: the possibility of the absurdity of God! Or might it be better to say that the text might be drawing attention to the absurdity of human portrayals of God or to the absurdity of human claims to have understood God?

But Sherwood's point about the interpretation of Jonah having become a forum for anti-Judaism also deserves further exploration. As Marcus has pointed out (p. 148), 'to the 18th century German founders of modern biblical scholarship ([Johann Salomo] Semler, [Johann David] Michaelis, [Johann Gottfried] Eichhorn), Jonah exemplified the Jewish fanaticism which begrudged God's mercy to the Gentiles'. Sherwood (2000, pp. 22–5) traces this thinking back to Augustine (354–430) and Martin Luther (1483–1546) but agrees that it comes to full, sustained and repeated expression in modern Christian scholarship that 'all too often sinks back into an essentially supersessionist reflex' (p. 3) that regards Judaism as superseded by Christianity. Jonah the character, 'created in the image of the stigmatised European shtetl Jew', in this thinking 'becomes iconic of all the tyrannical dogma and narrowness that the Enlightened scholar must by definition resist' (p. 27). However, having surveyed a welter of readings, Sherwood goes further, noting that Jonah, portrayed as a retrogressive, exclusivist and separatist ghetto Jew with xenophobic tendencies, becomes otherized, dehumanized and monsterized (pp. 28, 31, 72).[16] We find this monsterization encapsulated, for instance, in Leslie Allen's exasperated question (p. 229), 'What religious monster is this?', referring to Gerhard von Rad for a similar assessment.

Sherwood (p. 65) lists a barrage of unflattering terms that have been applied to Jonah the Jew, which includes but does not exhaust itself in seeing him as self-centred, hypocritical, inferior to the wonderful pagans, cantankerous, bad-tempered, narrow-minded, petty, bigoted, carnal, vindictive, arrogant, self-righteous, and a type of 'the narrow, blind, prejudiced, fanatic Jews' (the quote is from Bewer, p. 64). Quite a distressing list of 'anti-Semitic designations' this, which leads Sherwood to comment (2000, p. 85) that it is 'strangely telling' that 'it is not the Ninevites who epitomise the savage needy Other ... but the Jew [who] is the proto-Savage, the archetypal Other'. Polish sociologist and philosopher Zygmunt Bauman (1925–2017) calls this 'allosemitism', the othering of the Jew, which he regards as 'endemic to Western Civilisation' and a 'legacy of Christendom' (Bauman, p. 148). Having apparently also witnessed a fair share of this, LaCocque and Lacocque (p. 9) rather laconically note that 'anti-Semites have always found in this book a fertile ground for their poisonous seeds'. In contrast to Jonah the character, however, the author of the book has been styled by Christian readers as a 'liberal-minded pre-Christian Jew', a 'proto-Christian [this has been criticized by Magonet, 1992, p. 94], proto-Western author', a 'liberal intellectual and biblical scholar', says Sherwood (2000, pp. 28, 68, 84). Indeed, she speaks of 'the authoritative trinity of critic, author, and deity' (p. 77), noting that their identities all 'blur into one another' – thus pointing to the Western critic attributing their liberal proto-Christian understanding to the book's author, who is portrayed as expressing the attitude of an equally liberal proto-Christian God. This, she adds (p. 85), leaves 'Jewish Jonah' in 'the unenviable position of [being] isolated in his proto-Christian text'.

So where does all this leave us? Does the recognition of the book of Jonah's humorous elements inevitably lead us down a dark, anti-Semitic path? No, not only would this be an unwarranted conclusion, it also would not be doing the text much justice either. It is perhaps not entirely accidental that it is Yehuda Radday, a professor of Jewish Studies, who shows us a better way (p. 27) when he sees as mistaken only the kind of humour that 'is read into the text out of sheer, open and undisguised hostility', pointing out (p. 30) that what is needed to discover biblical humour is empathy – an 'empathy with Jonah *as human being, prophet, and as a member of a people*' that, as Sherwood (2000, p. 118) notes, has long been an 'integral part of Jewish interpretation'.

Jonah as a carnivalesque cartoon

At first glance, Sherwood's reading of Jonah seems to proceed along similar lines when she describes the book (1998, p. 49) as a 'cartoon, an adventure in the fantastic, a series of boldly penned word-pictures ranging from the prophet in the belly of a fish and the divinely ordained belching to the bizarre pageant of repentance at Nineveh and the surrealist tableau of the plant and the worm'. She goes on to note that the actions performed by the characters are frequently driven to excess. YHWH does not just send the storm in chapter 1 but hurls it (טול, *tul*), while the worm in chapter 4 does not nibble at the *qiqayon* but smites it (נכה, *nakhah*). Sherwood comments, 'the reader can almost see the words "pow," "biff" and "arghh" written in large over the text', which 'tips over into a kind of Theatre of the Absurd, in which animals don sackcloth and mourn for their sins, and Jonah sings a psalm in the fish's belly' (pp. 49, 50). So far, so very similar when compared to other humorous or satirical readings, and yet for the reasons outlined above, Sherwood is highly critical of interpretations that portray the book of Jonah as a satire. Over against these, she advocates a Bakhtinian dialogical reading (p. 62), which 'allows a subversive ideology to exist in intimate contact with the orthodox voice' – note how both the subversive and the orthodox voices are given space here – and sees 'the text as a mutually deconstructive and humorous struggle, which is less like a lesson and more like a game'. According to Russian philosopher and literary critic Mikhail Bakhtin (1895–1975) (1984b, p. 12), 'the satirist whose laughter is negative places himself above the object of his mockery, he is opposed to it ... The people's ambivalent laughter, on the other hand, expresses the point of view of the whole world; he who is laughing also belongs to it.'

As the above quote indicates, humour is here being used not negatively, not to put anyone down, but in an inclusive manner, in what McNinch (p. 5) describes as 'an inclusive critique, a laughing "with" the inherent absurdity of the world itself and not "at" a single, exteriorized target'. The point, McNinch goes on to explain, is not to identify any targets at all but for the text to function as 'a kind of literary laboratory in which to test ideas by pushing them to absurd limits'. Applying a Bakhtinian perspective to the book of Jonah, Sherwood believes that the story 'may be playing with and dialogizing God's usually uncompromising word'. The author of Jonah, she suggests (1998, p. 67), is 'creating fantastic stories around biblical texts', which is an allusion to the book's many intertextual references to other Old Testament texts. In practice, this means that the author is 'trying out the principle of universal mercy in the most extreme circumstances, asking a fantastic "What if" – What if Nineveh, the "bloody city" as Nahum puts it, the equivalent of [the] Berlin of the Third Reich, repents?' Sherwood notes (p. 78) that it is precisely the text's oddness that is 'a clue to the subversive, dialogizing role it plays within the prophetic canon'. The book of Jonah, in other words, is interacting critically with the prophetic tradition, a conclusion that has also been reached by Ehud Ben Zvi in his historical approach (see Chapter 2).

Sherwood in this context (p. 63) evokes the notion of carnivalesque literature, another Bakhtinian interest and a form that 'treats all perspectives (the tradition, the counter-tradition, God, Jonah, even the audience) with equal seriousness and equal levity'. In his recent article '"Who knows?" A Bakhtinian reading of carnivalesque motifs in Jonah', McNinch points out (pp. 3–4, 5):

> Seeing Jonah's humor through a carnivalesque lens invites the reader to revel in the dialogic dissonances of the book (rather than search futilely for a single, monologic 'point'), for in carnival fashion, the humor of Jonah counters the seriousness of a seemingly determined world with the liberating laughter of open-ended ambiguity ... that resonates deeply with the open-endedness of human experience.

Whereas monologic readings tend to regard the text as 'sacred and sacrosanct', seeking to suppress 'all rival perspectives', dialogical readings and texts, according to Sherwood, allow all characters to 'develop their positions to "[their] maximal force and depth"' (Sherwood, 2000, pp. 89, 177, referring to Bakhtin, 1984a, p. 69). Exalting in the 'contradictory and double-faced fullness of life' (Bakhtin, 1984b, p. 62), dialogical texts '[toy] with every perspective, every character, without exception' (p. 178). In the case of Jonah, this means that, as Etan Levine has pointed out, the author does not weigh the dialogue in either Jonah's or God's favour.

McNinch goes on to explore three characteristics of carnivalesque literature, the first of which is the *suspension of social hierarchies*. In Bakhtin's words (1984a, p. 123), during carnival 'all distance between people is suspended' as 'carnival brings together, unifies, weds, and combines the sacred with the profane, the lofty with the low, the great with the insignificant, the wise with the stupid'. Carnival thus has a social levelling effect while 'conventions of respect are ignored' (McNinch, p. 6). In Jonah, a Jewish prophet is brought together with gentile sailors, who address him frankly without regard for his social status. The sailors furthermore 'prove to be just as good (or better) at divination than the Israelite prophet' (McNinch, pp. 6–7). In carnival, as again Sherwood points out (1998, p. 63) with respect to the episode involving the great fish, 'vulgar and sacred language mix – in Jonah the language of being sick collides with the language of praise'. There is another erasure of social hierarchies at Nineveh where all society dresses in sackcloth and fasts, 'everyone, great and small' (3.5), with McNinch adding (p. 7) that 'the inclusion of beasts ... is consistent with the carnivalesque style'.

A second characteristic of carnivalistic literature is what McNinch (p. 8) describes as '*decrowning and debasing*', as bringing down the high and mighty and elevating 'the foolish and base'. Jonah is brought down from his elevated position as a divinely appointed prophet, which is emphasized in his continual descent (see our earlier discussion of the use of ירד, *yarad*, 'to go down'). Sherwood similarly notes (1998, p. 63) that 'carnival brings the "high spiritual and abstract" down to earth with a bump', which can be seen also in the abstract idea of 'descent into Sheol' being materialized in the form of Jonah's descent into the belly of the great fish, while the normally metaphorical sea imagery of the Psalms is 'crudely literalised as the prophet complains, "seaweed was wrapped around my head"' (2.6). Significantly, however, and entirely in line with Bakhtin's earlier words about carnivalesque literature offering an inclusive critique, Jonah is not destroyed by the way he is portrayed. His degradation rather 'brings him down ... to a plane where he, like the sailors, like the Ninevites, like all of us, is subject to the vulnerability and possibility of real life'. This brings us to those other human figures, the carnivalesque 'fools', who are 'crowned'. In Jonah, the gentile sailors and the Ninevites are consistently portrayed in a positive light as those who pray to Israel's God (1.14–16), repent of evil and violence (3.8, 10), and speak 'theologically – one might say prophetically – about the ways of God' (McNinch, p. 10).

McNinch's third characteristic is the '*grotesque and hyperbolic*'. According to Bakhtin (1984b, pp. 306–7), 'the interpretation of the grotesque image as purely satirical, that is, negative, is ... radically erroneous' because it completely neglects the text's ambivalence. Is the great fish good news or bad? Is it a penal or a salvific agent? 'Viewed through the dialogic lens of carnivalesque', says McNinch (p. 10), 'the answer is unhesitatingly: both!' And as for the 'constant barrage of hyperbole', which leads McNinch to comment (p. 12) that 'nearly every scene in the book is depicted as an extreme of one sort or another', we have already explored this earlier.

In another characterization of carnival, Bakhtin suggests (1984a, p. 160) that it is:

past millennia's way of sensing the world as one great communal performance. This sense of the world ... with its joy at change and its joyful relativity, is opposed to that one-sided and gloomy official seriousness which is dogmatic and hostile to evolution and change, which seeks to absolutize a given condition of existence or a given social order.

Bakhtin here captures several important aspects, including carnival's communal nature, its expectancy of change, and its 'joyful relativity' or ambivalence – in contrast to what he calls 'gloomy, official, dogmatic seriousness'. He thus captures a similar vibe to what Nigerian novelist Chinua Achebe (1930–2013) expressed in *Anthills of the Savannah* (p. 95) when he speaks of 'a genuine artist' feeling in their blood 'the ultimate enmity between art and orthodoxy'. As McNinch points out (p. 14), carnivalistic humour lays open 'the illusory nature of the rigid, official world', pointing instead to hidden possibilities for renewal or rebirth, saying with the Ninevite king in the story of Jonah, 'Who knows?' (3.9) because anything might happen. McNinch specifically points to carnival's hopeful attitude, expressed in Jonah by both the sailors and the Ninevite king, who are hoping that they might not perish (1.14; 3.9). And he concludes (pp. 14–15):

Jonah wrestles with the theological dissonances of a people whose experience of the world has not conformed to any predictable model. Therefore, the book of Jonah is not making a monologic point. Rather, it is wondering aloud: What if the world is not as simple, ordered and predictable as the prophetic voice often assumes?

For further reflection

1 What do you make of some scholars lamenting that we have largely missed the humour of the Bible – and the reasons given for why we missed it? What do you think of Walker's claim that to miss the humour of Jonah would mean to miss much of the book's essence, joy and meaning? Do you think the story of Jonah is a humorous one? If so, why?

2 What do you think of satirical readings of Jonah? And what about the rebuttals by those who see the story as 'too earnest for laughter' and the laughter itself as too unsympathetic? What about Jonah's potentially explosive challenge to God being silenced and him being presented in an anti-Judaic or anti-Semitic light?

3 What do you think of Sherwood and McNinch's reading of Jonah as a carnivalesque cartoon? In what ways does this differ from satirical readings? What about the story as a playful literary laboratory that tests ideas by pushing them to the limit (for example, God being merciful even to the Ninevites)?

4 And what about carnivalesque humour – and hence the book of Jonah – seeking to offer an inclusive critique, to unify people, to level social hierarchies, to decrown the high and mighty and crown the 'fools', to oppose gloomy, official, dogmatic seriousness with 'joyful relativity', adopting a 'Who knows?' attitude?

Reader-response criticism and the contribution of the reader

We saw earlier that narrative criticism assumes that textual signals guide readers in their making meaning. The focus is on the text rather than the author who plays such an important part in historical readings. But narrative critics, certainly in the early stages, also did not pay much attention to the text's readers, except for the implied reader who is, however, seen as a textual construct. According to narrative criticism, it is from the text that the implied reader emerges, a reader who, for instance, knows the locations of Tarshish and Nineveh and other cultural knowledge assumed by the book of Jonah. This focus on either the author (historical criticism) or the text (narrative criticism) has traditionally gone hand in hand with an underestimation of the importance and contribution of the actual reader, not the one inscribed in the text but the flesh and blood reader who reads the book of Jonah while eating an ice cream or attending a Bible study group.

And yet, in our discussion of satire, we noted Sherwood's claim that the satirical and frequently anti-Judaic or anti-Semitic interpretation of the book of Jonah is prescribed not by the author – nor, we might add, by the text – but by the reader. Readers actualize or perform the text, and their reading depends not only on the words of the text, the signs on the page as it were, but also on their background and personality, on who they are and where and when they live(d). The reception history of any (biblical) text – how that text has been read and understood – demonstrates how considerably its interpretation has varied over time and from one cultural context to the next, or even within cultural contexts depending on the knowledge, interests and world views of the readers. In the case of Jonah, this has been shown especially by Sherwood in *A Biblical Text and Its Afterlives*, which explores how the book and the prophet have fared in 'mainstream' Christian, Jewish, and in popular interpretation, and also by Lena-Sofia Tiemeyer in *Jonah through the Centuries*, which surveys interpretive trends in Jewish, Christian, Muslim and secular readings.

Ben Zvi notes (2003a, p. 130) that 'given the diversity of authorities and their theological, social and political agendas, the number of potential and actual readings of the book of Jonah may well be considered infinite for all practical purposes'. To be sure, he qualifies this by adding (p. 131) that '"infinite" does not mean unconstrained or unlimited', as all readings of Jonah 'share at the very least the fact that they have to relate in one way or another to the text of the book of Jonah'. There is, as we said, the text, and there is the reader, and meaning emerges in a dialogical process involving both text and reader. There is, of course, also the author, but as Canadian poet, novelist and literary critic Margaret Atwood suggests, the 'eternal triangle' of author, text and reader effectively lacks a base; there is no line connecting the author and the reader (see Figure 6). As Atwood puts it (p. 113), speaking of a 'writer' instead of an 'author': 'The writer communicates with the page. The reader also communicates with the page. The writer and the reader communicate only through the page.'

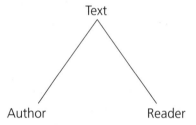

Figure 6 The 'eternal triangle' of author, text and reader.

And readers, as Sherwood and Tiemeyer and many others have shown, evidently read texts in different ways, in different contexts and with different interests and agendas. Realizing this for Jione Havea (2020, loc. 3038) frees the text 'from my control as reader', which, he adds, is 'a humbling confession because it makes me recognize the right of other readers to find and defend other readings, and reminds me that i[17] do not have the final say in determining the meanings and functions of the story'. In biblical studies, there has been a development from author- to text- to reader-centred approaches – although each of these orientations continues to have its advocates – with the latter being promoted by what has come to be known as reader-response criticism. A case could easily be made for this to warrant its own chapter, but as reader-centred approaches are given much space in what follows – this is most evident in Chapter 4 on contextual, liberationist and postcolonial readings, all of which are reader-centred – I will here only briefly sketch some of the conceptual underpinnings of this approach to biblical interpretation.

When we considered narrative criticism, we noted the building blocks of narrative: its plot or story line, the implied author and reader, the ways in which characters are presented, how settings are used in the story, and the impact of repetition. All these for narrative critics are textual phenomena that guide readers in the meaning-making process. However, what we did not consider – although this became increasingly apparent in our discussion of Jonah's genre – is the extent to which readers contribute to the construction of the text. To take just one example, the text clearly has a lot to say about its two main characters, Jonah and God, but what readers have made of their portrayal has varied enormously throughout the text's ancient and modern history and in different parts of the world. Why is that? It is here that some of reader-response criticism's main insights can help us gain more clarity.[18]

While readers approach texts from different perspectives, texts themselves are always underdetermined. One reason for this is the *polysemy* inherent in all language, the fact that words have multiple meanings so that linguistic expressions can never be completely unambiguous. Second, words are signs that represent what is *not* present, and they do this in an incomplete way. The sign, while representing something, at the same time creates a gap, which readers fill in in different ways. If, for instance, I were to talk about an 'elephant', you would immediately form a mental picture of said animal without necessarily realizing that I was thinking of a pink cuddly toy. Of course, the context in which the word 'elephant' appears would eventually help you fill in the gaps, but then that longer, 'more complete' text, what we might call a 'proliferation of signs', features a whole new set of gaps, creating yet further potential for varying interpretations. According to German literary critic Wolfgang Iser (1926–2007), these gaps created by the limited signs on the page call for the active participation of readers in the reading process; they challenge readers to get involved in the creation of the literary work. In the words of Havea (2020, loc. 2573), 'narrative gaps are thresholds that draw readers into the worlds of the text'; and it is in the act of reading that the literary work is created. The full significance of this only emerges once we realize that Iser distinguishes between the text, which itself has no meaning, and the literary work, which only comes into being as something meaningful in the reading process. And so it is, as Atwood notes (p. 44), that 'works of literature are recreated by each generation of readers, who make them new by finding fresh meanings in them'. This again has been amply shown to be true by Sherwood in her study of Jonah's history of interpretation, *A Biblical Text and Its After-lives*. Atwood goes on to illustrate the process of the actualization of the text – or the creation of the literary work in Iser's words – with the well-known analogy of a musical score, which, she says, 'is not itself music, but becomes music when played by musicians, or "interpreted" by them'.

Much has been said by reader-response critics about how reading is affected by a reader's context, but as that would seem to be evident to most readers nowadays – and is anyway illustrated abundantly by the readings of Jonah that follow – it does not require much comment here. One thing to note, however, is American literary theorist Stanley Fish's notion of the *interpretive community*, which briefly put is about readers adopting the conventional strategies of interpretation that are prac-tised and deemed to be acceptable by the community(ies) to which they belong, be it academia or a church community. Fish's theory thus empha-sizes that readers are affected by communal forces and conventions. Of course, as noted earlier, in our global context, which allows us to read the fruits of biblical readers and interpreters across the world, there now exists a global interpretive community alongside any local or regional communities to which we may belong. The dialogical nature of mean-ing-making accordingly now extends to this global context. However, as Louis Jonker (2010, p. 55) has flagged up, it is still all too frequently the case that 'certain perspectives and approaches (or interpretative contexts) are simply regarded as being more valid and important than others' – and these have tended to be the perspectives and approaches developed in Western biblical scholarship in the northern hemisphere. But as Jonker also notes, having understood that meaning is not simply something 'out there' to be read off the page but emerges in the reader's engagement with the text and their dialogical interaction with other readers, we are now in a better position to recognize and address the issue of the dominance or interpretive power of some readers over others.

Another concept worth highlighting is the notion of meaning as an event in time. As readers, we are never dealing with the whole text at once but are engaging with it bit by bit in what effectively is a series of events following one another in rapid succession. And what moves in this reading process is not so much the text but the reader, in that the reader's ideas and expectations change from one moment to the next. As we are negotiating our way through the different parts of the text, aiming to arrive at a meaningful whole, we are always looking both back and ahead. We are constantly orienting and reorienting ourselves, constantly assigning and reassigning meaning as in the example of that elephant, which turned out to be a cuddly toy.

Reader-response criticism has also devoted much energy to the characterization of the reader. While narrative criticism speaks of the implied reader, other concepts that have been put forward include the *ideal* reader (Booth), the ideal recipient of the text who is only *partially* inscribed 'in the text' and is constructed differently by different readers. For Iser, the implied reader takes shape only in the reading process and is located not *in* the text but *between* the text and the reader. Reader-response critics have also reflected on the varying competencies of readers, noting for instance that mere knowledge of the alphabet, grammar and semantics (the meaning of words) does not necessarily make a 'good reader'. Even in our mother tongue, we may be unable to fully understand certain texts, and two people sharing a language may read the same text with vastly differing degrees of insight: to one it means very little, while the other discovers an endless world of meaning and significance. However, we can work on coming close(r) to being a text's 'ideal' reader. When, for instance, Jonah says, 'That is why I fled to Tarshish at the beginning; for I knew that you are a gracious God and merciful, slow to anger, and abounding in steadfast love, and ready to relent from punishing' (4.2), the ideal reader would note straightaway that Jonah is quoting one of Israel's ancient 'creeds' (see Exod. 34.6–7). Indeed, that reader might also realize that the prophet Joel, encouraging the people to return to God, was using the very same creed when reminding them of Yahweh's grace and mercy (Joel 2.13). All of which makes the statement quite ironic in Jonah's mouth, given that the prophet perceives these celebrated divine properties as problematic.

Intertextual allusions are an area that tests a reader's competence like nothing else. *The Name of the Rose*, a novel by Italian philosopher, semiotician and novelist Umberto Eco (1932–2016), features a scene in which one of the monks makes love to a girl from the village, but what makes that scene so special to the informed reader is that it is written in language deriving from the Song of Songs; this is something that could not be captured in a film such as Jean-Jacques Annaud's 1986 thriller of the same name, but adds an additional dimension to the reading of the text. An even more extreme example is Eco's *Foucault's Pendulum*, which has been characterized as a work in which 'textual interactions ... are to be met at every step' (Juvan, p. 3), much as in the book of Jonah, as we noted in our exploration of Jonah as satire. Such allusions raise the question of readerly competence. Can readers understand the text if they fail to recognize the allusions? How much of the text's intertextual dimension must readers be able to grasp to perform a competent reading? As Slovenian literary critic Marko Juvan notes, Eco concluded that reading on the intertextual level enriches readers' engagement with the work, while 'the text also offers pleasure to a naïve "semantic reader" whose poorer encyclopedic knowledge does not allow her to recognize sophisticated citational items'. All of which, again, is true for a reader's engagement with the book of Jonah.

Coming back to the concept of the ideal reader, we should note that the American literary critic Jonathan Culler has questioned its usefulness, partly because it is a theoretical construct that can never be actualized, as no actual reader can ever be a text's ideal reader (Culler, 2002). Eco, in his novel *The Island of the Day Before*, plays with the notion of the ideal reader in an extraordinarily sophisticated text that at times defeats virtually any real reader. To quote a not entirely random example: 'Father Caspar describes it as a "Sphynx Mystagoga, an Oedipus Aegyptiacus, a Monad Ieroglyphica, a Clavis Convenientia Linguarum, a Theatrum Cosmographicum Historicum, a Sylva Sylvarum"' (Eco, 1996, p. 309) – and so the text continues for a few more lines. But the term 'ideal reader' also suggests that certain readings are better than others, which raises the question as to what it is that makes them 'better'. What about the readings we are going to meet in the following chapters? Which of them are 'better', and for what reasons? Culler prefers to speak of a 'competent reader', which allows for the possibility of different readings being equally competent, while Fish favours the term 'informed reader'. While some readers may be more informed than others, this does not mean that they necessarily achieve 'better' readings. What all these terms – 'ideal', 'informed' or 'competent' reader – do indicate, however, is that our readings are limited and that we never manage to actualize a text's full potential so that there is always room for us to grow, learn and develop in relation to any text and hence also the book of Jonah. And such learning, growth and development happen not least by engaging with the interpretations of other readers.

For further reflection

1 How do you understand the contribution of the reader to the meaning of a text? What do you make of the fact that the interpretation of a text such as Jonah has varied greatly over time, from one cultural context to another, and even within the same cultural contexts? And what about Havea's point concerning the right of other readers to find other meanings in the text?

2 What do you make of notions such as polysemy and the gaps in words/signs, and the readers' involvement in filling them?

3 What about interpretive communities and their influence on how readers read? What might be the advantages and/or disadvantages of that influence upon readers?

4 And what about reading as an event or a series of events in time, of the reader's ideas and expectations changing from one moment to the next?

5 Finally, what do you make of the notion of ideal, competent and informed readers? How might we go about developing our readerly competence? What might be the benefits of this?

4

Jonah's Challenge:
Contextual, Liberationist and
Postcolonial Interpretation

The historical-critical approaches to the Bible that emerged in the wake of the Enlightenment were striving for objectivity, for readers to leave their (dogmatic) prejudices behind and approach the text without bias. Philip Davies (pp. 11–14) in this context distinguishes between approaches that operate 'inside the canon', reading the biblical literature as 'scripture', and those operating 'outside the canon', which adopt the values of the 'critical observer'. It is precisely this kind of attitude that led George Aichele and colleagues (pp. 176–7) to note that 'during the era of objectivist scholarship, issues of theology and faith have been banned from critical biblical studies'. Liberationist readings, by contrast, do not believe in any pretence of objectivity. Exemplifying an ideological approach to interpretation, they read the biblical texts from a specific social location and with clearly defined and openly stated interests in mind, based on the understanding that objectivity in textual interpretation is either a false claim or an unfortunate delusion. As for the 'outside the canon' principle, liberationist approaches to biblical interpretation value the perspectives of the poor and the uneducated, who interpret the texts within the context of the church. Indeed, they see in them a modern manifestation of the type of faith community that produced the biblical writings in the first place. The readings we are going to explore in this chapter, therefore, are contextual, interested readings that approach the book of Jonah with usually very clearly defined aims and perspectives.

In what follows, we are going to make an essentially arbitrary distinction between contextual, liberationist and postcolonial readings. It is arbitrary in that a specific reading may be contextual, liberationist and postcolonial all at the same time. There will, therefore, be some inevitable overlap in our discussion. However, the distinction is important for heuristic reasons as it allows us to explore three separate issues – that is, that certain readings are:

- Self-confessedly and deliberately *contextual*, approaching the text from a clearly defined social location.
- An expression of a *liberationist* theology that seeks to offer biblical readings that are conducive to the liberation of its intended readership.
- *Postcolonial* in that they view the biblical literature from within an imperialist or (post)colonialist framework.

Contextual biblical hermeneutics

Vincent Wimbush (1989, p. 44) notes that 'every "reading" is, and must always be recognized as, culture-specific', while Jione Havea (2021a, p. 18) emphasizes that 'context is more than geography and location; ideas and biases are contexts as well ... contexts shape how we interpret texts, how some texts are *not interpreted*, and why some texts are *not even read*'. Of course, none of this is to say that the interpreter's cultural location and faith or other ideological commitments necessarily blind them to the biblical text's own perspective. Indeed, for Wimbush, what he calls 'historical and cultural criticism' are essential in that they can 'aid minority, culturalist readings of the Bible to stand with integrity against alien imperialistic readings' (p. 43). In other words, it is precisely by engaging critically with the biblical text that minority readings are enabled to enquire into the text's meaning and thus to question whatever imperialistic readings may have been imposed upon them.

As Jonathan Culler once said (1982, p. 128), 'meaning is context-bound but context is boundless'. We are dealing therefore – at least theoretically – with a boundless cornucopia of contextual readings. And yet in practice we can only consider a few selected examples, beginning with African or Afrocentric biblical interpretation.[1]

African or Afrocentric biblical interpretation

While Franziska Andrag-Meyer and Elna Mouton speak of 'African hermeneutics', Randall Bailey (2003) and Cain Hope Felder (2004), adopting Molefi Asante's notion of Afrocentricity, prefer the term 'Afrocentric biblical interpretation'. Felder (2004, p. 297) explains:

Afrocentricity is the concept that Africa and persons of African descent must be understood as making significant contributions to world civilization as proactive subjects within history, rather than being regarded as mere passive objects in the course of history. Afrocentrism requires reconceptualizing Africa as a center of value and a source of pride.

The phrase 'of African descent' is important here, as most of the contributors to the volume edited by Bailey are residents of the United States, who 'speak to the existential reality of being Black' in their North American context (Bailey, p. 2). Addressing the issue of biblical interpretation, Felder emphasizes the need for scholars and readers of the Bible to recognize the significant roles played in biblical history and literature by 'Africa, its people, nations, and cultures'.[2] He laments (2004, p. 301) that across the world biblical characters are perceived as white and 'somehow typical Europeans', and that the impression has been given that 'Europeans magically populated the entire region of ancient Palestine, rendering its inhabitants White'. Suggesting that the biblical writers, in common with Greek and Roman authors, had no notion of colour prejudice, Felder (p. 299) traces the recasting of 'the Bible into a religious saga of European-type people' to the period between the end of the fourth century and the time of the Enlightenment. A key factor in this was medieval and Renaissance art, which depicted biblical characters as contemporary Europeans. Indeed, so influential has this been that, as Felder points out, 'even Blacks portray biblical characters within their churches as totally unlike themselves'.

At least as disconcertingly, the Bible has frequently been used to denigrate and oppose African culture and religion. To mention only one example, the impact of Christianity and European colonialism upon Igbo culture in Nigeria has been eloquently explored by Chinua Achebe in several novels and short stories, including *Girls at War and Other Stories*, *No Longer at Ease* and *Things Fall Apart*, all exemplifying Salman Rushdie's notion of 'the empire writes back' (Jaggi, p. xi; Achebe, 2003, p. 75).[3] And when, for instance, black South Africans eventually did embrace the Bible, they often found 'their white South African brothers and sisters using the Bible against them in the guise of apartheid'. Thus Andrag-Meyer and Mouton (p. 207), who maintain that all African biblical hermeneutics needs to be understood against this postcolonial background, while Gerald West (p. 727) speaks of biblical scholarship as a useful resource for 'emancipatory work with particular communities of the poor and marginalised in African contexts'.

Andrag-Meyer and Mouton (p. 207) go on to say that 'the dominant strand in African biblical hermeneutics', therefore, 'is to use the Bible to reclaim what missionary and colonial forces have denigrated and destroyed' (see also West, p. 725). The Bible itself, however, has been perceived as a double-edged sword in that context. Some African scholars, such as Itumeleng Mosala and Tinyiko Maluleke, have highlighted the Bible's problematic legacy, while Lamin Sanneh and Kwame Bediako see it as an important tool and ally when it comes to repairing the damage done by colonialism. Given these perspectives, Andrag-Meyer and Mouton (p. 208) suggest that, in the eyes of indigenous peoples, the Bible was initially not so much simply a text as 'an object with power'. As Wimbush (1989, p. 45) notes:

> The point that the white slave-holding ... nation was conceptually wrapping itself in the 'Holy Book,' defining itself by 'the Book,' acknowledging its source of power (including imperialistic and racist hegemony) in 'the Book,' was not lost on the Africans. It did not take the Africans long to associate 'Book Religion' with power, with survival.

These dynamics have been captured rather powerfully in a painting by English painter Thomas Jones Barker (1813–82) depicting Queen Victoria presenting a Bible to a genuflecting African king. This painting features the telling and not inaccurate title 'The Secret of England's Greatness'.[4]

Hermeneutical repair work was undertaken by historical and sociological approaches. As Eric Anum has pointed out (p. 468), responding to 'missionaries who believed that African cultures were satanic and pagan', some African biblical scholars have been keen to 'identify similarities between the biblical world and African religio-cultural practices'. However, that is not to say that the dialogue between biblical text and contemporary African context would have been an uncritical one. As again Andrag-Meyer and Mouton note (p. 219): 'The text can and does have a voice over against the African context, critiquing and judging it. But the text also confirms and affirms the African context ... the African context does, occasionally ... critique the biblical text, declaring it to be inherently damaging to African interests.'

Unsurprisingly, biblical themes of liberation and/or reconstruction have proved to be particularly popular and helpful to African theologians. And just as Latin American liberation theologians have stressed the importance of the 'exegesis of the poor', Andrag-Meyer and Mouton highlight the role of ordinary African Bible readers, noting that they 'partially constitute African biblical scholarship' (p. 212). What that means is that 'the resources of the people's culture and historical life experience are used as complementary to conventional critical tools of biblical exegesis' (p. 213). Interestingly, the translation of the Bible into the vernacular, which itself already constitutes an affirmation of African culture, led to the adoption of indigenous criteria for its message; it led to what Andrag-Meyer and Mouton (p. 218) describe as 'a piece of radical indigenization'.

Of course, in speaking of 'Africa' and 'Afrocentricity', we have been guilty of perpetuating what Osayande Hendricks (p. 86) calls 'a mythical monolithic cultural construct called "Africa"', thereby:

> denying many peoples the grandeur of their own specificity, the wonder of their own sojourn, the rooty of they own tooty, and so on. *Guerrilla exegesis*[5] asks 'how can a white supremacist construct that disses and dismisses the political social economic ideological cultural meteorological topographical geographical particularity of diverse peoples of diverse circumstances, a rainbow of folk in a land mass three times the size of Europe; how can this historiographic equivalent of the insulting supremacist mode of address "you people" serve *our* needs?'[6]

For further reflection

1 What do you make of the notion of the Bible as 'an object with power' in the hands of missionaries and colonial forces?
2 What about the concept of identifying 'similarities between the biblical world and African religio-cultural practices'? Why might this be helpful?
3 One of liberationist criticism's key insights concerns the involvement of 'poor' and non-academic readers in the practice of biblical interpretation. Which groups of people might make a difference to how you read the Bible in your church community?

Reading Jonah from an African perspective

Andrag-Meyer and Mouton (pp. 215–18) sketch the contours of *one* African reading of Jonah. They note that African scholars have often seen the book as a text about mission, and that it was primarily for that reason that missionaries were keen for the text to be translated into the vernacular. But Jonah is also a book with which many African readers have an affinity, as it 'mirrors, in a mainly non-condemnatory way, elements of the African world-view' (p. 216). Examples include:

- The wind and sea acting as God's agents.
- God's message, like those of tribal gods or ancestors, not always being entirely clear, thus calling for an interpretation.

- The simple acknowledgement that different people worship different gods and that, in contrast to white missionaries but in line with traditional African custom, they show respect for the gods of others.
- The centrality of herds and flocks (3.7–8; 4.11).
- God's mercy being extended to the Ninevite 'herdsmen', which leads Andrag-Meyer and Mouton to comment (p. 217) that 'all African Christians would rejoice that God is merciful to such people'.

Elaborating on the incidents in Jonah 1, they furthermore point out (pp. 216–17):

> Here is a god of power that must be properly acknowledged by sacrifice and vows. For most Africans this makes perfect sense, and remains an important part of their lives, even if they are Christians (and even if they do their sacrifices 'by night') ... what is remarkable about this first chapter of Jonah is that there is no condemnation whatsoever of people worshipping different gods and of offering sacrifices to more than one god.

An element of tension does, however, arise when we get to Jonah's psalm where the prophet condemns those who worship 'vain idols' (2.8). Of course, as we saw earlier, there are questions as to how Jonah's prayer is best read, with some even suggesting that it is precisely his sickly sweet piety, including perhaps his condescending and condemnatory attitude towards the sailors, that leads to the prophet's sudden expulsion from the fish in a heap of vomit. Apart from this, Andrag-Meyer and Mouton (p. 218) see in the storyteller's non-condemnatory portrayal of the sailors a 'wonderful message ... for our African continent which is wracked by ethnic intolerance and conflict', suggesting that 'perhaps the most significant contribution of the book of Jonah to the recovery of African culture is its very strong anti-xenophobic stance'. However, they also note (p. 217) that:

> the tension in Jonah between the universalistic narrator and the more parochial perspective of Jonah himself would find resonances among many African Christians who find themselves torn between a respect for their inherited traditions and the legacy of the post-missionary missiological imperative to reject indigenous practices.

Cossi Ahoga's short commentary in the *Africa Bible Commentary* illustrates how local customs or sayings can enrich the engagement with the text. Commenting, for instance, on Jonah's flight, Ahoga, who is Beninese, writes (p. 2781) that the prophet 'was hoping to escape from God, but forgot that, as the African proverb says, "there is nowhere on earth where the wind does not blow"'. Reflecting on the question as to whether the story presents a true historical incident or is best read as 'a fable intended to convey a message to the Jews', Ahoga maintains (p. 2783):

> There is no point in giving a detailed account of the different positions, for all spring from a mindset and an approach to literature that is at odds with the African oral tradition that gives precedence to the spiritual significance of events and sees the Creator revealing himself through the relationship between humans and nature. Thus Africans have no problem with the intervention of an animal ... and are far more interested in Jonah's reaction to his experience, as expressed in his prayer.

Turning to Jonah's prayer from the belly of the fish, Ahoga notes that we can call on God from anywhere. 'Nor', he adds, 'do we need to take our troubles to diviners and magicians, as many Africans do.' As for the fact that Jonah cannot avoid his Ninevite mission, he wryly comments (p. 2784) that 'God's command will be carried out whatever happens, as is clear from 3.1–3, for "okra cannot grow bigger than the one who plants it".' Reflecting on the business of the plant and the worm, Ahoga says (p. 2788): 'God then chose to teach Jonah using an object lesson, a common technique in African stories.'

For further reflection

1 What do you make of those aspects of the text highlighted by Andrag-Meyer and Mouton as being particularly appealing to African readers?
2 Specifically, what do you think about the non-condemnatory way in which Jonah's narrator portrays the sailors' worship of other gods?
3 How would you characterize Ahoga's approach to Jonah?

Asian biblical interpretation

Having considered some African or Afrocentric readings, we now turn to Asian approaches to biblical interpretation, our second example of global hermeneutics. Given the tremendous racial, cultural and religious diversity that characterizes the Asian continent, it goes without saying that there is no uniform Asian method of biblical interpretation. Instead, Asian approaches have creatively applied the Bible to their varied and distinctive cultural settings. Having observed how the Bible has frequently been used as a tool of domination, some Asian theologians and biblical scholars have been at pains to stress that it is essential to 'avoid superimposing a European framework on the development of Asian hermeneutics, which must remain rooted in its own specific cultural context' (Kwok, 1995, p. 39). Indeed, Taiwanese scholar C. S. Song urged Asian Christians to develop theological reflection that expresses a direct Asian relationship to God's redemption, thus bypassing Western Christianity altogether. In line with this, Kwok Pui Lan (1989, p. 25) has called for biblical reinterpretation conceived as a 'creative act of dialogical imagination'. The critical hermeneutical principle for her does not lie in the Bible but 'in the community of women and men who ... through their dialogical imagination appropriate it for their own liberation' (p. 37). More specifically, this means that Asia's poor, women and other marginalized groups are wanting to know whether the Bible can help them in their struggle for liberation. Biblical interpretation in Asia, Kwok points out (p. 30), 'must create a two-way traffic between our own tradition and that of the Bible'. She adds (p. 29): 'Chinese philosophical tradition ... is more concerned with the moral and ethical visions of a good society ... most Chinese ... can only judge the meaningfulness of the biblical tradition by looking at how it is acted out in the Christian community.'

One of the key issues for Kwok, therefore, is how Chinese Christians might 'hear God speaking in a different voice – one other than Hebrew, Greek, German or English' (p. 25). In the background here lies the problem that the Bible has frequently been used to emphasize 'a basic deficiency in the "heathen" [Asian] culture' (p. 27), and thus to demonstrate that Western culture is both the norm and superior.[7] In connection with this, Kwok notes (p. 36) that Chinese Christians find it difficult to accept a scriptural canon that excludes their own great cultural teachings and traditions. Indeed, she adds (p. 35) that 'once we recognise the Bible is one system of language to designate the "sacred," we should be able to see that the whole biblical text represents one form of human construction to talk about God.' In this context, Kwok also cautions (p. 30):

Our fellow Asians who have other faiths must not be considered our missiological objects, but as dialogical partners in our ongoing search for truth. This can only be done when each one of us takes seriously the Asian reality, the suffering and aspirations of the Asian people, so that we can share our religious insights to build a better society.

It is impossible to speak about Asian biblical interpretation without mentioning minjung theology, which, as Jeffrey Kuan says (p. 306), 'emerged as a theological voice of Korean Christians in their struggle for democracy and human rights'. The term 'minjung' refers to 'the masses' or 'the people', those who are oppressed politically, exploited economically, marginalized sociologically, despised culturally, and condemned religiously. As Kwok (1989, p. 33) points out, 'Minjung is a very dynamic concept: it can refer to women who are politically dominated by men, or to an ethnic group ruled by another group, or to a race when it is ruled by another powerful race.' Especially well known is the work of Cyris Moon who, in his book *Korean Minjung Theology*, sought to bring the social biography of the Hebrew people and the Korean minjung story into dialogue with each other. Commenting on Moon's work, Kwok (1989, p. 34) regards social biography as 'a promising hermeneutical tool because it reads history from the underside and, therefore, invites us to read the Bible from the underside as well'.

For further reflection

1 Asia's poor, women, and other marginalized groups want to know whether the Bible can help them in their struggle for liberation. What does this mean? How is liberation understood here? Can the Bible help?
2 What does it mean for God to speak in a voice other than Hebrew, Greek, German or English – in other words, what is the point behind that notion?
3 What do you make of the Bible being only one system of language to designate the sacred?

Reading Jonah from a Taiwanese perspective

Chen Nan Jou, Professor of Christian Ethics and Director of the Center of the Programs of Indigenous Theology and Mission, in his essay on Jonah in the *Global Bible Commentary*, focuses on the interfaith context in which Taiwanese Christians find themselves. His concern is that 'influenced by old missionary fundamentalist evangelical thoughts, many Taiwanese Christians tend to think that there is nothing of value in non-Christian religions'. Arguing from a creation-theological perspective, Chen maintains:

> If God is the God who created the heaven and the earth, the God who rules the world, and the God who is the Lord of history, God must have been with us in Taiwan from the beginning, before the arrival of the Christian missionaries ... The history and the cultures of Taiwan must possess traces of God. They must possess theological significance and relevance.

The book of Jonah, written to contrast the xenophobic attitude found in the books of Ezra and Nehemiah, has something to say about this, Chen believes. Commenting on God's question addressed to the prophet, 'Is it right for you to be angry?' (4.4, 9), he suggests that 'the storyteller asks people who are not pleased about God's compassion and concern for the followers of other religions, "Is it right for you to be angry?"' Noting furthermore that non-Jews, the sailors and the Ninevites, are 'depicted as devout, religious people', he adds that while pious people are not necessarily righteous before God:

> acknowledging people's piety and the merits of other religions is a necessary attitude for relating to followers of other religions. If we envision other cultures and religions from the perspective of creation, we might recognize that they also manifest God's mercy and love in familiar ways.

Chen believes that 'the storyteller wants all hearers/readers to know that God's mercy and love transcend the boundary of ethnicity and religion, and to respond to this merciful and loving God.' He urges that 'we *must* be aware that God's mercy and love extend to all', before concluding that:

> Following the teaching of the book of Jonah, Christians should participate in God's mission not because they think that they hold all the truth

and that all other religions are evil, but because they have experienced God's compassion and salvation for all. Bringing this good news to other people does not involve denying their culture and religion, and thus their identity. Rather it involves appreciating the merits of other religions and acknowledging what God has done among their followers before they ever heard about the gospel.

For further reflection

1 Do you agree with Chen that 'God must have been with us in Taiwan from the beginning'? Do you agree that Taiwan's history and cultures 'must possess traces of God', 'theological significance and relevance'? What does this mean?
2 Do you agree that 'If we envision other cultures and religions from the perspective of creation, we might recognize that they also manifest God's mercy and love in familiar ways'?

Islander criticism, or reading islandly

Our third example of contextual interpretation is least well known in Western biblical interpretation, despite the highly prolific efforts of Havea, whose work is particularly interesting for our purposes, as he has written not only on islander criticism and theology[8] but also on the interpretation of the book of Jonah from several perspectives. Our focus here is on his articles on 'Engaging scriptures from Oceania' (2014a), 'Reading islandly' (2014b), and 'Islander criticism' (2018a). But to begin with we might note a more general point made by Havea in connection with the interpretation of Jonah. Employing the traditional Samoan storytelling concept of *su'ifefiloi*, which denotes the weaving together of different flowers and leaves or analogically of different stories or perspectives – it has been used, for instance, by Sia Figiel in her novel *Where We Once Belonged* – Havea notes (2018b, pp. 43, 44) that this 'provides an opportunity to read the ... narrative in the interests of different, including minoritized, characters'. Elsewhere, he says (2021a, p. 12): 'i read *for* minoritized subjects and *against* cultures of minoritization in Scripture, in society and in biblical scholarship'. And he points out (2018b, p. 43) that 'the Jonah narrative reads differently when read in the interest of the sailors, in the interest of the moana/sea, or in the interest of the people of Nineveh'. Reading with the sailors and the people of Nineveh, for instance, encourages us 'to sympathize with the working class and their duty of care, with the vulnerability of travelers and migrants ... to love foreigners and the people for whom one does not usually care' (p. 44).

As for contextual reading, Havea observes (2014a, p. 9) that this is usually associated with 'minority cultures and subalterned races and classes' only to emphasize that no reader and no reading is 'context-free' (see also Jonker, 2010, p. 49). Every interpretation is 'contexted' but 'not all contexts receive the attention of biblical scholars' (p. 10). While some readings, especially those from white, male interpreters in Western academia, have claimed to be of universal significance, 'native and indigenous voices are pushed to the contextual corner' (p. 11). Indeed, Havea (2014b, p. 90) speaks of a tendency among biblical critics to 'privilege the ways of white men but look down on indigenous and native ways', with the former being associated with civilization and the latter 'demonized as backward, pagan, and defiling'. He characterizes these Western influences as what he calls 'Westoxification' (p. 77), pointing out that this has led to islander criticism being suffused with 'heavy doses of contextual, liberation, and postcolonial moves'. Havea notes (2018a, p. 7) that one of the key challenges for minoritized peoples such as islanders is a feeling of inferiority, instilled by Western myths of superiority, which 'tame the mind and break the soul'. He identifies protest as an 'opportunity for minoritized people to shout their voices into the silences of the inferiority complex and into the halls of power' (p. 8) but also speaks of the challenge of 'getting the masters to hear, to be engaged, and to be accountable'.

Havea's comments on native and indigenous voices being pushed to the contextual corner chime with concerns expressed by those who have reflected on reading the Bible in today's global village. Justin Ukpong, for instance, notes (p. 35) that this is made impossible while non-Western biblical scholarship is still 'consigned to the margin of biblical scholarship'. Knut Holter (pp. 87–8) takes issue with the phrase 'voices from the margins' being applied to 'alternative or resistant interpretative strategies' by 'mainstream' guilds of biblical interpretation, arguing that those voices articulate 'central interpretative concerns'. Others have embraced their minority position as one that provides unique perspectives and opportunities. This was famously expressed in *Voices from the Margin*, a volume of articles on interpreting the Bible in the two-thirds world, edited by R. S. Sugirtharajah and first published in 1991 and reissued in revised form in 1995 and 2006, before being rereleased as a 25th anniversary edition in 2016. Havea himself (2012, p. 178) suggests that minority biblical criticism is well placed to be 'attentive to processes of minoritization that are based on race and color'. Randall Bailey, Tat-siong Benny Liew and Fernando Segovia, in another important volume on minority biblical criticism, see its importance in demonstrating that from the margins, the periphery, or the boundary emerges the possibility of radical newness (Bailey, Liew and Segovia, p. 7).

Coming back to Havea's islander reading, it is worth noting that one of its exciting features is his creativity in approaching the texts from a range of often very fresh perspectives. For him (2014b, p. 80), texts are 'open for fishing'; they are 'deep and fluid'. In his article 'Reading islandly', he connects this with the notion of orality, which characterizes islander storytelling and foregrounds values and practices that have typically been missing from Western interpretation. Orality, as Havea emphasizes (pp. 86–7), is 'about presence, relationships, and fluidity. One cannot be oral without being present(ed) – without being in relationships, which requires reciprocity – and without being fluid (flexible)'. He elaborates (p. 87):

> Orality requires presence and at once pushes subjects to cross over boundaries. You accompany your words, but your words take you beyond where you are … orality makes you present in a specific space in an event in which you cross into the space of others. They, in return, are drawn by your words into your space. When the presence and border-crossing aspects of orality are seriously taken into account, the hierarchical (power) axis in relationships is lowered.

This again connects with the concerns of scholars who have been reflecting on global interpretation. As Louis Jonker notes (2010, p. 50), the problem does not lie in the diversity of interpretations or the range of approaches but in 'the power plays that we keep alive in our hermeneutical endeavours'. Elsewhere, Havea too had focused on this (2012, p. 178), characterizing biblical interpretation as 'a field in which many interests and powers exercise and jostle, establish and empower, draw lines and exclude, resist and subvert, reconsider and repress, and more'. His effort to reorient 'ways of reading toward being relational, reciprocal, and fluid' (2014b, p. 88) takes on special significance against that kind of context. Jonker (2010, p. 55) similarly longs for 'communality' rather than for interpretation to follow 'agendas of control and influence'.

For further reflection

1 What do you make of Havea's concept of reading the Jonah story from the perspective of minoritized characters such as the sailors or the people of Nineveh? What difference might this make?

2 And what about the notion of Westoxification? How does Havea characterize this, and what does it say about how we read the Bible?

3 What do you make of native and indigenous readings being marginalized in the global village? What can we do to become more inclusive in our reading of the Bible? Should that be of concern to us?

4 Finally, what about power plays in biblical interpretation? Have you come across this? How can we ensure our practice of biblical interpretation is relational, reciprocal and fluid? Why might fluidity be important in this context?

Reading Jonah from a Tongan perspective

An intriguing example of an islander reading has been provided by Nāsili Vaka'uta. As an islander from Tonga, Vaka'uta is especially interested in the depiction of the ocean space, the *moana*, in Jonah 1. *Moana* for him is home, it defines his identity, it is a source of food, it links the islands, it is 'an accommodating space ... of difference', and it is vast, in marked contrast to 'the continental (or land-based) view of islands as small, peripheral, and insignificant' (p. 128). All this leads him to reject the construction of *moana* in Jonah 1 'as a destructive force, an instrument of God's wrath'. Vaka'uta instead focuses on the opportunities that the sea affords (p. 129), noting that:

> the ocean offers a different space of encounter. Boarding the Tarshish-destined ship, Jonah has the company of people who were different from him in terms of faith, and perhaps culture. The sea serves as a multi-religious (and multicultural) space. Whereas in-land Yhwh demands conformity and conversion, everyone at sea worships his own god.

The ocean thus 'links and connects' rather than just being an instrument of God's wrath. As Vaka'uta underlines, 'a *moana* reading focuses on the connections and links that the ocean allows'. Another feature attracting his interest is Jonah's request to be cast into the sea, which leads Vaka'uta to comment (p. 129) that 'like an islander, [Jonah] prefers to make the ocean, the *moana*, his home'. Indeed, he adds that while the narrator is keen to 'take Jonah on to dry land, out of the *moana*, toward Nineveh ... as an islander, [he] would rather remain in the ocean – the place where difference is accommodated, and freedom is not compromised'.

Liberationist readings

Liberation theologies have played an important role in many parts of the world. Some of the better-known examples include Latin American, Asian (Dalit[9] in India, minjung in South Korea), *mujerista*,[10] African American, South African, feminist, womanist,[11] and gay and lesbian theologies. Reflecting perspectives concerned with issues such as class, gender, sex, race and ethnicity, these 'readings from below' interpret the biblical texts out of their own concrete political, economic and social circumstances. This makes for great diversity among liberationist readings, as each reflects their proponents' unique historical context. Indeed, these 'interested' readings, as Barbara Green points out (p. 102), 'allow some who would not have been welcome at the interpretation table to take their place there, to have their opportunity to interpret from their stance, skill, and experience'. Liberationist readings push against the boundaries of the text, asking questions that challenge the given social order by questioning its dominant myths, values and practices. Liberationist readers tend to state their political purpose up front. Yet while other types of biblical criticism may refrain from doing so, liberationist critics maintain that all readings are ideological, including those that seek to maintain the status quo.

Tina Pippin (p. 169) reflects on the need for liberationist and contextual readings in connection with 'the white supremacy of biblical textbooks'. As she points out (p. 170):

The dominant, normative voice in these introductory textbooks remains the historical-critical method as performed by predominantly Anglo-European males. Even though I continue to supplement these dominant voices with various critical voices from African American biblical hermeneuts, feminists, womanists, postcolonials, and popular culture, I spend way too much time on 'the basics,' with all the other material representing the marginal voices ... The few introductory textbooks that do let in other voices tend to control the (white) space in various ways that nonetheless continue to privilege white, male voices.

Writing in the aftermath of George Floyd and the Black Lives Matter demonstrations, some brief comments on whiteness, white privilege and white supremacy would appear to be pertinent. Educational theorist Peter McLaren (p. 66) defines whiteness as 'a sociohistorical form of consciousness, given birth at the nexus of capitalism, colonial rule, and the emergent relationships among dominant and subordinate groups'. Rather more trenchantly, he goes on to say: 'Whiteness is also a refusal to acknowledge how white people are implicated in certain social relations of privilege and relations of domination and subordination.' Michael Hardt and Antonio Negri, for their part (p. 194), focus on the notion of white supremacy, which, they point out, functions 'through first engaging alterity and then subordinating differences according to degrees of deviance from whiteness'. Whiteness, in other words, functions as the norm against which everything else is judged or measured and established as deviant or deficient. Focusing on people's lived experience, Norman Gottwald (2003, p. 181) is somewhat ironically but perfectly reasonably concerned about a different kind of superiority. He is worried about the 'asymmetrical relationship in which black scholars know white culture(s) experientially in a way that white scholars by and large do not know black culture(s) experientially'.

Widening out her concerns and moving beyond issues of race and skin colour, Pippin emphasizes (p. 174) that academia is 'certainly not a democratic space', which raises the question to what extent this is true of the church and of theological education undertaken within its context.[12] What we are doing here – biblical hermeneutics or interpretation – Pippin regards as a political act. As she points out (p. 175): 'I believe, with bell hooks, that all the spaces we inhabit are political spaces and that our academic languages are highly politicized ways of keeping or challenging privilege or power.' American author, feminist and social activist bell hooks (1952–2021) described all human language as 'a place of struggle' (p. 145), while Pippin notes (p. 175) that, for instance, the academic language employed in Afrocentric biblical interpretation is specifically involved in the struggle 'to remember and create spaces of resistance'. Biblical language and biblical texts can help in that struggle, but surveying the contributions to *Yet with a Steady Beat*, a collection of articles on US Afrocentric biblical interpretation, Gottwald (2003, p. 178) reflects on 'the near unanimity with which they caution against assuming that the Bible is uniformly and reliably supportive of liberation'. For that reason, 'a hermeneutic of suspicion toward the biblical text has steadily grown in black theology', which has led to the Bible being 'sharply interrogated and evaluated in terms of criteria for liberation formulated out of black experience'.

Indeed, as has now long been recognized, 'not even all "liberation" theologies ... are liberating for all peoples' (Wimbush, 1989, p. 43). In an article entitled 'Canaanites, cowboys, and Indians', Robert Warrior reads the biblical exodus and conquest stories from the perspective of the Canaanites, the indigenous people conquered and subjugated by the Israelites. As an Osage Indian, Warrior provides a Native American liberationist interpretation grounded in a different experience from the 'normative' liberationist readings of the exodus story. This supposedly liberating text, he notes, is not nearly as hospitable to the Canaanites, whose language, culture, religion and heritage are presented as the negative 'other', as foreign and dangerous, as something to be avoided at all costs. Coupled with the notion of being chosen, these Old Testament narratives provided European settlers with a biblical warrant for the destruction of indigenous peoples. The ideology of one liberationist reading has thus paradoxically become the dominant ideology against which another liberationist reading reacts. Indeed, Warrior concludes (p. 289): 'As long as people believe in the Yahweh of deliverance, the world will not be safe from Yahweh the conqueror.'

For further reflection

1 What do you make of Tina Pippin's observation regarding the white supremacy of biblical textbooks, including her point about marginalized voices being controlled by privileged white, male ones?
2 What do you think about the wider issues of whiteness (as the norm), white privilege and white supremacy? How should the church respond to them?
3 Are the church and theological education democratic spaces? How could they become more democratic?
4 What do you make of Pippin's portrayal of biblical hermeneutics as a political act and bell hooks's view of language as 'a place of struggle'?
5 And what about Warrior's point about the subjugated Canaanites and their modern-day equivalents being regarded as the negative 'others'?

Holding the empire to account

In 2007, Miguel De La Torre, a Cuban refugee and Professor of Social Ethics at Iliff School of Theology, published *Liberating Jonah: Forming an Ethics of Reconciliation*, in which he presents Jonah as a model for the under-represented and oppressed, whom he sees as being called to be instruments of reconciliation today. De La Torre's starting point (2007, p. ix) is the observation that 'the discourse on reconciliation is often reduced to how those with power and privilege within the social structures can reconcile with those who are marginalized, and to how harmonious co-existence can be created while preserving the power of the dominant culture.'

There are, in other words, two key dynamics at play. First, talk about reconciliation is usually undertaken from the perspective of those with power and, second, such talk is designed to preserve the established power structures. The book of Jonah, by contrast, presents us with a 'story of the marginalized called by God to bring the "good news" of God's grace to an oppressive empire' (p. x). Jonah, a representative of tiny, oppressed Israel, is sent to Nineveh. While the city had been beautified by King Sennacherib to resemble 'an ancient Versailles' (Allen, p. 221), the Assyrian empire, which it represents, was infamous for its intimidation, oppressive violence, merciless brutality, cruelty, malice and sadism in mocking, mutilating and slaughtering captured enemies. Chaim Lewis (p. 162) describes them as 'the Nazis stormtroopers of the ancient world', while Peruvian Catholic priest and liberation theologian Gustavo Gutiérrez (1991, p. 38) highlights that the term for violence (חמס, *khamas*) used in Jonah 3.8 'signifies the extensive and severe injustices that one people commits against another as well as the oppression that the powerful practice against the weak'. Daniel Timmer (p. 6) draws attention to the religious motivation (probably better described as justification) for Assyrian imperialism, quoting one of the royal inscriptions of Ashur-nasir-apli II (883–59 BC):

> By the command of Ashur (and) the goddess Ishtar, the great gods my lords ... I erected a pile in front of his gate; I flayed as many nobles as had rebelled against me (and) draped their skins over the pile; some I spread out within the pile, some I erected on stakes upon the pile, (and) some I placed on stakes around about the pile. I flayed many right through my land (and) draped their skins over the walls. I slashed the flesh of the eunuchs (and) of the royal eunuchs who were guilty (quoted from Grayson, pp. 123–4).

Referring to Isaiah 36.10, 18–20, David Blower offers some further observations on the arrogant Assyrian imperial rhetoric. In Isaiah 36, we find the Rabshakeh, King Sennacherib's spokesperson, delivering the following message:

> Moreover, is it without the LORD that I have come up against this land to destroy it? The LORD said to me, Go up against this land, and destroy it ... Do not let Hezekiah mislead you by saying, The LORD will save us. Has any of the gods of the nations saved their land out of the hand of the king of Assyria? Where are the gods of Hamath and Arpad?

Where are the gods of Sepharvaim? Have they delivered Samaria out of my hand? Who among all the gods of these countries have saved their countries out of my hand, that the LORD should save Jerusalem out of my hand?

Blower comments (p. 47) that 'the rhetorical invocation of one god against another was entirely within the imperial mindset. It was all part of imperial bravado, and it still is.' According to De La Torre (2007, pp. xii, 124, 147), Jonah's task now is to hold this brutal, arrogant Assyrian empire answerable to the principles of justice. As Blower spells out (p. 29), 'the Book of Jonah calls upon the powerless, and asks them for nothing less than proactive compassion for the utterly tyrannical despots of empire' in a mission that involved holding the empire account-able for its injustice, calling on the people to rediscover their souls and humanity, and bringing to them the good news of God's grace, salvation and liberation. Jonah, for his part, only very grudgingly goes about his task, and yet we witness an astonishing conversion. Perhaps Stephen Riley (p. 124) is right to see a subversion of the empire's power here, achieved 'by imagining a world where the empire ... represented by the Assyrian city of Nineveh, did not strike back when confronted with its evil, but rather repented and worshipped YHWH'.

The prophet, however, is outraged that his 'unjust' God simply for-gives the ones who had been subjugating the Jewish nation. Does God not side with the oppressed and marginalized, standing in solidarity with them rather than those who benefit from empire, those whose privilege comes at the expense of the oppressed? It is this that occasions Jonah's death wish, and the booth, the *sukkah* (סֻכָּה) he built, was an intentional reminder of the covenant that God had made with the Israelites (De La Torre, 2007, p. 22).[13] Contrary to other interpretations we reviewed earlier, the prophet's death wish is here taken with utmost seriousness, as Alyssa Walker observes (2015, pp. 14–15), pointing out that liberationist and postcolonial readings move 'away from a tendency in recent scholar-ship to view Jonah as petty and ridiculous and find humor in virtually every move he makes'.

Perhaps Jonah was worried that the sparing of the Ninevites, what De La Torre calls the 'redemption of the oppressor', would lead 'to the destruction of the oppressed'. After all, with the story being set in the eighth century,[14] the original readers would have been only too aware of how the spared Assyrians subsequently conquered Israel, leading its people into exile. And yet this story makes it clear that while Jonah assumed 'that God would execrate and renounce those whom Jonah execrated and renounced, and that God's doctrines and beliefs would correspond to his own', both the oppressed and the oppressor 'are subject to God's mercy and God's grace' (De La Torre, 2007, pp. 60–1). Indeed, Riley notes (p. 122) that in the story of Jonah 'every major character, or group of characters, ends up in relationship with YHWH'. He adds (p. 125): 'if we can begin from the standpoint that God desires relationship with all humanity, we can forge an important starting point for the work of healing and reconciliation'. De La Torre (2007, p. 126) speaks of reconciliation as involving all of creation, which of course connects with God's concluding question as to whether God should not be concerned about all those people – and also the many animals (4.11).

As will be apparent from what has been said thus far, De La Torre's reading, even though he begins by retelling the whole story (2007, pp. 9–24), effectively focuses on the events in chapters 3 and 4 and their implications for marginalized people today. In this it differs from other approaches that seek to offer a coherent reading of the narrative in its entirety. That said, De La Torre's interpretation is a good illustration of a theological, ideological, liberationist reading that approaches the text from a clearly acknowledged 'interested' perspective. Following feminist biblical scholar Elisabeth Schüssler Fiorenza, De La Torre describes his approach as a 'hermeneutics of creative imagination', in contrast to the 'standard' reading, which he argues (2007, p. xi) 'imposes on a text a theological view that tends to normalize and legitimize the power and privilege of a dominant culture'.

Writing as someone of Hispanic origin living in the United States and applying Jonah's message to that specific context, De La Torre concludes (2007, p. xii) that 'the people who suffer in the shadows of the U.S. empire, whether within or without, are called to bring a message of salvation to the center of power and privilege'. Adopting a somewhat wider but similar perspective, Blower (p. 37) suggests that 'the West is the epicenter of empire today', and that 'we have as much blood to answer for as the Assyrians did'. Parts of De La Torre's book (2007, pp. 25–58) are devoted to a discussion of the United States understood as 'today's Assyrian empire', its economic, racist and religious faces, and the ways in which it exploits its economic, military and technological superiority. Empire, Joerg Rieger (pp. 2–3) suggests, 'has to do with massive concentration of power [and] ... forms of top-down control that are established on the backs of the empire's subjects'. Commenting on today's global context, De La Torre refers to Hardt and Negri (pp. xi–xii), who describe the modern form of empire as a 'decentered and deterritorializing apparatus of rule that progressively incorporates the entire global realm'.

Looking at 'the religious face of empire', De La Torre (2007, pp. 48–58) offers some critical observations on 'the merging of Christianity and empire', on the issues of Christianity having been co-opted by the state, on the one hand and, on the other, of it freely cooperating with the state. As American Baptist minister and civil rights activist Martin Luther King (1929–68) once said (p. 59): 'The church must be reminded that it is not the master or the servant of the state but rather the conscience of the state.' Just as the Ninevites did 'not know their right hand from their left' (Jonah 4.11) or lacked a properly calibrated moral compass, so, De La Torre maintains (2007, p. 2), 'those who benefit from the present power structures cannot be relied upon to define reconciliation, or to determine how to go about achieving it.' The reason for this is that 'their social location legitimizes unjust social structure as normative', thus rendering them 'unable to be objective about the reality of their privileged positions'.

Any hope for reconciliation must therefore rest with the disenfranchised. They, after all, are the ones who yearn for justice (p. 7). As French historian, literary critic and philosopher of social science René Girard (1923–2015) once pointed out (p. 21), it is only the victims who can reveal 'the truth of the system, its relativity, its fragility, and its mortality'. As victims of oppression, they understand both the causes of their disenfranchisement and the ways in which their oppressors benefit from the prevailing power structures. De La Torre (2007, pp. 88–9), therefore, maintains:

> Any definition of reconciliation must arise within marginalized communities ... Reconciliation must always start with the victims of abusive power structures. This is why Jonah was sent by God ... to call the Assyrian empire to repentance ... reconciliation must originate from within the marginalized communities.

All this is very much in line with the thinking of Brazilian educator and philosopher Paulo Freire (1921–97), who has argued (p. 44):

> This, then, is the great humanistic and historical task of the oppressed, to liberate themselves and their oppressors as well. The oppressors, who oppress, exploit, and rape by virtue of their power, cannot find in this power the strength to liberate either the oppressed or themselves. Only power that springs from the weakness of the oppressed will be sufficiently strong to free both.

However, the Ninevites' defective moral compass notwithstanding, the story of Jonah speaks of a God who seeks the salvation of everyone, including those benefiting from the empire's unjust power structures, and it is for that reason that Jonah is commanded to go to Nineveh. And he is given no choice either because, 'if the people of Nineveh are lost from YHWH's grace, it is not because they are sinners but because those who live on the margins of empire refused to reach out to them with YHWH's good news' (De La Torre, 2007, p. 18). But, as De La Torre puts it (p. 5), 'separation from neighbors brings about separation from God' – in this case, Jonah's or Israel's separation from their God, or indeed the separation from God of today's marginalized. In King's words (p. 50): 'We must love our enemies, because only by loving them can we know God.' Or, as Gutiérrez insists (1988, p. 85), 'salvation – the communion of human beings with God and among themselves – is something which embraces all human reality [and] transforms it.' It is important for the oppressed and marginalized to see, as again King once put it (p. 45), that 'the evil deed of the enemy-neighbor, the thing that hurts, never quite expresses all that he is. An element of goodness may be found even in our worst enemy.'

According to De La Torre, the book of Jonah presents us with a model for disenfranchised communities that are committed to working for justice. But of course, as for Jonah, the resistant, disobedient character in the story, so for De La Torre (2007, p. 1), this raises the question of how the oppressed and marginalized can possibly 'relate to those who bring subjugation, misery, and death to [their] people, [their] loved ones, and [themselves]'. 'Can those who are oppressed reconcile with forces that produce death? Forces that are satanic? Forces incarnated as empire?' (p. 58). De La Torre's answer is that reconciliation:

- Requires acknowledgement of wrongdoing and repentance.
- Requires justice: 'claiming God's care and love for the oppressor should never be an excuse to ignore or exclude the requirements of social, political, and economic justice' (p. 67).
- As 'the intersection of mercy with truth' requires the kind of justice that leads to *shalom*, which 'connotes solidarity, well-being, and wholeness' (p. 115).
- Requires addressing the causes of oppression – that is, for the dominant culture to crucify its 'power and privilege on the cross', to die to its 'complicity with oppression' (p. 76).
- Is thus 'the process of moving ... from alienation to communion' (p. 141).
- Requires countercultural churches that do not merely emulate the values of the dominant culture.

De La Torre further comments on a range of important issues, such as:

- Forgiveness as a subversive 'act of self-empowerment, self-healing, and self-preservation' (p. 108).
- Healing and public recognition of the victims' dignity and oppression having to occur for forgiveness to become possible.
- Premature forgiveness preventing offenders from recognizing their complicity in structural and institutionalized violence.
- The disenfranchised needing to learn how to love their enemies, while seeking to foster liberating justice for all and refusing to submit to oppression.
- Members of the dominant culture standing in solidarity with the marginalized in their struggle towards reconciliation and justice.

All these issues, however, would take us far beyond our exploration of the book of Jonah and into more wide-ranging considerations of how the oppressed and marginalized may go about Jonah's task of confronting empire with God's demands of justice and proclaiming the message of God's grace.

For further reflection

1 What do you make of the suggestion that the powerless, by holding the powerful to account, can help them rediscover their souls and humanity? Can you think of any examples where that might be the case today?

2 Do you agree that those benefiting from the present power structures cannot be the ones to define reconciliation, or to drive the process towards realizing it? If so, why might this be problematic? Why does Girard suggest that only the victims can reveal the truth of the system?

3 What do you make of the demand upon the powerless to meet the forces of empire with compassion and thus to liberate both themselves and their oppressors? What is the church's role in all this? What do you think about King's point that the church ought to be the state's conscience, not its master, nor its servant?

4 What have you learned about the book of Jonah from De La Torre's reading, which combines biblical interpretation and theological reflection? How does he go about the practice of biblical interpretation and theological reflection?

Jonah as an archetypal Palestinian liberation theologian

Another liberationist reading of Jonah has been suggested by Palestinian Anglican priest and Arab citizen of Israel Naim Stifan Ateek in his book *A Palestinian Christian Cry for Reconciliation* (2008). Tracing his own journey as a reader of the book, Ateek (p. 71) notes that, having over time come to see it 'in a more radical and revolutionary way', he now treasures it as 'a significant resource for peacemaking and for arriving at a solution to today's Middle Eastern conflict'. As the title of Ateek's book indicates, he reads from a Palestinian Christian perspective – and with an eye towards texts that reflect Christ's 'inclusive and nonviolent message', as he points out (p. 54). One of these texts he finds in the book of Jonah whose author he describes as 'an archetypal Palestinian liberation theologian' who manages to be 'very consistent in his inclusive and universal message', criticizing 'any religion that reflects a tribal and xenophobic god' as non-genuine (p. 55). More specifically, Ateek (p. 163) argues that the book of Jonah promotes 'the inclusive nature of the one God, an inclusive theology of the people of God that embraces all of humanity, and an inclusive theology of the land that opens the way for the sharing of the land between Israelis and Palestinians'.

Elaborating on these points, Ateek notes, first (p. 73), that God is presented as the creator of the world who 'is not limited to one country' and does not show any 'partiality to any culture or nation or race or ethnic group'. Second (p. 74), in the book of Jonah, 'God's people are not restricted to Israel' when even the savage and brutal Assyrians, Israel's worst enemies, can be embraced by God 'who shows concern for their well-being'. And third, as the exile had already told the people, God and his presence, and God's activity, could not be limited to Israel. God was no tribal god. To drive home these points, the writer of Jonah chooses as his main character a 'patriotic prophet who represented a narrow Israelite jingoism', a 'prophet with a nationalistic streak', 'an ardent nationalist who harbored deep contempt for the Assyrians' (p. 69) – these characterizations are based on Ateek's reading of the portrayal of Jonah in 2 Kings 14.23–25 and in the book of Jonah itself. For Ateek (p. 72), it is to the credit of the Hebrew religion that such a radical and self-critical book was included in the canon of scripture. Dating it to the late fourth century BC, Ateek sees Jonah as standing 'as the zenith of Old Testament theology' from where it addresses post-exilic disputes between voices that favoured universalism and diversity, on the one hand, and those that expressed bigotry, xenophobia, racism and a narrow nationalism, on the other (pp. 72–3).

For Ateek, the book of Jonah is of great relevance for the contemporary situation in Israel-Palestine where even today a tribal form of religion 'insists on a special Jewish god, on the privileges of a special people of God, and on a unique Jewish right to the whole land of Palestine' (p. 76). All this, Ateek maintains, leads to the oppression and dehumanization of the Palestinians as well as to the negation of their claims to the land where their families have lived for centuries. The book of Jonah, which 'refutes and condemns all narrow, restrictive, or exclusive theologies', for Ateek and his fellow Palestinian Christians is therefore a 'spiritual and theological life line' (p. 77).

For further reflection

1 What do you make of Ateek's reading of Jonah as an archetypal Palestinian liberation theologian? Why does he characterize Jonah in this way?
2 Why does Ateek see the book of Jonah as a resource for peace-making and as pointing towards a solution in the Middle Eastern conflict?

Postcolonial biblical interpretation

Postcolonial biblical interpretation covers a wide range of approaches and perspectives that reflect different races, empires, colonies, geographical locations and times, which, as Musa Dube notes (2004, p. 361), only goes to illustrate the pervasive spread of imperialism.[15] It is worth pointing out that I will be using the unhyphenated terms 'postcolonial' and 'postcolonialism' as the hyphenation of 'post' and 'colonial' is contested by those who see it as 'implying a transcendence of colonialism and a movement somehow "after" and "beyond" the past' (Donaldson, 1996a, p. 5). Timmer points out (p. 3) that manifestations of imperialism and colonialism go back to the earliest times of human civilization, arguing that the Old Testament is to a large extent 'literature of the colonized'. Colonialism has, of course, taken different forms, including military, ideological, cultural, economical and ecological ones, and concerns issues such as culture, race, class and gender (Donaldson, 1996a, p. 8). But what has been stressed as well is that in our post-independence era we still see ongoing domination by former colonizers and the concomitant dependence of the formerly colonized nations.

As we already saw, one form of colonization has been the imposition of foreign canons, especially the Bible but also other Western texts; these are understood as the universal standard for all cultures, through which local cultures were interpreted and assessed. Dube emphasizes (2004, p. 361) that this, together with the imported Western European and North American interpretation of the biblical text, 'hewn from imperial contexts and serving the interest of these empires', led to the denigration of 'the colonized peoples and their lands through texts that serve to uplift the colonizer'. Focusing on the Asian and African contexts, she outlines (p. 363) how people were subjected to imperial attitudes 'that elevated Western cultures, claimed racial superiority, and discounted native cultures, races, and languages'. And she notes (p. 362) how 'the voice of biblical scholars of former imperial centers and settler colonies remained largely silent during the perpetration of international crimes of colonialism and holocaust'.

However, decolonizing reading practices, such as biblical interpretations of resistance, collaboration or nativism, have begun to emerge from a range of places, especially in Africa, Asia and Latin America. These adopt a range of strategies, including: (a) reading biblical texts in connection with other local texts or cultures, thus upholding the validity of those cultures; (b) involving base communities of non-academic readers in biblical interpretation; (c) theological interpretations that emerge out of readers' own socioeconomic contexts; and (d) critical interrogations of the biblical texts with respect to their complicity or compatibility with colonialist processes. In an essay entitled 'Guerrilla exegesis: "Struggle" as a scholarly vocation', which Dube (p. 364) describes as 'one of the boldest postcolonial biblical readings ever to be published in a Western scholarly journal', Hendricks talks about the struggles and strategies of the colonized against the colonizer. Published in an issue of the journal *Semeia*, entitled *Taking It Personally*, it is a highly autobiographical piece of writing. Having 'lived a childhood punctuated by racial insults, racial rejections, racial assaults, and weekly recountings of racially motivated murders, lynchings and castrations', Hendricks (p. 75) points out that 'struggle' is the lens through which he views the biblical text and the world, that for him 'writin' is fightin''. He maintains (p. 74) that 'biblical interpretation today continues to be a field of contestation and struggle between unstated, but no less real, neo-colonial white supremacist sensibilities and various resistance responses to the casual, everyday horror of white supremacist domination'. It is in this contested context, where 'there is no objective methodology just as there is no objective military' (p. 79), that Hendricks's guerrilla exegesis operates.

Turning to a description of what guerrilla exegesis as an approach to the biblical text entails, Hendricks (p. 76) talks about 'the bringing or leading out of oppressed/suppressed/don't-get-no-press meanings by sabotage, subversion or other non-traditional appropriations of hegemonic renderings, by independent non-conventional means of struggle and attack'. Summing up the reasons for the guerrilla exegete's struggle, Hendricks says that (p. 82):

> s/he struggles because her/his people are bibliocentric, their lives devotedly focused on a Bible whose liberatory power has been defused and confused by dominationist interpreters. S/he struggles for the lives of those lovingly dedicated to a Bible whose strategically imposed hegemonic readings militate against their own fragile well-being. S/he struggles because the Bible continues to stand as the foremost tool of oppression and hegemonic domination in human history ... Used to justify slavery. Lynching. Segregation. Genocide. Rampant militarism. Gender oppression. Myriad exclusions ... A gospel of liberation debauched to a rationale for oppression. A proclamation of freedom perverted to promulgation of dominationist rhetorics.

What the guerrilla exegete fights against is interpretation from above. Taking on that fight (pp. 83–4), guerrilla exegesis is:

> Not afraid to say big ugly words like 'white supremacy' and 'Eurocentric.' Not afraid to demystify 'whiteness' as an identity of unjust color privilege rather than an ethnicity. Not afraid to call white supremacy demonic. Evil. Godless. Demonic ... Likewise, Guerrilla exegesis is not afraid to call Eurocentrism demonic ... a white supremacist historiographic distortion casting Europeans as subjects and the rest of the world as objects, mere dark props on a white stage. The European as the chosen, the non-European 'other' as the wretched. The European as civilized, the dark 'other' as savage.

Guerrilla exegesis and Afrocentricity are a response to 'the myths of blk inferiority, attenuated intellectuality, out-of-control sexuality, and innate basketballity ... to racist biblical interpretations and racist exegeses purveyed by racist preachers and racist scholars' (p. 84). Afrocentric biblical interpretation focuses 'on models and issues of liberation and domination in the Bible for the express purpose of raising an oppressed peoples' bibliocentric consciousness' (p. 86). For Hendricks, however, Afrocentricity cannot capture everything he is concerned about, and so he also speaks of 'Negrocentricity' and 'Ghettocentricity' (pp. 87–8), identifying the latter with brutality without measure, unsung softness, truly marginalized existence, alienation and exploitation – all seen as the effects of white supremacy. In his epilogue, also described as 'the guerrilla's call to arms', Hendricks notes (p. 88) that 'white supremacy in its various guises continues to inject the lives of African-American people with casual horror, everyday horror'; and writing, as we saw, in 1995 he worries that 'those who would deny our humanity seem now to gain a new momentum'. The Bible, for Hendricks, is crucial in all this, as he points out in his concluding thoughts (p. 88):

> Because the Bible and its interpreters remain central to the lives of this beleaguered people, because white supremacist readings of the Bible continue to tie our people's hands, blind their eyes and cloud their minds, we *must* explicate biblical models of domination and liberation, hegemony and counter-hegemony ... We must claim the Bible as our site of struggle and our field of contestation. As guerrillas. As freedom fighters. As solid but subversive scholars. As reappropriators of the biblical logic of justice.

For further reflection

1 What do you make of Dube's point about Western biblical interpretations having served imperial interests while denigrating the colonized peoples? What does this tell us about biblical interpretation?

2 What do you think of alternative reading strategies that (a) focus on reading the biblical texts in connection with local cultures, (b) involve non-academic readers, (c) emerge out of the readers' socioeconomic contexts, and (d) read the Bible critically in terms of its complicity or compatibility with colonialism?

3 And what about Hendricks's 'guerrilla exegesis' and his notion of biblical interpretation as a 'field of contestation and struggle'? What are he and his community struggling against?

4 How would you describe Hendricks's goals as a biblical interpreter or guerrilla exegete? How does he view the Bible?

Jonah un-deconstructed by postcolonialism

In a 2009 article exploring Jonah from a postcolonial perspective, Timmer notes (p. 3) that the book 'affords a unique perspective on the relation of the colonized to the colonizer'. The colonized, of course, being Israel, represented by the prophet Jonah, while the colonizer features in the form of the Assyrian city of Nineveh whose violence, highlighted by Timmer, we already briefly noted in connection with De La Torre's liberationist reading. Timmer (p. 8) describes postcolonial criticism as 'a style of inquiry, an insight or perspective', which he sees as applicable to various forms of 'reactive resistance discourse of the colonized'. As we shall see, it is of course equally applicable to the critical engagement with colonial discourse itself. Timmer (pp. 8–9) goes on to say that post-colonial studies are concerned with identity, either 'the identity that the colonizer projects onto the colonized or the various means the colonized use to preserve their identity and freedom'.

Looking at the book of Jonah, Timmer finds strong intertextual con-nections with other parts of the Hebrew Bible whose primary function, he suggests (p. 9), is 'to create identities for the book's main characters', Hebrew identities, that is, and thus 'to formulate a Hebrew response to Neo-Assyrian colonialism'. Jonah is, therefore, portrayed as 'a colonized individual identifying himself first ethnically, and then religiously' (p. 10). However, being fundamentally opposed to Yahweh treating the Assyrians with grace and mercy, Timmer suggests (p. 12) that Jonah, 'the colonized, is fundamentally a colonizer', except that 'the political and military weakness of Israel has not afforded him the opportunity to enact his ideology'. However, Timmer argues against seeing the book of Jonah as an imperialistic text. He devotes a good deal of attention to the sailors and the Ninevites and their respective responses to God. For instance, commenting on the phrase 'the men feared YHWH with a great fear' (1.16), he understands it as signifying 'whole-hearted con-version to Yahweh' (p. 15) because 'to fear/revere God' in the Hebrew Bible describes 'a healthy relationship with Yahweh'. Indeed, he goes on to say (p. 20) that 'in light of the religious transformations evident in the sailors and the Ninevites, it is important to note that nothing is *imposed* on them'. We will turn to an alternative reading below, but it may be helpful to ask whether Timmer might be underestimating the text's potential propagandist dimension. He does, however, raise some interesting questions when he asks (p. 20):

But were not the transformations of the sailors and the Ninevites both forced upon them, given the danger of the storm in the first case and the threat of divine judgment in the second? Indeed, did not Yahweh act in much the same way as an imperialist nation toward these gentiles in using his unlimited power to get them to do what he wanted? In other words, while Yahweh seems to deconstruct colonialism in the Book of Jonah, does postcolonialism deconstruct Yahweh?

These are difficult but highly pertinent questions. Indeed, they are just the kind of questions a postcolonial approach would ask. That said, Timmer is quick to respond (pp. 20, 21) that the sailors 'come to revere the Creator without having any assurance that he will deliver them from their life-threatening predicament', while the Ninevites' repentance 'is not presented as being motivated by self-interest'. Surely, though, fearing the divine judgement and potential annihilation and desiring to survive these must count as a form of (perfectly legitimate) self-interest, while the sailors end up fearing or 'revering' – to go with Timmer's preferred term – a deity whose life-threatening display of power they had just witnessed. Timmer is certainly quick to eliminate the ambivalence created by the wordplay on 'fear', which can mean either fearing or revering God. He is equally quick to conclude (p. 21) that 'the Book of Jonah portrays human freedom as inviolate in the context of divine intervention', which, given the demonstration of irresistible divine power in the storm and the threat of divine violence against Nineveh, would not appear to be self-evident. When Timmer goes on to suggest (p. 21) that 'threats of punishment in Jonah … function as epistemological aids designed to help those in violation of the Creator's will remedy the situation before they meet the fate that attends such behavior', he operates with a take on (the threat of) divine violence that has been challenged by other postcolonial readings.

For further reflection

1 What is your take on Timmer's suggestion that nothing is imposed on the sailors and the Ninevites, that human freedom is inviolate in the book of Jonah?
2 What do you make of the underlying threat and/or the display of divine force or violence throughout the book?

Jonah as imperialist discourse

In contrast to those interpretations that read the book of Jonah as an expression of the colonized – that is, the people needing to come to terms with their experiences at the hands of imperial powers such as the Assyrians – Steed Davidson in his postcolonial commentary focuses on the colonizing power of the text of Jonah itself, on the ways in which *that* text seeks to dominate the 'other'. He notes, for instance (loc. 7937), that:

the claim of the Ninevites as wicked positions [Jonah's] intended proclamation as adversarial, condemnatory, and condescending. The prophetic task presupposes the prophet to be the bearer of a morally superior ethic that the recipients through ignorance or weakness have abridged. Positioning the Ninevites as wicked in a generic sense enables the text to call attention to Jonah's special claim to be the bearer of this morally superior message.

However, not only is the message presented as morally superior, the people of Nineveh are also being confronted with a 'superior power that has the capacity to destroy aberrant nations and to make the world in its image' (loc. 8001). Davidson in this context suggests (loc. 8017) that Nineveh's foreignness is a key factor for the book of Jonah to work: 'travel to a foreign space and the construction of spaces become integral aspects of the book's design and interpretation'. It is this that 'clearly draws the line between "us" and "them", and that line proves critical for imperialist discourses'. In what Davidson sees as a typically imperialist move (loc. 8032), 'foreign spaces are constructed through Judean perceptions about those spaces from partial knowledge or even ignorance as geographies of otherness that are distinct from "our own" or known geographies'. All this contributes to the 'production of otherness'. Indeed, as Davidson elaborates (loc. 8049), a 'geography of danger, strangeness, and depravity' further adds to the evocation or construction of otherness. To justify the colonizer's civilizing mission, Nineveh must be represented as different, other, and standing outside of the normal. Being a degenerate place, full of 'insufficiently discerning residents', it also becomes 'a marginal space rather than a central space, as would be expected of an imperial city'. And it is construed as an 'environmentally determined' place. Environmental determinism conceives of people as products of their environment, with, for instance, 'the Ninevites' moral depravity deriving from the expanse of urban spaces' (loc. 8065). Davidson notes that environmental determinism is another characteristic feature of imperialist discourses, leading to the contention that change can only come from the outside – which in this case is through Jonah's intervention.

In our discussion of narrative criticism, we noted how authors make use of different types of characters, including round and flat ones, with the latter also known as stereotypes. In Jonah, we said, the sailors and the Ninevites are flat characters or stereotypes, designed to prompt the reader to focus on Jonah and God, the story's main characters. Davidson highlights (loc. 8174) that all the 'foreign bodies' are stereotypes, with 'the narrative space provid[ing] little room for their fuller development'. The implication, of course, is that this is a deliberately tendentious type of characterization. Mention of the animals adds to this, he suggests (loc. 8190), by associating the Ninevites with 'wildness' and 'animality', in contrast to the imperialist's 'civilization' and 'humanity', thus providing further justification for imperial action against them. The text's colonizing power is further exercised by means of Jonah's prophetic words, which Davidson describes (loc. 8206) as 'one of the weapons of imperial military technology', maintaining (loc. 8221) that 'the divine technology seeks to conform the world to its order, here to transform different, dissident, and non-conforming bodies into versions of acceptable humanity that still fall short of the ideal'. He adds that although the Ninevites are ultimately spared, 'God's callous comment about [them] at the end of the book indicates the perception of their incapacities that derive from their ontological inferiority'.

Based on the rhetoric of violence found in oracles against foreign nations in other prophetic texts (for example, Amos 1—2; Isa. 13—23; Jer. 46—51; Ezek. 25—32; Obad.; and Nahum) and on God's change of mind in 3.10, Davidson surmises (loc. 8237) that God's initial response to Nineveh involved violence. Indeed, he highlights (loc. 8306) what he calls the book's 'specter of actual and potential violence'. Examples of this include the great wind of chapter 1, which illustrates 'God's willingness to use violence in pursuit of Jonah' (loc. 8254), and the 'gratuitous display of violence' against the *qiqayon* (4.7), which offers an opportunity for instructing both Jonah and the book's readers about the nature of divine violence (loc. 8288). Davidson calls the latter incident 'the farce in the desert', suggesting (loc. 8387) that it 'reveals a moral order that lacks a coherent articulation for the use of violence other than an expression of its sovereignty'. Davidson in this context mentions Cameroonian historian and political theorist Achille Mbembe's notion of 'necropolitics', the sovereign's right to determine who dies and who lives. In the end, Davidson maintains (loc. 8357), 'the divine violence in its imperialist representations is indistinguishable from the violence of empire, despite claims of moral superiority'. He adds that to negate violence, as the book ultimately does, 'may provide mercy but this negation does not abolish the violence that serves as an operating principle of imperial configurations'. It is for this reason that Davidson deems the book of Jonah to be 'inadequate to inform anti-imperial practices'. In fact, because it 'participates in the discourses of exceptionalism that fueled and continue to support imperialist logic' (loc. 8357), he concludes (loc. 8372) that the book must itself be regarded as imperialist discourse. Indeed, for Davidson (loc. 8387), the presentation of Jonah 'as the messenger of a morally superior order that violently shapes the world' exemplifies the fallacy that is at the heart of the Old Testament's prophetic literature.

In my summary, I have focused on Davidson's observations on the depiction of Nineveh, but his discussion includes the sailors as well. One comment seems particularly pertinent here, simply because it contrasts so starkly with Timmer's reading discussed above. For rather than as converting to Israel's God, Davidson sees the sailors as 'eventually *succumbing* to YHWH's power, praying to YHWH and offering a sacrifice and pledging vows' (1.14–16). He understands this as no more than an outward submission to 'overwhelming imperial power' (loc. 8143), something that many colonized people feel compelled to do.

Rebecca Lindsay has made the case that Nineveh, in the book of Jonah, has become marginalized and at least partially 'Israelitized' (2016, pp. 51, 53), adopting a term also used by Ben Zvi (2003a, p. 75), as we saw earlier. Or, to put it differently, 'the multilingual and cross-cultural reality of Jonah's encounter with a city from a different cultural milieu is ignored' (Lindsay, 2016, p. 53). Indeed, as Yvonne Sherwood has observed (2000, p. 264), the Ninevite king is presented as speaking 'perfect accentless Hebrew' and being familiar with Scripture, which leads Havea to suggest (2012, p. 182) that 'the narrator of the Jonah story operates like someone from a dominant language group, who expects others to learn and understand his language'. He adds that 'this is especially critical given that the story circles around YHWH demanding Jonah to deliver a message against/to a non-Hebrew speaking people'. For Havea, such disregard for different tongues amounts to a 'power move' on the narrator's part.

Havea shares some of Lindsay's perspectives, especially her focus on Nineveh, and invites his readers to imagine 'how YHWH's message to and desire for Nineveh might be perceived by the *Tāngata whenua* of Nineveh' (p. 177). The phrase, which has been borrowed from the Māori in Aotearoa–New Zealand, means 'people of the land'. Havea himself, as he points out, approaches the book of Jonah 'as a Polynesian, reading on behalf of Nineveh and its people' and standing in solidarity with them. His reading, therefore, is a cross-cultural one that resists the thrust of the biblical text, favouring Nineveh rather than Israel (p. 185). It is also an example of minority biblical criticism, which Havea describes as 'committed and biased' (p. 179). He takes it as a given that most readers sympathize 'with the cause and people of Israel', which makes Nineveh a 'city of minoritized subjects', as indeed it is in the biblical text, which favours Israel while disfavouring Nineveh. That, however, for Havea, 'does not mean that readers should do the same' (p. 180).

Turning to the portrayal of Nineveh, he notes that the nature and extent of Nineveh's 'wickedness' are never revealed. Was it perceived as wicked, he wonders, simply because it was a non-Israelite city? It is worth noting that the Jonah text itself shows the Ninevites' behaviour not to be exclusively evil and perhaps also not quite as evil as God made it seem at first (1.2). This is suggested especially by the portrayal of the people's repentance in 3.5–8. Moreover, as Lindsay adds, the harsh task of crying out *against* Nineveh (1.2), expressed with the preposition עַל (*'al*), is later softened when Jonah is told to go to Nineveh and proclaim God's message *to* the city (3.2); here, the preposition אֶל, (*'el*) is used. Lindsay comments: 'the change of language suggests a subtle softening of God's perspective. God seems to turn away from anger' (2016, p. 55; see also Havea, 2012, p. 181). That said, however, the portrayal throughout the book minimizes Nineveh's complexity, depicting it as a unified whole. As Lindsay notes, 'the vulnerable subjects of the city, those who receive rather than perpetrate its evil, are kept voiceless and unseen' (2016, p. 55). Indeed, she goes on to maintain (p. 57):

> Such generalisations of places and their inhabitants are difficult to sustain. Labelling a city 'evil' does not open up the myriad situations of inhabitants, the power differences between the later mentioned king and his subjects, even the way the animals are drawn into the story. In refusing to acknowledge that there might be those within Nineveh who do not engage in 'evil,' those who may be trapped within a system of domination, Jonah himself becomes a figure of domination.

Staying with Jonah, who is aware of God's decision not to destroy Nineveh but in his fierce anger waits to see what will happen to the city (4.5), Lindsay suggests (p. 58) that he places it under his gaze, thereby objectifying it from a position of power. Although he, the speaker of God's words, knows God's mind, he does not communicate his knowledge to the Ninevites but rather marginalizes the city. 'Some voices', notes Lindsay (p. 50), 'have power to push others to the periphery', while for Nineveh, 'there is only silence. The city is left to wait, in a moment of perpetual wondering of when and if the prophecy would be fulfilled' (p. 58). But Nineveh is not only marginalized. It is also Israelitized, its culture and language ignored by a narrator who expects everyone to speak and understand his language. Havea comments (2012, p. 182) that 'from the standpoint of the *Tāngata whenua*, the favoring of a language that is not one of the local ones can be seen as an attempt to strangle and suffocate the native and local languages'. Emphasizing the close connection between language and identity, Havea goes further in his criticism when he maintains that 'the Jonah narrator's disregard for the local languages of Nineveh is ... insensitive and disrespectful, and wicked'. Commenting on the final verse, which depicts the Ninevites as stupid, and compares them to beasts, Havea suggests that this disrespect, shared by the narrator and Yahweh, may be attributed to 'ethnic and racial biases' (p. 183). He compares this to the reception Jonah was given by the people of Nineveh, which indicates that there was 'a culture of hospitality' (p. 184):

> Jonah came with the words of destruction, and the people of Nineveh received him with open minds ... I am intrigued that the people of Nineveh welcomed and accepted Jonah, a stranger with a strange message, which reflects a culture of hospitality similar to that of the people of Oceania ... His language, his message and his smelly body would have been offensive to the people of Nineveh. Yet, they embraced his message.

In the end, Havea could only conclude 'how smart the fish was: it spit out what it did not want' (p. 185).

A positive assessment of Nineveh is also expressed in Jesus' message, as depicted by Matthew (12.41) and Luke (11.32), according to which 'the people of Nineveh will rise up at the judgment with this generation and condemn it, because they repented at the proclamation of Jonah'. Lindsay comments: 'Jesus was praising as righteous a city long since destroyed, and one deemed to be the enemy of God's people within other portions of the Hebrew Scriptures' (2016, p. 53). And she refers to Dutch cultural and literary theorist Mieke Bal, who once suggested that characters who are repressed within the text need readers to help them return (Lindsay, 2016, p. 51, referring to Bal, 1988, p. 239). Taking her cue from Bal, Lindsay notes that 'if the Nineveh of the Book of Jonah has been marginalised, then reading along with this character works to open up ... new cracks for learning, compassion, alongside new possibilities to seek out justice' (pp. 51–2). And that this might have repercussions beyond our reading of the story of Jonah has been suggested by Sara Koenig (2011, p. 6), who believes that how we engage with the characters we encounter in texts 'can similarly condition our response to the human "characters" we meet in the world'.

For further reflection

1 What do you make of Davidson's point about the construction of otherness, of drawing a line between 'us' and 'them', of constructing a 'geography of strangeness and depravity' as critical for imperialist discourse? Can you think of any examples where such strategies are at work today? What is their aim? Is Davidson right to characterize the book of Jonah as imperialist discourse?

2 And what do you think of Davidson's take on the spectre of actual and potential divine violence in the story? Do you agree that the book of Jonah exemplifies a sovereign's right to determine who dies and who lives? Is divine violence indistinguishable from the violence of empire?

3 What do you make of Lindsay and Havea's suggestions that Nineveh has become a marginalized, objectified, generalized and Israelitized character in the book of Jonah whose culture, language and social realities have been ignored? What do you think of the move to favour Nineveh rather than Israel in one's reading of the story? Are there any textual signals that allow for such a reading or even call for one?

4 And what about Koenig's belief that how we engage with textual characters might condition how we engage with people in the real world? What does that suggest for how we should read?

Jonah, Nineveh and the emerging British imperialism

In a discussion of sixteenth- and seventeenth-century sermons by Bishop John Hooper (c. 1495–1555), Protestant Reformer John Brentius (1499–1570), and English divine George Abbot (1562–1633), as well as the work of cartographer John Speed (1551/2–1629), Simon Staffell investigates their use of the story of Jonah to fuse scripture with developing national and imperialist ideologies, firmly tying the sacred to the English nation. Speed, who produced a map of Canaan ('Canaan as it was possessed both in Abraham and Israels dayes with the stations and bordering nations', 1595)[16] showing a huge fish, a ship, and a figure plunging into the Mediterranean, imagined Canaan as Britain, thereby 'asserting [the] divine and antique inevitability' of the emerging imperialism (Staffell, p. 488), while Nineveh, 'the great city', was seen as 'a paradigm of imperial strength and virtue' (p. 489). Abbot, similarly, celebrated imperial civic space, thinking of Nineveh as 'the greatest Citie that was upon the earth' (Staffell, p. 497). Brentius, in turn, presented Nineveh as 'a precursor to the English civic space, the powerful centre of political and social order' (Staffell, p. 494). In his thought, Nineveh represents the imperial centre, and he uses divine authority to silence the majority.

'The powerless are dismissed', notes Staffell (p. 496), 'because they are impious, by nature of being peripheral', just like Jonah. Hooper, in a 1550 sermon delivered in the presence of King Edward VI (1537–53), specifically focused on Jonah and the 'Jonasses' of his time, those who contested his anti-Catholic world view and 'whose immorality [presented] a danger to the nation and commonwealth'. In Hooper's hands, too, the biblical text becomes 'a pretext for crushing dissenting voices' (pp. 490, 491), with dissidents, the Jonasses who have been rocking the boat, being expulsed from the storm-tossed ship of state (Sherwood, 2000, pp. 39–40). 'Can you live quietly with so many Jonasses?' asks Hooper (1550, p. 480). 'Nay then, throw them into the sea.' In Hooper's sermon, Sherwood notes (2000, p. 50), the book of Jonah turns into 'an ideal-ised picture of dissident forces being pitched overboard and turbulent social storms calmed'. Jonah effectively serves as a 'tractate about the production of docile bodies', with the message being: 'Don't rock the boat' (pp. 41, 42).

Another notable interpretive move by Abbot is to see the notion of 'chosen-ness' as having been transferred from Israel to England. Recog-nizing that 'the previously favoured lands and peoples were in the Orient', he claims that 'chosen-ness' has now 'moved northwestwards' to the 'new imperial centres', as Staffell puts it (pp. 497, 498), who ends by concluding, rather sardonically, that 'the Bible can – and does – underpin imperialist ideologies' (p. 500).

For further reflection

1 What do you make of the interpretations advanced by Hooper, Brentius, Abbot and Speed, who used the book of Jonah to support British national and imperial ideologies?
2 And what about the book being used to silence dissenting 'periph-eral' and 'immoral' voices?

Reading Jonah in Polynesian (many islands) style

'I, a saltwater person from the poly-lingual sea of islands in Oceania, offer this reflection in Polynesian (many islands) style', says Havea in the opening lines of his article on 'AdJusting Jonah', thus expressing his interest in reading the book 'with an island twist, attending to the currents and vibes in [his] region' (2013a, pp. 44–5). Some of Havea's key start-ing points are his emphasis on the fluidity of meanings and the way he draws on 'talanoa', which he describes (p. 47) as 'a cross-cultural pro-cess of storytelling derived from Pacific islands traditions' that helps to 'build inter-subjective understandings'. It may be helpful to note the key differences between Havea's 2012 article discussed earlier and this later one. While the starting point in both cases is Havea's own cultural context, his earlier pro-Nineveh stance has here been replaced by an interest in Jonah's desire for justice and how this may be read against Havea's Polynesian context. In pursuing this, he offers a striking demonstration of what I am seeking to show in this book – namely, that the same text, in this case the book of Jonah, can be read in illuminating ways from a good number of perspectives.

Drawing on Havea's article on 'islander criticism' allows us to pinpoint further characteristics of his approach. As he points out (2018a, p. 10), islanders expect biblical texts and their interpretations to be 'fluid. Wet. Flexible. Unstable. Shifting. But also powerful. Substantial. Crushing. And so forth'. For him, this means that 'dominating and minoritizing readings can be resisted, protested, revoked' (p. 11). Another metaphor favoured by Havea is that of dancing, which, he says (p. 14), 'is groovy and bodily', only to add that 'so should be the reading of biblical texts'. As he explains, 'the aim of islander reading is not to divide, claim, and control a biblical text but to dance with it. To tease the text so that meanings leap in front of one's eyes.'

Coming back to his article on 'AdJusting Jonah', we might also note that Havea here reads Jonah from a position of solidarity with imprisoned islanders, who, because of their skin colour, cannot get justice and wonder whether God 'is colour-blind' (2013a, p. 48). Havea follows Catherine Muldoon (p. 150), who believes that the book's original readers, still under domination in the Persian era, may have read Jonah doubting 'Yhwh's commitment to them, or to the principle of divine justice'. Muldoon, therefore, in her reading of Jonah 4, is unwilling to give up on the need for justice. As Havea points out (2013a, p. 48), they both 'seek to bring justice to the surface. Muldoon reads justice in G*d's response to Jonah; i hear justice in Jonah's anger'. Havea also refers to African American biblical critic Valerie Bridgeman, who saw Jonah as worrying that God's mercy would not just temper justice but override it completely (see Bridgeman, locs 3540–53).

For Havea, too, Jonah's problem is that Yahweh is too quick to pardon Nineveh. Such sparing of a colonial power, he posits, would not be endorsed by anyone with any 'post-colonial inkling', which is why, for instance, in the eyes of Oceania's imprisoned islanders, who see wrath against authorities as cries for justice, Jonah's anger is entirely justified. As Havea points out (2013a, p. 49; 2013b, p. 131), a colonial power such as Nineveh 'should not be let off the hook but called to account for its past and ongoing violent actions', adding that, 'in relational cultures, the premature pardoning of wrongdoers is insulting' (2013a, p. 51). Indeed, as he puts it (p. 50):

it rubs salt into my native eyes when mercy trumps justice for desperate and colonized peoples [when] mercy benefits those who have done wrong more than those who are desperate. If i have to choose between mercy and justice, i pick justice because it benefits those who have been wronged and with whom i am in solidarity ... So in this instance, i stand with Jonah.

Havea recognizes that his context conditions his reading. He notes (pp. 50–1): 'my reaction to the sparing of Nineveh in the text is precisely how i react to claims that G*d is merciful toward the "Ninevehs" who still roam in Oceania [where] post-colonialism exists in the comfort of rhetoric more than on the paths of locals'. He makes a similar point in his article 'Engaging scriptures from Oceania' (2014b, p. 84), maintaining that 'the colonial era ... has not ended for many islanders in Oceania', which he substantiates by referring to the occupation of West Papua by Indonesia, Tahiti and New Caledonia by France, Rapa Nui by Chile, and Guam, Marshalls, and American Samoa by the United States. All this leads him to conclude that it is 'impossible to be fully postcolonial in islander criticism'.

Coming back to the issue of divine mercy in Jonah, Havea emphasizes (2013a, p. 51) that it is important to note who has been wronged, and that they 'have a say in when and how pardon is given. One cannot pardon for another.' He therefore wonders, given that Nineveh's wickedness was against Israel, if it is for God to forgive Nineveh on Israel's behalf and suggests (p. 52) that 'the justice in Jonah's wrath is in the interest of those who were/are wronged'. That said, commenting upon Nineveh's ready repentance, Havea approvingly refers to Lindsay's recognition of 'Nineveh not as evil empire or as repentant gentiles *only*, but as textually marginalized subject *also* that awaits reviewing, reconsidering, and reengaging' (Havea, 2013a, p. 53, referring to Lindsay, 2012). Nineveh, in other words, is not *only* wicked.

Returning to the figure of Jonah, Havea notes that in a wild story world, in which stuff is 'hurled here and there, in the sea and on land', Jonah ends up sitting down (4.5), a position that Havea sees as significant (p. 53), suggesting that it 'was not that of a savage but that of a grounded native'. In line with his own cultural context, Havea interprets Jonah's positioning as a sign of him having been at peace, which he describes not as the absence of anger but as involving engaging with passion: 'peace does not shut questions down or substitute for justice, but it privileges the voices of dissent and opens the path for justice', seeking a 'weaving of justice into mercy and peace' (p. 54). After all, 'is justice real if peace is suppressed? What kind of peace reigns if justice is denied? When justice reigns, what kind of peace is there?' In his 2018 article on 'islander criticism', Havea relates 'Jonah's protest against God for letting Nineveh off the hook' to a modern context, such as Indonesia's occupation of West Papua and the complicity of the United Nations, Australia and other neighbouring nations which, by ignoring 'the genocide of over 500,000 black native West Papuans', let 'the Indonesian government off the hook' (2018a, p. 15).

For further reflection

1 Having explored a range of interpretations of Jonah, what do you make of Havea's concept of the fluidity and instability of meanings and of him here offering a reading that completely contradicts the one we reviewed in the earlier section on contextual readings? What about the notion of dancing with the text?
2 And what about Havea's comments on mercy and pardon on the one hand, and wrath and justice on the other?

A silent prophet resisting the rhetoric of the strong

Chesung Justin Ryu writes from a Korean perspective, being mindful of Korea's oppression by imperial Japan and offering a reading that sympathizes with Jonah's original readers, who also had experienced oppression and colonization. Ryu (p. 196) is critical of Christian anti-Jewish readings that portray 'Jonah as the personification of a narrow-minded Jew ... blamed for his nationalism or particularism'. He regards it as unreasonable, insensitive and dangerous for 'outsider' Christian readers to expect the book's original readers to embrace a call for universalism and an emphasis on God's universal love that 'makes the voice of the weak and the marginalized' – the voice of the colonized Jews, who were still suffering under their oppression – disappear (pp. 199, 204). Such an approach only demonstrates that its adherents fail to understand the feelings of the colonized. 'As long as the oppression or colonization and its painful memories are ongoing, how can the oppressed hide their anger in learning that their oppressors and colonizers are saved by their God – the God of the oppressed?' Ryu asks (p. 198). After all, God's special favours on their behalf and them being chosen by God had been fundamental for their very survival. How could these favours possibly be available to their oppressors? Where does that leave God's justice?

Ryu draws attention to the 'extremely negative' characterization of Nineveh in many biblical texts (2 Kings 17.6; 2 Chron. 32.9–32; Nahum; and Zeph. 2.13–15), noting that this was unchanged even several hundred years later, as can be seen for instance in Tobit, and Josephus' *Antiquities*. And he quotes John Collins as pointing out (pp. 325–6) that 'no regime in the ancient world was more brutal, even granted the pervasive brutality of ancient (and modern!) warfare'. For Ryu (p. 206), it is evident that a colonized audience that had been at the receiving end of that brutality would have regarded Nineveh's repentance as hypocritical, especially as it lacked 'the compensatory actions to the people that they had sinned against'. Nor is God's response to that repentance in line with what one might expect. Ryu in this context refers to the death of David's son, conceived with Bathsheba. Like the king of Nineveh, David fasts and, like him, he has the same hope:

He said, 'While the child was still alive, I fasted and wept; for I said, "*Who knows* (מִי־יוֹדֵעַ, *mi-yode'a*)? The Lord may be gracious to me, and the child may live."' (2 Sam. 12.22)

When the news reached the king of Nineveh, he rose from his throne, removed his robe, covered himself with sackcloth, and sat in ashes ... '*Who knows* (מִי־יוֹדֵעַ, *mi yode'a*)? God may relent and change his mind; he may turn from his fierce anger, so that we do not perish.' (Jonah 3.6, 9)

However, while David's innocent child died, the Ninevites' lives were spared. Ryu comments (p. 209) that although Jonah's anger in 4.1 might seem absurd to some Christian scholars today, it would have made perfect sense to a colonized audience. Similarly, Jonah's death wish is no 'childish whim'. After all, 'where is the Auschwitz survivor', ask André LaCocque and Pierre-Emmanuel Lacocque, 'who would go to Berchtesgaden or Berlin carrying God's salvation?' (1994, pp. 121–2).[17] And that takes us to Ryu's focus on Jonah's silence, brought about by the rhetoric of the strong. Whereas in 4.4 God did not enquire about the reason for Jonah's anger, in 4.9 God is quick to identify it as the *qiqayon*. But, asks Ryu, 'was Jonah really angry to death because of the plant?' He sees this as a clever move by God, who makes everyone focus on the plant, and comments (pp. 216–17):

This is [an] example of the rhetoric of the strong, who like to de-historicize and de-contextualize. Whatever the oppressor did to the oppressed in the past, the oppressor wants to wipe out shameful past events and to demand that the oppressed talk only about current situations.

In fact, Ryu goes on to say that the weak cannot avoid the rhetoric of the strong, partly because it is they who dictate the 'social and rhetorical norms for conversation' and partly because the weak 'do not have the skill to … invent their own rhetoric'. This disadvantage means that they 'cannot help answering in an impetuous mood', and that is how they get 'trapped' (p. 217). Was God not supposed to be on their side? Why does God suddenly extend his mercy to the brutal empire, while ignoring justice and the fate of the weak? Questions such as these should have been asked, but 'Jonah is trapped in the rhetoric of the strong … The only thing he could do was to remain silent' (p. 218). Ryu adds that 'a colonized audience would have understood what the silence of Jonah meant because they were with Jonah there, in silence'. At the same time, however, that very silence must also be understood as 'resistance on the part of the weak over against the rhetoric of the strong' (p. 198).

For further reflection

1 What do you think of Ryu's focus on the oppressed, colonized original readers whose understanding of being chosen by God had been fundamental for their survival and who struggle with their oppressors and colonizers being saved by their own God – the God of the oppressed?

2 Do you agree that it is unreasonable for 'outsider' Christian readers to expect the book's original readers to embrace God's universal love that makes their own voice, the voice of the weak and the marginalized, disappear?

3 And what about the silencing of the weak by the rhetoric of the strong on the one hand, and that silence becoming the weak's resistance against the strong on the other?

4 Having seen these different postcolonial (contextual and liberationist) readings of the book of Jonah, what are your thoughts? Do you prefer some readings over others? If so, what are the reasons for your preferences? Can you see why readers have approached the book of Jonah in different ways?

5

Jonah's Depths:
Psychological Biblical Criticism

Dennis Shulman (p. 331), in an article entitled 'Jonah: His story, our story; his struggle, our struggle', describes the Bible as 'our culture's heart, psyche, and soul'. Writing as a biblical scholar, a rabbi and a psychoanalyst, Shulman furthermore regards the Bible as 'a masterpiece of psychological genius', noting that 'in its myriad narratives there is ancient wisdom concerning the texture and complexity, the feel, taste, and smell of human experience'. The Bible, he adds, 'is *our* story. In its pages, it is *we* – our struggle with ourselves, our struggle with our humanity, our struggle to be human – who is revealed.' It is that ancient biblical wisdom about human experience and, to use a modern term, human psychology that invites a psychological approach to the biblical texts, an approach that Wayne Rollins (1999) and Andrew Kille (2001) prefer to describe as psychological biblical criticism, hence the title of the present chapter. Despite its increasing prevalence in academic biblical studies, psychological biblical criticism is still not commonly taught in theological education, even though German Lutheran theologian and Hebraist Franz Delitzsch (1813–90), in *A System of Biblical Psychology*, first published in 1861 (English translation: 1867), described 'biblical psychology' as one of the oldest sciences of the church.

Although Delitzsch's work predated the emergence of depth psychology, as developed especially by Austrian neurologist and psychoanalyst Sigmund Freud (1856–1939) and Swiss psychiatrist and psychoanalyst Carl Gustav Jung (1875–1961), he already referred to dreams and worked with concepts such as archetypes, the 'I' (ego), and conscious and unconscious experiences. For Delitzsch, the application of a psychological approach to biblical studies was advisable because of the human capacity to grow and develop by means of self-investigation. However, following a period in the nineteenth century during which psychological interpretation of biblical texts was quite popular, biblical scholars in the first half of the twentieth century became increasingly critical of those endeavours.[1] One of the main problems had been the application of a naïve psychologism, which Kille (2001, p. 141) describes as 'reducing a phenomenon [in this case, the interpretation of the biblical text] to purely psychological categories'. To mention only one example, German theologian, philosopher and physician Albert Schweitzer (1875–1965), in his 1913 work *The Psychiatric Study of Jesus*, vehemently objected to some medical studies that, based on psychological analysis of the New Testament Gospels, had concluded that Jesus was 'mentally diseased'. Schweitzer, himself a physician and theologian (among other things), saw both the medical and the historical-critical value of those studies as 'exactly zero'.

It is important to see that Schweitzer objected on both medical/psychological and historical-critical grounds, thereby drawing attention also to the naïve way in which those studies had moved from the textual representation of Jesus to the historical figure. Other studies similarly sought to come to conclusions about the historical figures of Moses, Jeremiah, Paul and others. In contrast to those endeavours, the focus more recently has been on 'the literary construct of the biblical figure rather than presuming to deal with the historical figures themselves'. Thus Rollins (1999, p. 85), who goes on to say that the concomitant desire 'to find in the figure or story a positive or negative model for human behavior' can be fruitful. Kille (2001, p. 15) similarly suggests that the power of literature, including biblical literature, lies precisely in the construction of characters that 'accurately reflect human experience and behavior'.

Psychologism, according to Rollins (p. 53), can be averted if psychological inquiry focuses on the narrative rather than on the presumed psychological state of the author who produced the text. Another way of avoiding psychological reductionism is to ensure that the historical, social, sociopolitical and literary contexts of the texts are taken seriously. As we shall see, some approaches to Jonah have combined psychological biblical criticism with careful attention to the book's historical context and the issues faced by its author and the community for whom the text was ostensibly written. As Andries van Aarde notes (p. 487), psychological biblical criticism thus understood investigates the texts 'methodologically in a complementary fashion together with historical-critical, social-scientific critical, and literary-critical methods'. After all, psychological aspects are just one of the factors that affect textual meaning. Psychological interpretation, therefore, is not a replacement for other approaches but a supplement that affords us additional insights. That said, Kille (2001, p. 135) has rightly emphasized that 'psychological methods are essential for getting at unique dimensions of a text'. And in doing so they add yet more layers to the multiple meanings of the book of Jonah that we have already explored.

Indeed, it is important to note that psychological biblical criticism helps to restore precisely 'those levels of meaning lost to a rationalistic and literal-minded culture' (Rollins, 1999, p. 120). As we shall see, there has been a strong emphasis in psychological interpretation of Jonah on approaches that focus on the unconscious, the pre-rational – and even the irrational. And as Rollins (1999, p. 212) has pointed out, the rejection of psychological interpretation of biblical texts may at times have been a rejection of just such levels of meaning and thus an attempted suppression of the kinds of issues they have raised.

We must also briefly consider the objection that the use of modern psychological categories is anachronistic, as the biblical authors would not have been familiar with these concepts and could, therefore, not have produced texts that deal with them. Responding to this point, Kille (2001, p. 11) concurs that it would be anachronistic to simply read psychological theory into the biblical texts, as their authors 'did not inhabit [our] world of the "psychological human"'. Nor did they use our modern categories of psychological language or thought. Interestingly, though, as Ilona Rashkow has remarked (2012, p. 239), it was no other than Freud himself who acknowledged that 'most of his discoveries about the unconscious mind had been anticipated by the poets of the past'. This leads Rashkow to conclude that 'it should not be surprising that psychology in general (and psychoanalytical approaches in particular) have been used in an effort to explain the origins, character, and effects of biblical literature'.

The rejection of ostensibly anachronistic psychological concepts is also in danger of ignoring 'the continuity of the human psyche which links the modern reader to the ancient author' (Kille, 2012, p. 15). In connection with this, it is worth adding that the mechanisms of the unconscious, which we are going to explore more fully in what follows, apply to ancient authors just as much as to modern readers. As, for instance, Rollins so aptly affirms (1999, p. 146), 'any text [ancient or modern] is in part constituted, shaped, and informed by factors of which the author and the author's community are not consciously aware'. It is for this reason that a text 'often "means" more than either author or reader suspects'. Ultimately, George Aichele and colleagues (pp. 222–3) are, therefore, probably correct to suggest that we must avoid any 'naive dismissal of psychoanalysis as irrelevant to the critical reading of literary and religious texts'.

Finally, before we take a closer look at Jungian textual interpretation, we should note that there is quite a broad spectrum of psychological theories and methods. Back in the 1990s, the American Psychological Association already listed no fewer than 58 different fields within the discipline of psychology (Rollins, 1999, p. 6). Rollins notes (p. 116) that the areas of study for psychological biblical criticism are also varied and include:

> the psychology of symbols and archetypal images; unconscious factors at work in the history of biblical motifs and cultic practices; psycho-dynamic factors in biblical narrative; the psychology of biblical personalities; the varieties of biblical religious experience or the phenomenology of biblical religion in psychological perspective; the psychology of biblical ethics; and biblical psychology.

To fully appreciate the wide remit of psychological biblical criticism, we should also note that, according to Rollins (pp. 111–14), these approaches seek to revision aspects such as:

- The biblical origins – for example, whether certain movements and texts might have been caused by some 'psychic event', such as a special experience of God.
- The biblical texts – for example, how they occasion meaning, how they came to be accepted as 'sacred scripture', and how they mediate both conscious and unconscious factors.
- Biblical interpretation, focusing, for instance, on 'the act of reading as a psychic event' and on how different readers interpret the same text in different ways depending on their psychological type.[2]
- The biblical history, including its pre- and post-histories, and its cata-lytic or therapeutic effects (for example, of actuating individual and communal consciences, wills and imaginations for right moral action) as well as the pathogenic ones (of triggering, for instance, prejudice, animosity, inquisitional paranoia, racial suppression and, we might add, the suppression of women, violence against LGBTQIA+ people, and other forms of abuse and violence).
- The fundamental purpose or telos of the Bible, 'an artefact of the human soul', which psychological biblical criticism sees as essentially therapeutic.

For further reflection

1 Before reading on, what kind of contribution do you think psycho-logical biblical criticism might make to our engagement with the biblical texts?

---

2 What do you make of the argument that psychological readings might be anachronistic on the one hand, and the counterclaim that these readings should not be dismissed as a result of the 'continuity of the human psyche' on the other?

Psychoanalytical (Jungian) textual interpretation

Notwithstanding the spectrum of psychological approaches that have been applied to biblical interpretation, we are here going to focus specifically on Jungian readings, which have been the most prevalent in the interpretation of Jonah. That said, there have been some early psychological readings that took their lead from Freud; and we should note that while some scholars applied a wholesale Jungian approach, others, influenced by Jung's thought, combined this with a range of additional interests. A key aspect of Freudian, Jungian and related approaches is the focus on what Douglas Lawrie (2005b, p. 174) calls the revolutionary notion of the unconscious. While this was one of the pioneering elements of Freud's work, Jung built on it by distinguishing between the personal and the collective unconscious, thereby making the point that both individually and collectively we are influenced not only by our conscious rationality but also by unconscious and pre-rational or irrational factors. Applied to textual interpretation, this includes the observation that a text's 'manifest content' – what we might call its surface text, the words we can see on the page – is not all there is to it. As Rollins notes (1999, p. 92), 'conscious and unconscious factors are at work in the biblical authors and their communities, in the texts they have produced, in readers and interpreters of these texts and in their communities, and in the individual, communal, and cultural effects of those interpretations.'

So to focus exclusively on the text's surface level, as most critical biblical interpretation has traditionally done, keeps that other dimension hidden from sight. It has even been suggested that authors, texts and readers habitually collude, either deliberately or perhaps subconsciously, to keep it hidden. As again Rollins explains (1999, p. 157), given that the text is here understood as the 'product of, and participant in, a complex psychic event, riddled with conscious and unconscious factors ... [its] meaning can no longer be reduced simply to what the author intended'. Psychological biblical criticism therefore aims to uncover 'the unconscious meanings of the words' (Laplanche and Pontalis, p. 367). With this focus on the unconscious, Freudian and Jungian readings are effectively drawing attention to what we might call the world *beneath* the text. In doing so, they add yet another perspective to those readings that focus on the worlds 'behind', 'in' or 'in front of' the text.

The contribution that psychological biblical criticism makes to our understanding of biblical texts has been helpfully sketched by David Clines and Cheryl Exum (p. 18), who note that it allows us to 'search for the unconscious drives embedded within texts', helping us to 'uncover the psychology of characters and their relationships within the texts, and ask what it is about the human condition in general that these texts reflect, psychologically speaking'. Jungian interpretation focuses on archetypal patterns and symbols, which link the conscious with the unconscious by communicating emotions or pre-rational data alongside rational content. In line with this, Rollins (2004, p. 401) sees the text as 'the voice of the unconscious' whose function it is to 'complement or correct the one-sidedness of conscious life either for the individual reader or for the entire culture'. Or as Margaret Atwood (p. xx) put it, summarizing some of the reasons given by writers for why they write, 'To create a national consciousness, or a national conscience ... To serve the Collective Unconscious.'

This is an interesting concept given that the texts now included in our biblical canon were preserved not least because of the corrective function they exercised for the communities that preserved them. Rollins (2004, p. 401) adds: 'the mode in which these "truths anchored deep in the psyche" are expressed is the language of symbol and archetypal image' – in Jonah, for instance, water, the most primal of all archetypes, plays an important role. Kille similarly notes (2012, p. 13):

> Symbols enable us to remain connected to transcendent experience, they are bearers of moral underpinnings of culture and civilization, and they work as catalysts within us to lead us into the next steps of our personal and cultural development. Symbols always point us beyond where we are.

Archetypes are part of what Rollins (1999, p. 117) describes as a 'self-regulating system that calls on the "wisdom" of the unconscious to compensate for the one-sidedness of conscious life', aiming to provide direction and facilitate the health of individuals and communities. In connection with the psychological interpretation of biblical texts, it is also worth saying that archetypal images are frequently mediated precisely in the form of literature – not just the biblical literature, but also in important works of fiction and poetry today. As such, both in biblical times and now, they can function as a corrective to 'the psychic attitude of an entire culture' (Rollins, 1999, p. 54).

In contrast to Freud's focus on human psychosexual development, including the Oedipus complex about a boy's desire for the mother and the concomitant wish to be rid of the father, Jung, a pupil of Freud, developed a different model of human development. Concretely, this means that Jung was less focused on sexuality and less inclined to approach human development from a strongly pathological perspective. For Jung also, a person's psychic development is not completed at an early age but remains possible in later life. In fact, Jung's approach seeks to stimulate personal growth or integration and, ultimately, individuation, with the conscious and the unconscious, the individual and the community, all being brought into harmony (Lawrie, 2005b, pp. 180, 188).

The issues to be overcome in this process are 'intrapsychic conflicts' (van Aarde, p. 488) or 'psychodynamic factors', such as projection, repression, transference and so on (Rollins, 1999, p. 44). It may be helpful in this context to remind ourselves of some of Jung's terminology and key concepts, which include the *ego* with its self-centred concerns; the *persona*, which is the image of ourselves we seek to project; the *shadow*, which is our rejected alter ego; and the *self*, which propels us to integrate the various components of our psyche. Kille (2001, p. 83) describes the self as 'the source of the inner drive to psychic growth', adding that 'one often experiences an encounter with the Self as a meeting with the divine'. Commenting further on the shadow, he notes that it has not just personal but also collective dimensions, denoting 'the totality of what society denies, rejects or considers "evil"'. This is important since biblical texts typically are not just interested in personal transformation but in that of society, both then and now. This, then, takes us back to Jung's model of psychological development, which aims at individuation, becoming our own true self, and involves recognizing and assimilating the unconscious dimensions of our personality, the undeveloped and often undesired aspects of the self. Rollins (1999, p. 109) somewhat understatedly comments that all these 'patterns of inner conflict and personal development that psychoanalytic theory finds in the structure and processes of the self are not foreign to patterns intuitively rehearsed in biblical stories and narratives'.

There have been many who have applied a Jungian model to the interpretation of Jonah, some examples of which we are going to explore in the next section. One who sought to integrate a Jungian hermeneutical method with traditional biblical scholarship was American biblical scholar, theologian and activist Walter Wink (1935–2012), who endeavoured to interpret the biblical texts in such a way (pp. 1–2) that 'the past becomes alive and illumines our present with new possibilities for personal and social transformation'. Wink's statement demonstrates his interest in relating the biblical text to the personal and social lives of its readers. Rollins has made a similar point. We noted earlier that the Bible and its interpretation have had both pathogenic and therapeutic effects. In connection with this, Rollins suggests (1999, pp. 177, 180–1) that Jungian readings can serve therapeutic ends by nourishing 'the development of the self in the process of individuation' – for instance, by 'deploying the biblical stories and characters as associative devices for identifying the reader's conscious and unconscious complexes, fears, ideals and needs' and providing them 'with liberating and inspiring models for future action, perception, and behavior'.

Jungian psychological interpretation thus seeks to analyse psychic habits or strategies that can be observed as being operative in the characters of a biblical narrative, either consciously or unconsciously. Reading with an interest in personal and social transformation, it allows us to detect in the texts psychodynamic processes such as repression, denial, sublimation, projection, displacement or transference. On the other hand, the texts may also present biblical characters as people involved in a process of transformation or, indeed, as models of individuation.

For further reflection

1 What do you make of the notion of the 'world beneath the text', of unconscious, pre-rational, and perhaps even irrational forces operating underneath its surface? What does that mean for how we engage with it?

2 And what do you think of the concept of the biblical text and the archetypes found within it as 'the voice of the unconscious', a voice that seeks to 'complement or correct the one-sidedness of conscious life either for the individual reader or for the entire culture' and to facilitate direction, growth, integration, individuation and health for both?

3 What might it mean for us to read the biblical texts with an eye (a) to personal and social transformation, and (b) to countering potential pathogenic effects while activating their catalytic or therapeutic ones?

Psychological approaches to the book of Jonah

Having considered psychological biblical criticism in general, we now turn to look at how this has been applied to the book of Jonah. Our starting point is the observation of the book's rich symbolism. André LaCocque and Pierre-Emmanuel Lacocque (pp. 39–40) even go so far as to maintain that 'everything in the book of Jonah is symbolical, even the prophet's name'. German social psychologist and humanistic philosopher Erich Fromm (1900–80), who understood symbolic language as language in which the outside world stands for our souls and minds (1951, p. 22), similarly believed that the book of Jonah 'is written in symbolic language and all the realistic events described are symbols for the inner experiences of the hero' (p. 12).

Cursory comments on Jonah's psychology have been offered by traditional biblical commentators for some time – but will not be rehearsed here (for examples, see van Heerden, 2003, p. 718) – while several professional psychologists have provided us with psychological characterizations of Jonah's behaviour and personality. Some of these (especially Freudian ones and contributions from the perspective of object relations theory) will be summarized in the following section before we then turn to more comprehensive reviews of Jungian readings, existentialist psychological interpretations, Avivah Zornberg's psychological and midrashic approach (and the responses it occasioned) and, moving beyond the psychoanalytical perspective that has been pervasive in readings of Jonah, an analysis of the book from the perspective of trauma theory. However, before we begin, we might like to take note of Stuart Lasine's threefold caution (2016, p. 247; 2020, pp. 120–1):

- That the book's 48 verses do not allow us to construct any definitive psychological profile of Jonah.
- That our interpretations of his personality may say more about our own 'personalities, expectations, values, academic paradigm, and group identity' than about Jonah.
- And that people's behaviour (including that of literary figures such as Jonah) may be affected not only by their psychological state but also by the situations and circumstances in which they find themselves (p. 138). It would therefore be mistaken to reduce Jonah's behaviour to an outcome of his perceived psychological problems.

From Sigmund Freud until today: a kaleidoscope of psychological perspectives

The purpose of this section is to offer a brief overview of a range of psychological perspectives on Jonah before we then consider some readings in more detail. As Shulman (p. 337) has pointed out, there is only a single reference to Jonah in Freud's written oeuvre (2001, p. 274), which relates the episode of the big fish to the process of giving birth, as did psychoanalyst Michael Eisler (1882–1944), whose professional interests included pregnancy and childbirth. According to Eisler (p. 279), 'the archaic conception of oral birth is most impressively represented in the biblical story of Jonah, where the hero is spat forth by a whale'. English paediatrician and psychoanalyst Donald Winnicott (1896–1971), best known for his work in object relations theory, somewhat similarly noted (1967, p. 367) that 'as a student of unconscious symbolism, I knew ... that the sea is the mother, and on to the sea-shore the child is born. Babies come up out of the sea and are spewed out upon the land, like Jonah from the whale.' We might also note Rosa Ching Shao's comment (p. 43) that 'the images of swirling currents and seaweed wrapped around his head are recalling a baby inside her mother's water bag with the umbilical cord around her'.

An interpretation of Jonah from the perspective of Winnicott's object relations theory has been pursued by Ellen Martin (1993), who reads the book as an elemental story of human language acquisition and how that process forms a child's relations with those who bring it into language. This for her means that God, who is seen to be instructing Jonah, acts like a mother. In 2.1, the fish is suddenly and somewhat surprisingly female (feminine דָּגָה, *dagah*, is used instead of masculine דָּג, *dag*), which Martin sees as no mere accident, pointing to 'the maternal subtext of Jonah's education'. And if Jonah's behaviour appears childish at times, this is because he *is* a child. Commenting on Jonah's psalm in chapter 2, Martin suggests 'one might speculate that the psalm and its densely beautiful images of the deep are the verbal counterpart to the child's discovery of bodily sources of pleasure, in hands, genitalia, skin, and wriggling. Hence the optimism and sensation of liveliness in images supposedly of drowning.'

There is more to Martin's reading, but we must turn to Austrian-born psychologist Bruno Bettelheim (1903–90), who understood Jonah's struggle from a psychoanalytical perspective (1976). He found the key to the story in Jonah's psalm in chapter 2 where the prophet discovers his 'higher morality' and is 'wondrously reborn'. In what follows, Jonah then reaches his 'full humanity' and is no longer dependent upon his *id*,[3] the 'pleasure principle' that had urged him to run away to Tarshish. Instead, he finds himself ready to meet the demands of his *superego* and go to Nineveh. The first detailed Freudian analysis of the book was undertaken by psychoanalyst and psychiatrist Hyman Fingert (1909–99), who read it 'as an oedipal family crisis involving the triad of Jonah/son, mother/water, and father/God' (Shulman, p. 339). According to Fingert (p. 55):

> The Lord's command ... is interpreted as anger against the mother. In flight from this conflict, Jonah seeks refuge in a ship bound elsewhere (mother symbol) but is thrown into the sea (union with mother) and swallowed by a whale (return to the womb). After oral rebirth he makes his peace with the father.

As this quote indicates, Fingert had a tendency of seeing, in the words of LaCocque and Lacocque (p. 51), 'mother symbols in practically all events in the story (e.g., Tarshish, the ship, the fish, Nineveh, even the king)'. Fingert concluded that Jonah's behaviour revealed an emotionally disturbed person. Applying Freud's focus on human psychosexual development, he read the story in terms of the prophet being angry with his mother (symbolized by Nineveh) for preferring his father over him, seeing this as 'the wickedness of Nineveh that Jonah feels called upon to denounce' (p. 58). The sparing of the Ninevites, accordingly, stands for Jonah's renunciation of his sexual longing and his 'wishes for the mother and her destruction' (p. 61). To those not persuaded by Freudian concepts of human psychosexual development, Fingert's interpretation might seem bizarre. LaCocque and Lacocque are critical of the fact (p. 51) that his reading makes no reference to the historical or Old Testament context of the book of Jonah or the issues facing Israel at the time. Kille (2001, p. 32) adds that Fingert in his psychoanalytical analysis completely ignores 'the difficulties of discerning whether Jonah is a historical figure or a literary one'.

Another psychoanalytical reading is that of Joseph More, who maintains (p. 3) that when the book's puzzling aspects 'are considered in the light of modern psychodynamic theory, they do fall into place'. For More (p. 5), however, the key issue is not oedipal but concerns sibling rivalry. While the city of Nineveh stands for 'the "bad" mother whom Jonah wants to destroy because she mothers others' alongside him (p. 7), the people of Nineveh refer to his rival siblings whom he wishes to be rid of, as he does not want to share his mother's love with them (p. 8). Jonah's feelings for the plant that had been giving him shelter reveal his wish to have all his father's love to himself (p. 8). According to More, the plant combines 'oral wishes for comfort' with erotic fantasies, which leads him to describe it as a 'breast–penis composite' (p. 10). Its withering is highly significant, indeed necessary, 'for eliciting Jonah's feelings', for it is only now that he becomes aware of his great anger or can verbalize it. 'Without this', More adds (p. 11), 'any insight he might have gained would have been a purely intellectual one.' We might also note that More sees the book's concluding dialogue between God and Jonah as bearing 'some striking similarities to what takes place during the process of psychotherapy' (p. 5).

In his book on *Psychological Biblical Criticism*, Kille offers an assessment of Freudian readings, in which he points out (2001, p. 126) that they tend to disregard the existing story as story, which is approached instead in an atomizing way 'in which a few details are made to serve as the key to the story'.

For further reflection

1 Do you agree that there might be a symbolic dimension to the language of the book of Jonah?
2 What do you make of the themes that some interpreters deem to have detected, such as the whale as a womb and Jonah being birthed, various entities symbolizing the mother and father, the oedipal family crisis, and sibling rivalry?
3 Given the brevity of the summaries above, this is perhaps not the moment for a proper assessment of these interpretations. That said, what are your initial impressions?
4 What do you think of the concerns of LaCocque and Lacocque, Kille and Lasine that such readings (a) fail to engage with the book's biblical/historical context, (b) reduce Jonah's behaviour to his psychological state rather than taking into consideration the situation and circumstances in which he found himself, and (c) deal with the story in an atomistic way?

Jungian readings of Jonah

Having garnered some initial impressions of Freudian interpretations of Jonah, we now turn to consider the Jungian readings offered by M. A. Corey (1995), Edward Edinger (2000),[4] Jongsoo Park (2004), and Maria Kassel (2012). According to the latter (p. 411), a reading from the perspective of depth psychology suggests itself, 'since even a cursory look shows that the protagonist is faced with an inner struggle of the soul ...

that can bring him through developmental stages of progress, stagnation, or regression'. It was the book's unrealistic features and mythical elements that led Park to read it psychologically and symbolically, understanding it as 'a therapeutic myth' (p. 276). Virginia Ingram (pp. 140, 142, 153) similarly speaks of Jonah as a therapeutic text and, like Park, finds that a psychological reading makes its puzzling features 'disappear', while also fostering a deeper understanding of the text. For Park again, the use of mythological motifs is significant in that they address 'the collective unconscious of the readers who had similar experiences to those of Jonah' (pp. 276–7).

Corey (pp. 1, 2) focuses specifically on the unconscious, which for Jung is 'numinous, or spiritually oriented' and for many religious writers represents 'the psychospiritual interface between the human world and the Divine'. He suggests writers like Jung have shown that 'the single most effective means of interpreting religious phenomena is in terms of the unconscious', which Corey regards as 'God's world-based means for helping us become fully individuated in the world' (p. 3). In a chapter entitled 'Jonah and the unconscious', he seeks to decipher the book's 'hidden meaning in terms of the principles of modern depth psychology', convinced there is 'a wealth of deeply symbolic material that is directly applicable to many of the spiritual troubles that afflict us today' (p. 6). Edinger, for his part, begins from the general understanding of the book of Jonah as a 'psychological gem' (p. 120). They both see the figure of Jonah as representing the human ego, which is called by Yahweh, who stands for the Self as the 'integrative center of the human soul', to the task of individuation or 'psychospiritual wholeness' (Corey, pp. 6–7; Edinger, p. 120). Corey also describes this as 'the development of a higher behavioral regulatory center within the mind' (p. 14). According to him, the opening of the story is about the spirit of God acting through the Self and seeking to instigate 'a reconciliation between the ego and its rejected Shadow', the repressed aspects of the personality.

Nineveh's profound wickedness, according to Corey (p. 11), represents 'the pathological wickedness that is inevitably generated whenever the Shadow is repressed', while its threatened destruction by God, the Self, 'is directly symbolic of the profound self-destruction that will eventually take place in an individual's life if the ego doesn't come to terms with its Shadow'. God's command that Jonah preach to Nineveh is similarly 'symbolic of the Self's relentless push for reconciliation within the mind'. However, Jonah, the ego, flees from this task, which leads Corey to comment on the human condition, noting (p. 16) that 'this lack of courage on the part of the ego is almost certainly responsible for generating much of the moral evil that exists in the world'. It is this flight that leads to the Self sending 'a variety of psychological disturbances upon the ego' in another attempt to drive it towards reconciliation with its Shadow. Jonah's behaviour and the consequences it occasions for Corey (p. 17) demonstrate that 'anyone who consistently turns his back on the inner callings of the Self runs the risk of complete self-destruction'. After all, in our story, the storm was directly caused by Jonah refusing to follow the divine command.

The sea, in this reading, represents the unconscious, which leads Edinger to comment (p. 126) that 'if the [ego] goes to sleep [which often signifies repression], then that puts the unconscious in a terrible uproar'. Corey (pp. 17–18) is more specific when he sees the violence of the sea as depicting the 'tremendous amount of anger ... exhibited by the unconscious whenever the ego forces it to conceal an important part of the larger personality'. For Corey, Jonah having gone 'below deck' points to the 'subterranean nature of the repressive process'. Park (p. 280) regards Jonah's sleep as 'another example of his running away ... as he falls into a numb state without any thought'. Bypassing the actions of the sailors and the captain (for relevant comments, see Corey, pp. 19–20), we note that Jonah, the ego, having been quite aware of the storm's cause, only agrees to be thrown into the sea and thus face his own unconscious under ultimate duress, in a moment that Edinger (p. 126) regards as the story's turning point. That Jonah, instead of drowning, finds himself in the belly of the great fish leads Corey to comment (p. 23) that God, the Self, 'will provide a safe haven for the ego once it decides to immerse itself within the "raging sea" of the unconscious'. Edinger (p. 128) describes this as 'a purposeful descent into the maternal womb of the unconscious for the purpose of transformation and rebirth', only to add that:

> The monster represents the primordial psyche in its natural, elemental and undifferentiated state. It is untamed animal energy, not yet available for the conscious civilized functioning of the ego. As long as that monster has not been entered and dealt with from within, the ego is in constant danger of being swallowed up by it.

He further notes (p. 129) that the transformation process is only activated if the ego actively descends into the unconscious. If this happens passively, then, far from being transformative, it constitutes 'a dangerous regressive phenomenon of being swallowed up' (p. 132). Commenting on Jonah's prayer (p. 24), Corey highlights terms such as 'the deep' or 'engulfing waters', noting that anyone 'who is seriously intent on reaching wholeness must persevere through the immediate pains and fears of the journey'. Park (p. 282), who also sees this part of Jonah's journey as him meeting 'the inner voice of the unconscious', suggests that the belly of the fish, 'as a womb of the truth, is the place where Jonah sees God'. Edinger, for his part, reflects on the fact that Jonah's psalm essentially is little more than a combination of various quotations from the Psalms, which he interprets as Jonah speaking in an 'archetypal voice' rather than in his own personal one (p. 130). This leads him to maintain (p. 132) that sometimes 'the only safe attitude to have is one that is founded on archetypal reality as opposed to ego reality'. Corey (p. 25) interprets Jonah's being freed from the fish as having been caused by his humility as demonstrated in his prayer. As Willie van Heerden (2003, p. 723) notes: 'the only way we can re-emerge in one piece from our inner neurotic suffering is to develop enough meekness of heart to allow us to become reconciled with the Shadow side of our personalities'.

This, then, takes us to the second part of the story where the city of Nineveh, according to Corey (p. 26), 'represents the unconscious part of the mind', which is so important that 'it takes three solid "days" just to see it all'. For Corey, this points to our reconciliation with our Shadow being a time-consuming process as we 'cannot reintegrate back into consciousness a lifetime of repressed pains and fears overnight'. The wickedness of the Ninevites for him symbolizes 'the pain and suffering that is routinely produced by the Shadow when the ego fails to include it within the overall matrix of the personality' (p. 27). However, once the ego seeks to come to terms with the Shadow, the latter's 'wickedness' quickly disappears, as is depicted in the story by the Ninevites' eagerness to repent. And once God, the Self, realizes 'that the Shadow has been transformed and reintegrated within the personality, it will simultaneously relax its previous threat to destroy the personality' (Corey, p. 27). Crucially, of course, it was the actions of Jonah, the ego, that made possible the repentance and conversion of the Ninevites, the Shadow, which allowed them/it to be saved. Van Heerden comments (2003, p. 724) that 'metaphorically speaking, it means that the Self would not be able to bring harmony between the different parts of the psyche, had the ego not reached a stage when it finally confronted the Shadow'.

Concerning the episode of the plant, which withers as quickly as it had grown, Park (p. 283) suggests that this reflects Jonah's unstable psyche as someone who easily becomes happy only to just as quickly fall into depression again. Van Heerden (2003, p. 724) wonders: 'did the Self use the comparison between the Nineveh experience and the new sources of anger, namely the plant-worm combination, to remind the ego of the vital importance of dealing with the Shadow?' Commenting further on Jonah's behaviour, Edinger notes (p. 134) that while Yahweh, the Self, loses his wrath, the wrath and wickedness are now transferred to the ego as reflected in Jonah becoming furious at Yahweh's decision to spare the Ninevites. While the Self is now able to manifest its loving and compassionate side, the ego is still vengeful and depressed, but all that is now out in the open rather than being repressed and hidden away in the unconscious. Lastly, Park (p. 277) offers an intriguing reading of the book's incomplete ending when he suggests that it 'reflects the process of ongoing life'. Thus, while on the story's symbolic level a process of transformation, integration or individuation has been set in motion, that process is clearly not yet complete, as indeed it never is for any of us for as long as we live.

Kassel's approach to the book, while also drawing on Jung's psychoanalytic theory, differs from the other Jungian readings reviewed in this section. She is less interested in applying such a perspective to every stage in the unfolding story, reads from a feminist perspective, and pays particular attention to what she describes as 'psycho-*theological* processes and conflicts' (p. 412). Her focus, therefore, is on 'the inner development of human beings, *into which faith in God is integrated*' (emphases added). More specifically, Kassel considers Jonah's image of God, noting that such images 'are always tied to the status of [a person's] psychic development'. Jonah, she points out (p. 415), 'is so identified with his image of God – that God must punish, even destroy, sinners – that to change his image of God would utterly destroy the world he inhabits'. His faith, even his very identity, require this merciless God, and any challenge to that image of God drives Jonah to despair, which expresses itself in his repeated death wish. Is this Jonah not a fundamentalist, asks Kassel, 'whose faith is not (any longer) integrated with his rational abilities'? She goes on to suggest that Jonah is fixated on a simplistic view of life and the world, that 'he denies the diversity and nontransparency of life and tries to avoid adulthood and its responsibilities'. In line with all this, Kassel (p. 417) views the book's ending as 'a challenge to Jonah to make room in his life not only for the angry God but also for the kind God, and in so doing to move forward in his development toward more complete personhood'.

These Jungian approaches to the book of Jonah, especially as exemplified by Corey, Edinger and Park, have been criticized by Lasine. One of his objections (2016, p. 249; 2020, p. 132) – that Jonah does not appear to have been transformed by his experience with the fish – seems however to have been rendered moot by the combined readings of Corey, Edinger and Park summarized above. After all, they see the transformational process to cover Jonah's entire journey as presented throughout the book – and indeed beyond it – rather than limiting it to just the episode with the fish. We might also note the observation – expressed, for instance, by Janet Gaines (p. 62) – that characters that have come through an initiation of some watery ordeal (whether in ancient Greek mythology or in the films of George Lucas) regularly fail to live up to 'sustained perfection' as they get on with their lives. Lasine's other point, which picks up a comment by Jungian literary critic Terence Dawson (2008) – namely, that these types of readings often ignore textual aspects that do not fit with their perspective, thus reading the work selectively – is however worth pondering. In his fuller study, Lasine (2020, p. 137) adds that 'any persuasive psychological study of Jonah must take into account all the features of the text, both what is – and is not – said by the narrator and how it is said'.

For further reflection

1 What do you make of the interpretations of Corey, Edinger and Park that see the book's symbolism as addressing issues such as the unconscious, repression, transformation, integration and psychospiritual wholeness?

2 What do you think of Kassel's reading, which stresses that a person's image of God is related to their psychic development? Is Jonah a fundamentalist, who denies the diversity and non-transparency of life and thereby resists his own personal growth?

3 And what about Lasine's criticism of Corey, Edinger and Park for reading the text selectively, for ignoring those aspects that do not fit with their perspective? Is the only acceptable reading one that can make sense of all textual data? Or might there be value in interpretations that offer additional perspectives – missed by other interpreters – without necessarily being fully comprehensive in their engagement with the text?

Existentialist psychological interpretations of Jonah

In his review of psychological interpretations of Jonah, van Heerden (2003, p. 719) lists two existentialist psychological interpretations: *Jonah: A Psycho-Religious Approach to the Prophet* by LaCocque and Lacocque (1990) and Ze'ev Haim Lifshitz's *The Paradox of Human Existence: A Commentary on the Book of Jonah* (1994), to which we might add Gaines's *Forgiveness in a Wounded World: Jonah's Dilemma* (2003). Also worth mentioning in this context, even though the author departs in important ways from these readings, are the works by Lasine: 'Jonah's complexes and our own' (2016) and *Jonah and the Human Condition* (2020).

LaCocque and Lacocque (p. xviii) refer to several influences on their approach, such as Sigmund Freud, C. G. Jung, Austrian-British psychoanalyst Melanie Klein (1882–1960), Donald Winnicott, Swiss psychologist Jolande Jacobi (1890–1973), German-Israeli psychologist and philosopher Erich Neumann (1905–60), pioneer of psychiatric medicine Harold Searles (1918–2015) and others. Among these others is American psychologist Abraham Maslow (1908–70), references to whom recur repeatedly throughout their study – more frequently, in fact, than to some of the named influences. Maslow, the founder of humanistic psychology, was profoundly influenced by the philosophies of humanism and existentialism. His reference to the book of Jonah was in connection with what Maslow originally called the 'Jonah syndrome' (1967) while subsequently preferring the term 'Jonah complex' (1993), by which he meant the '"fear of one's own greatness", the "evasion of one's destiny", or the "running away from one's best talents"' (1993, p. 34). The phrase 'Jonah complex' describes the reality that 'many of us evade our constitutionally suggested vocations (call, destiny, task in life, mission)'. Maslow adds (p. 37) that the notion includes the 'fear of being torn apart, of losing control, of being shattered and disintegrated, even being killed by the experience', while Gaines points out (p. 39) that 'frightened Jonah is the opposite of a self-actualized person'.

For LaCocque and Lacocque (p. 217), 'the story of Jonah is ... a psychological tableau of the human condition. Jonah is not just a Jew of Palestine ... He is human, he is everyone.' And by being human, Jonah exemplifies what LaCocque and Lacocque call our human 'call to task'. As 'Everyman', he 'is under the commandment to respond to his human vocation' (p. xxiii), but like most of us he runs away from that commandment (p. 61), which is meant to pull us up 'from animality to humanity' (p. 190). The call at the beginning of the book is a 'call to go "beyond," ... an exhortation to have the courage to be separated from the crowd' (p. 69) and 'to go *beyond* one's own limits' (p. 71). LaCocque and Lacocque quote Austrian psychiatrist and philosopher Viktor Frankl (1905–97), who suggests (p. 9) that a 'man ... finds identity to the extent to which he commits himself to something beyond himself, to a cause greater than himself'. LaCocque and Lacocque (p. 70) describe this as an 'existential conflict', before going on to refer to Maslow and the Jonah syndrome.

Jonah himself, being unable to follow the call, 'brings about the sea storm; he is at the same time its author and its victim. He *cannot* have a safe trip because the turmoil of his soul finds an echo in the turmoil of his environment' (p. 71). Having understood that his vocation involves facing the unknown and potentially even death, Jonah, by fleeing,

'resorts to a sheer instinct of survival' (p. 73). In choosing inconspicu-
ous Jonah rather than one of the Old Testament grandees, the author
'underlines the universal character of the vocation to self-transcendence
... to become fully human' (p. 74). Jonah, LaCocque and Lacocque go
on to say (p. 75), is 'our "alter ego"'. Ironically, though, it is by seeking
to avoid risk and death that Jonah not only evolves from 'one state of
alienation to another' but also ends up laying his life on the line. Indeed,
Jonah's engulfment in the 'shark', as LaCocque and Lacocque call the big
fish, 'is synonymous to entering a state of disintegration' (p. 79). That
said, they also quote Fromm, whose humanistic psychology combined a
Freudian interest in individual psychology with existentialist philosophy
and a concern for social interactions. For Fromm, the fish's belly, alongside other symbols of enclosure, had quite a different connotation. As he
suggests (1951, pp. 22–3), Jonah's various retreats – 'going into the ship,
going into the ship's belly, falling asleep, being in the ocean, and being
in the fish's belly' – refer to 'a condition of being protected and isolated',
a desire for 'safe withdrawal from communication with other human
beings'. And again (1949, p. 46):

> The central theme of this symbolic, dreamlike story is Jonah's desire for
> complete seclusion and irresponsibility – a position which at first was
> meant to save him from his mission, but eventually is turned into an
> unbearable, prisonlike existence ... Being inside the whale has brought
> this experience (of isolation and protection) to such a final intensity that
> Jonah cannot stand it any longer; he turns to God again; he desires to be
> freed, to go on with his mission.

A similar reading has been proposed by David Gunn and Danna Fewell
(p. 133), who 'see Jonah seeking security in "enclosure" ... [aiming]
to escape the challenges and ... the contradictions of the "real", the
"outside", world'. Lasine (2016), while not agreeing with Maslow's
humanistic Jonah complex interpretation, finds the focus on metaphors
of enclosure helpful, as these are quite prominent in the story of Jonah. In
addition to the ones already mentioned by Fromm, Lasine (2016, p. 247;
2020, p. 129) points to 'the belly of Sheol', 'the heart of the seas', the
'deep', the 'pit', the 'sheltering *sukkah*', and the '*qiqayon* plant'. In an
article, titled 'Inside the whale', English writer and critic George Orwell
(1903–50) similarly commented on the enclosures, averring that 'being
inside a whale is a very comfortable, cosy, homelike thought'. Indeed,
says Orwell: 'there you are, in the dark, cushioned space that exactly fits
you, with yards of blubber between yourself and reality, able to keep
up an attitude of the completest indifference, no matter *what* happens'.

'Short of being dead', he concludes, 'it is the final, unsurpassable stage of irresponsibility.'

LaCocque and Lacocque's discussion of engulfment motifs and the fear of the disintegration of one's personality, of the loss of self, of death (pp. 53–61), follows Jung in alluding to various hero myths even while noting that Jonah 'has no recourse to heroic acts'. They interpret the engulfment motifs as symbolizing a desire to 'regress to an anxiety-free state reminiscent of how it must have felt to be in [the mother's] womb: nurtured, protected, and held' – the Hebrew term for the fish's belly, מֵעֶה (me'eh), is used for an embryo's shelter in the mother's womb in Genesis 25.23 and Ruth 1.11. Interestingly, while the ship in Hebrew is feminine (אֳנִיָּה, 'oniyyah (1.3–5); סְפִינָה, sefinah (1.5)), the fish is usually masculine (דָּג, dag (1.17; 2.10)), except, as we saw earlier, in 2.1, where it is also suddenly feminine (דָּגָה, dagah). Arthur Boyd and Peter Porter's 1973 collection of poetry and art inspired by the story of Jonah features a poem ('Recitative', p. 26) that suggests that 'the storm was a metaphor to Jonah, who dreamt he was with his mother'. This is followed a few pages later by a drawing carrying the caption 'J. with his mother' (p. 38).

In line with this theme, LaCocque and Lacocque (p. 101) interpret the symbolism of water as representing 'first and foremost the water inside the womb' but also as 'a sign of non-development and to a certain extent of nonbeing' as well as 'the primordial milieu full of promise where life begins'. Commenting on Jonah's prayer inside the fish, they note (p. 104) that 'in the depth of the abyss ... he has torn himself away from introversion and has turned toward *another*'. LaCocque and Lacocque see the psalm as a highly significant turning point, expressing an attitude that they describe (pp. 105–6) in terms of an acceptance and an affirmation of the meaningfulness of existence, a 'cathartic collapse of the negative into the positive', a breaking out of isolation, a giving birth to oneself,[5] a transformation of 'absurdity and death into meaning and life'.

It is, however, important to note that LaCocque and Lacocque's reading differs from many other psychological interpretations in that they pay careful attention to the book's historical context, which they date to the third century BC. They see it as imperative to offer what they describe as a 'balanced integration of hermeneutics, exegesis, politics, and psychology' (p. xix). While we can explore neither their wider interests – for instance, in Jonah as a Menippean satire aimed at the intellectual isolationism of certain conservative ideologists in Jerusalem (pp. 26–48) – nor the ramifications those interests have for their psychological interpretation of the book, it is worth noting that, for LaCocque and Lacocque, the vocation from which Jonah is fleeing is specifically his priestly vocation as a Jew in the world (p. 84). In connection with this, it might be interesting to note that, for instance, their interpretation of the enclosures in the story in terms of the motherly womb becomes concretized when they describe this (p. 174) as the womb 'of the land where he was born'. However, they do also generalize, quoting American cultural anthropologist Ernest Becker (1924–74), who asked (p. 82): 'What is one's true talent, his secret gift, his authentic vocation? ... How can the person take ... the great mystery that he feels at the heart of himself ... to enrich both himself and mankind with the peculiar quality of his talent?'

What Jonah's specific Jewish vocation and our general human vocation have in common is that the individual's calling is meant to benefit the wider group. But if that is the aim, then Jonah's failure is ours. Humanity, as LaCocque and Lacocque put it (p. 90), 'sinks with him as a result of similar panic in the face of vocation, responsibility, and authenticity'. For them (p. 180), 'human self-actualization ... is not "an end-state"' but rather a by-product of fulfilling the potentialities of one's vocation vis-à-vis the world – which in Jonah's case is the specific vocation of a Jewish prophet vis-à-vis his own people. Turning to the end of the story and focusing on Jonah's anger, LaCocque and Lacocque (p. 143), on the one hand, note that 'psychology sheds light on the common human denominator between him and us. Jonah's anger is a feeling that we immediately understand. We can appreciate its intensity.' But, they add, 'it is within the concreteness of his Jewish involvement that we must understand it', a concreteness that concerns Jonah's anger about a God who extends his mercy to Nineveh, 'the destroyer of Jerusalem,[6] the concentration camp for God's people' (p. 139).

Gaines's interpretation shares several features with that of LaCocque and Lacocque. She sees Jonah as 'everyone' (pp. 9, 10, 111, 136), as an 'antihero' (pp. 9, 112, 127), as our 'alter ego' (p. 10), and as representing humankind throughout the ages' (p. 152). She is critical of Fingert's Freudian interpretation (p. 119), according to which Jonah is struggling with incest taboos, but Jungian stimuli are evident at various points (see, for instance, her discussion of the readings of Jonah by Jung, and Corey, pp. 33–4). A Maslowian influence is furthermore apparent in comments such as that 'Jonah evades his vocation' (p. 10) or seeks to 'escape the reality of his prophetic calling' (p. 47). In line with Jungian interpreters, Gaines (p. 44) sees the storm – 'symbolic of the ruckus we raise when we try to avoid our true selves' – as having been caused by Jonah himself. She adds that Jonah's environment is 'an echo of his interior self'. For Gaines, the sea serves more than one function. On the one hand, it is symbolic of the amniotic fluid inside the womb, which is a sign of human immaturity but also stands for the potential for growth. On the other hand, the sea also represents the demands of the unconscious, and its raging is indicative of the agitation caused by the ego's repression of parts of its fuller self (p. 45).

The reason Gaines's reading is discussed here is that, like LaCocque and Lacocque, she combines psychological concerns with historical and theological ones. Her specific interest is in Jonah having been called to offer forgiveness in a wounded world, as the title of her study puts it; it is this that Gaines sees as constituting the prophet's vocation. She notes, for instance (p. 10), that 'as Everyone, Jonah shoulders the burden of our unresolved conflicts about accepting those around us who look different, hold different values, and follow different belief systems'. In a biblical text that serves as a 'window into the human soul' (p. 20), Jonah plunging into the sea points to him undergoing 'a psychological metamorphosis' that helps him overcome his human limitations (pp. 11–12), which are precisely about that enormous struggle to forgive. Given that focus, Gaines's following words (p. 58) about our internal demons and the necessary maturation process are also best read in connection with Jonah's and our own all-too-human struggle to forgive:

> If ... the fish is a Leviathan-type monster, the message of the book of Jonah is that our threatening, internal demons can be transformed into saving graces. A hero must undergo a maturation process, a rite of passage. Typically, the challenge is to defeat the monster that represents the unconscious ... It represents our internal struggles, our daily battles that we are capable of overcoming.

Lasine, for his part (2016, p. 251; cf. 2020, p. 145), reads Jonah's experience in connection with the 'crises of childhood and adulthood', suggesting that the book's plot 'evokes crucial challenges faced by children, and the continued relevance of these issues for adult life'. Facing ambivalent, threatening or hostile parents, a child's perceived threat to the integrity of their self or identity, according to Lasine (2016, p. 252; 2020, p. 147), 'can prompt a mortal fear of being swallowed and eaten up, and thereby "reengulfed"'. Jonah's great fish, in this context, resembles the monsters that feature in various fairy tales. Jonah's behaviour has sometimes been seen as childish. Gaines (p. 38), for instance, portrays him as a two-year-old who 'throws a temper tantrum and defies authority'. Lasine (2016, pp. 252–3; 2020, p. 148) interprets this behaviour as 'a struggle for power and control'. Control, he notes (2020, p. 159), 'is also a key factor if one views Jonah as a mature adult who is attempting to keep his integrity in Yahweh's world'. As for the episode involving the big fish, Lasine (pp. 148–9) compares this to figures such as Carlo Collodi's Pinocchio and the Brothers Grimm's Little Red Riding Hood, suggesting that the issue is 'living entombment' and thus the 'child's' prevented development. He adds (p. 149) that:

> Even though Jonah expresses no desire to be sheltered in the big fish and does not experience the fish's belly as a welcome shelter, once he has been swallowed, it is still possible that readers of Jonah's story might find themselves reminded of the primal threat to selfhood evoked by being swallowed, even if that fear has long since sunk down into the depths of their psyche.

Turning to the ending of the story, Lasine (2016, pp. 252–3; 2020, p. 148) notes that Yahweh may be seen as a father who is 'patiently leading his pouting child toward the recognition that the father's course of action was correct, and that the "child's" anger and sense of moral outrage were inappropriate'. That said, however, in the earlier episode involving the plant and the worm, Yahweh comes across as patronizing, talking down to, and toying with Jonah's emotions, thereby infantilizing him and invalidating his complaint (Lasine, 2016, p. 254; 2020, p. 160). More generally speaking, the book of Jonah confronts us with the disquieting aspects of the human condition, such as our lack of control over our lives, the possible disintegration of our identity, and the threat of death (p. 255).

For further reflection

1 What do you make of Maslow's notion of the 'Jonah complex', of the book addressing the issue of the prophet – and us – running away from our vocation vis-à-vis the world, of Jonah being everyone, and the book, in that sense, addressing the human condition?
2 What about the big fish offering 'safe withdrawal', seclusion from the real world, and a state of irresponsibility, 'with yards of blubber between [ourselves] and reality', as Orwell put it?
3 What do you think of the ways in which LaCocque and Lacocque and Gaines combine psychological concerns with historical and theological ones, thus connecting the story with its historical context and/or some wider biblical-theological themes? Is that a 'better', more satisfying, reading of the story? Why?
4 And what, finally, about Lasine's focus on the story exemplifying 'crises of childhood and adulthood', such as Jonah facing a perceived threat to the integrity of his self or identity and thus struggling for power and control? If so, as what kind of father figure is God portrayed in this story?

Avivah Zornberg and the discussion in Psychoanalytic Dialogues

In 2008, the journal *Psychoanalytic Dialogues* published an article by
Scottish Torah scholar Avivah Zornberg, entitled 'Jonah: A fantasy of
flight', which was subsequently reissued in her book *The Murmuring
Deep: Reflections on the Biblical Unconscious* (2009). In the journal,
Zornberg's contribution was followed by several articles offering commentaries and responses to her paper (see Aron; Fishman; Salberg; and
Shulman) as well as Zornberg's response to the respondents (Zornberg,
2008b). Apart from their common interest in psychoanalysis, the contributors all approach the book of Jonah from a Jewish perspective.
Zornberg specifically combines an interest in literary analysis and
midrashic and talmudic[7] interpretation – or the 'rabbinic unconscious', as
she calls it – with psychoanalytical readings of biblical texts. In the introduction to *The Murmuring Deep* (2009, pp. xi, xii), she talks about her
focus on 'narratives of rupture and reconnection in three kinds of relationships: between self and other, between self and God, and within the
self', relationships that correspond to 'three spiritual registers – social,
religious, introspective'.

Turning to the book of Jonah, which she regards as 'the most enigmatic of biblical narratives', she notes (p. 77) that 'its central mystery
– Jonah's flight from God – haunts the narrative till the end'. 'What
does Jonah imagine he is doing in evading the omnipresent, omniscient
God?' she wonders, only to comment that 'it is striking that the theological absurdity of such an attempt never arises in the text'. Psychologist
and psychoanalyst Jill Salberg, one of Zornberg's respondents, who
approaches the book from a 'British Object Relations and Relational
theoretical approach'[8] (Salberg, p. 319), reflects on Jonah's mental state,
which she describes as one of agitation and despair. It is 'a despair so great
that he seeks out death'; and it only gets more and more desperate until
Jonah at last can only plead with God to let him die (p. 320). Zornberg,
however (2008b, p. 369), expresses some concerns about Salberg taking
her 'diagnostic thrust' too far, for instance, when she diagnoses Jonah's
'paranoid-schizoid anxieties' (Salberg, p. 320). But what should be noted
here is how seriously Jonah's death wish is taken from a psychoanalytical
perspective, especially when compared to interpreters who saw it as an
indication of the prophet being mocked by the author.

The first part of the story quickly takes Jonah into the hold of the
ship where he is soon fast asleep (1.5). The verb used here (רדם, *radam*)
corresponds to תַּרְדֵּמָה (*tardemah*), the deep sleep or coma-like state that
God caused Adam to fall into when creating Eve (Gen. 2.21). Zornberg
comments (2009, p. 79) that 'the wordplay subtly involves him in a

project of withdrawal from consciousness, as his trajectory carries him down into the ship's hold – a womblike enclosure – from which he is roused only to ask to be surrendered to the sea'. Salberg, for her part, asks (p. 324): 'is [this] sleep, or could it rather be dissociation, a deadening of awareness'? In fact, she suggests that the scenes on the boat and in the fish's belly might be Jonah's dream: 'Recognizing that he has endangered the crew, Jonah then dreams of an escape [that is, being tossed into the sea] that will not injure anyone else.'

Whereas both God (1.2; 3.2) and the ship's captain (1.6) had urged Jonah to 'cry out' (קרא, *qara*'), for Zornberg (2009, p. 83), Jonah's refusal to do so is a 'withdrawal from himself, from his own voice, his own depths'. Psychotherapist George Fishman (p. 309) sees it as a withdrawal from everyone else, noting that Jonah 'through most of the book ... does not engage in meaningful dialogue with God, the captain, his fellow sailors, or the Ninevites'. Quoting from Pirke de Rabbi Eliezer[9] 10, which has the ship's captain say to Jonah, 'Behold, we are standing betwixt death and life, and thou art slumbering and sleeping', Zornberg (2009, p. 84) interprets Jonah's flight as a refusal to cry out, 'to stand between death and life'.

In Jewish tradition, standing before God is 'the essential posture of prayer', and 'to cry from deep wounds of grief and need, to allow hollow places to open up within him, would be to stand in God's presence' (Zornberg, 2009, p. xxviii); but this is what Jonah refuses to do. American psychoanalyst and psychotherapist Lewis Aron (1952–2019) similarly suggests (p. 304) that 'arguing with God is a Jewish tradition ... Prayer is about standing up to and before God. Jonah seems incapable of engaging in dialogue and so he flees ... Jonah is the anti-hero, the one who cannot take a stand.' Instead, Jonah 'sinks into unconsciousness, suppressing the human cry. ... Sleep and silence are his flight response' (Zornberg, 2009, p. 84). Having gone down to Joppa, down into the ship, and down into its hold, Fishman (p. 310) understands Jonah's sleep as a further descent. Preferring 'death – the foregone conclusion – to the anguish of the human place between ... Jonah urges the sailors to throw him into the sea, into that condition of unconsciousness' (Zornberg, 2009, pp. 85–6). Again, Zornberg's interpretation here develops a theme found in traditional Jewish exegesis, for in Mekilta Shemot[10] 12.1.4 Rabbi Yochanan is quoted as saying: 'Jonah went (on that voyage) only to cast himself into the sea.' Mekilta Shemot in the same passage comments on Jonah's flight with reference to Psalm 139.7–10:

'And Jonah rose to flee to Tarshish, etc.' Now can one flee from the L rd? Is it not written (Psalms 139:7–10) 'Where can I flee from Your presence ... If I ascend to heaven, You are there, etc. If I take wing with the dawn, there, too, Your hand will lead me ...'

Zornberg comments (2009, p. 88) that 'the mystery that obsesses the Psalmist is the mystery of the soul that desires to flee, to be hidden from God's eyes, to be unfound, even as it rejoices in being touched, seen, found'. And she quotes Winnicott (2018, p. 187) as saying:

> Although healthy persons communicate and enjoy communicating, the other fact is equally true, that each individual is an isolate, permanently non-communicating, permanently unknown, in fact unfound ... At the center of each person is an incommunicado element, and this is sacred and most worthy of preservation.

For Zornberg (2009, p. 89), the psalmist's cry, 'Where shall I flee from your face?', therefore expresses 'an inexpressible and profoundly human dilemma'.

Having been thrown overboard, Jonah finds himself mortally surrounded by the deep (תְּהוֹם, *tehom*; 2.5), the chaos waters of Genesis 1.2. However, based on the words of his prayer, Zornberg (p. xxix) believes that Jonah resists their impact. His experience of the depths of the sea is having little effect on him. 'Unlike the Psalmist, who uses the depths of the sea as a metaphor for his spiritual anguish, Jonah plumbs literal depths without touching any chord of mystery in his soul ... he sleep-walks his way through the adventures of his life' (pp. 83–4). The prayer, after all, is couched in the past tense. It is 'a prayer of thanksgiving for a resolved existential crisis. The *tehom* is not permitted to be present, profoundly experienced within him' (p. 383). This is, Zornberg says (p. 93):

> a strange prayer for one who needs salvation *now*. What is missing is any religious or moral awareness of his situation: he confesses no sins, nor does he pray for forgiveness. The existential terror of his condition remains quite unexpressed in this formulaic prayer of gratitude for past salvation.

She adds (p. 94) that people crying out to God in times of crisis:

> will confess, entreat forgiveness, pray for salvation from the terror of now and here. But this standing place is closed to Jonah. Instead, he flees to the past moment of salvation ... What he cannot encompass is the transitional moment of danger and desire, when one is lost, the future obscure. The experience of *not knowing* ... is too terrible to bear.

Zornberg calls Jonah an 'emotional plagiarist', quoting literary critic, psychoanalyst and psychoanalytic critic of literature Albert Hutter (1941–2004), who notes (pp. 75–6) that 'one way to protect ourselves … is to hide behind someone else's words'. This is what Jonah is doing. Using the language of the psalms, he:

> assumes a false identity, substituting what is felt to be someone else's more authentic experience for one's own fragmented sense of self. In this sense, Jonah uses borrowed words to express a classic stance of gratitude, instead of speaking, or crying, out of his own unresolved situation of terror (Zornberg, 2009, p. 94).

Zornberg in this context again reads the story in connection with Pirke de Rabbi Eliezer 10 where, being admonished to pray, Jonah quotes from Hannah's song of triumph (1 Sam. 2.6): 'The LORD kills and brings to life; he brings down to Sheol and raises up.' Zornberg regards it as highly ironic that it is Hannah's song of triumph that Jonah quotes rather than emulating her urgent plea, which she expressed to Eli in these words: 'I am a woman deeply troubled … I have been pouring out my soul before the LORD … I have been speaking out of my great anxiety and vexation all this time' (1 Sam. 1.15–16). This for Zornberg illustrates 'true prayer, the cry from the depths of pain and perplexity', whereas Jonah, in the interpretation of Pirke de Rabbi Eliezer, 'is exploiting [Hannah's] resolved situation to give him borrowed assurance in his unresolved one. His prayer becomes an act of emotional plagiarism, covering an emptiness' (p. 95).

One of the sections of Zornberg's article is entitled 'The trauma of survival'. It follows another midrashic route in picking up a tradition, found in several sources (J. Sukkah 5.1; Midrash Tehillim 26; Pirke de Rabbi Eliezer 33; Yalkut Shimoni 550),[11] according to which Jonah is the son of the widow of Zarephath, who was brought back to life through Elijah's prayer (1 Kings 17.17–24). We are not here going to engage with the more specific claim that Jonah's trauma is that of survival. However, that Jonah's behaviour displays the marks of trauma has been found to be persuasive by some of Zornberg's respondents as well. Fishman (p. 311), for instance, notes that it is because of trauma having injured Jonah's capacity to feel that his capacity to relate to both self and others has become compromised. Aron (p. 303), in turn, speaks of fragmentation, connecting it with prayer and noting: 'A victim of trauma, Jonah … could not stand and talk to God because he could not bring the various aspects of himself into dialog, he could not stand in the spaces … nor could he stand up for himself and therefore he could not engage in a genuine meeting.'

When Jonah later insists on how right he was to flee, Zornberg suggests (2009, p. 78) that 'he is still fleeing'. It is this flight that leads to his prayer for death (4.3), which verbalizes a death wish that had been there all along. While in the scene with the sailors, death might have been Jonah's 'heroic choice, his sacrifice to save the sailors', it now becomes clear that 'it is also his profound desire' (p. 78). Commenting on 4.2 ('I knew that you are a gracious and compassionate God ...'), Zornberg (p. 80) notes that Jonah here inverts the celebration of God's gracious and merciful attributes:

> Moses first articulated them in pleading for the lives of his people ... they have become consecrated liturgical recitative in the prayer lives of the Jewish people. Indeed, on Yom Kippur, they play a central role in every service of the day, not simply as descriptions of God's loving ways, but as invocations, invitations, performative pleas that allow the loving face of God to emerge.

Who, Zornberg asks, is this Jonah, who 'demonically repudiat[es] love while desiring death and calling it good'? She interprets his actions as enacting 'the human desire to know and to control the Other [in this case God], to evade uncertainty and affirm mastery'. Jonah flees because he is unable to acknowledge God, as that would mean 'acknowledging the Other within oneself, as well as the enigmatic human other' (p. xvi) – in this case, the Ninevites. Part of the human condition, for Zornberg, is that we must 'acknowledge "the excess of the other – the other's *intrusiveness*"' (p. xxii). However, this is what Jonah is unable to do.

Jonah's flight, therefore, is also a flight into what Zornberg (p. 89) calls 'compulsive knowingness', which leads Fishman (p. 312) to reflect on 'our becoming aware of the Jonah in all of us, the part of our soul that cleaves to the safety of familiar knowledge in the face of agonizing uncertainties'. Jonah knows that the storm is endangering the ship and the crew because of him (1.12), just as he knows that God is compassionate and gracious (4.2). In both cases, this knowledge makes Jonah want to die. It 'is knowledge to die by, not to live by', Zornberg comments (2009, p. 90); and the platitudes of his knowledge also defend him 'from the terrifying space where he might speak what cannot yet be understood' (p. 99). Jonah's knowledge does not lead him to further interpretation:

> Too much knowledge becomes trivial knowledge, no longer dynamic or transformative ... Jonah will need to lose some of his knowledge so as to rouse himself to his own distance from God ... Jonah is transfixed

by what he already knows; he assumes that the future will be like the past (p. 92).

American philosopher and psychoanalyst Jonathan Lear connects 'know-ingness' with societal norms, which, he says (p. 4), 'try to shut down the question of how to live by giving a packaged answer ... norms often serve as a defense against living openly with the fundamental question'. 'To live openly with the fundamental question', by contrast, 'is to avoid assuming that there are any fixed answers which are already given.' The sailors and the Ninevites know that they do not know. 'Perhaps the god will spare us', the captain says (1.6). 'Who knows? God may relent', the Ninevite king wonders (3.9). Zornberg (2009, p. 90) comments that 'a sense of mystery, of standing in a Presence, shapes the responses of all the characters in the narrative ... The only exception is Jonah, whose know-ledge remains unshadowed by wonder.' She adds (pp. 90–1):

> Ultimately, 'dangerous Perhapses' inform not only human relations with God and with others but also the relationship with oneself. The enigma of oneself, the 'motivated irrationality'[12] with which one may feel and act – this awareness is hard to evade. But Jonah allows no qualms to trouble his certainties.

The notion of motivated irrationality concerns action and belief, such as action demonstrating weakness of will or deficient self-control and belief that may be motivationally biased and may also include self-deception (Mele). Motivated irrationality is precisely what Zornberg detects in Jonah's behaviour (2009, p. 92), 'in his flight from God, in his desire for death that dissolves into joy in the shade of the gourd, in his avoidance of the standing place *between*'. But some developments do eventually take place, as Zornberg's comments on the book's final chapter indicate. Here, she says (p. 80):

> the phenomena of the external world that are so often – fourteen times – called *great* ... yield place to the climate of Jonah's inner world, where there is, now, 'great evil,' and later, 'great joy.' His world up to now has been inhabited by a great city, a great wind, a great storm, a great fish, the great fear of the sailors. He has been a small figure, overwhelmed by gigantic forces, a child who shrinks to fetal size as he withdraws into his stupor in the ship's hold. Now, for the first time, he experiences great forces *within* him – great evil and great joy.

Many an interpreter has been wondering about the strange events of chapter 4, not least the plant and the worm. Zornberg (p. 101) sees a clear intention at work here, maintaining that 'God stages the life and death of a non-descript plant in such a way that Jonah becomes aware of the quick succession of intense feelings.' And it is these feelings that move him 'to the depths of his being.' Now, for the first time, he can be said to *have* depths to his being (p. 102). It is at this point that Jonah can, for the first time, talk to God about his flight. Still fleeing God, he is at least in dialogue with God, finding himself able at last to articulate that, for him, death is better than life. God's question in response to Jonah's anger (4.4) Zornberg (p. 101) sees as a therapeutic question that is designed to examine:

> the emotional reality of the human being who is still in flight. Apparently, it is important for Jonah to acknowledge his own anger. Unlike the reader, who has been informed by the narrator ('And he was angry' [Jonah 4.1]), Jonah is unconscious of the nature of the 'great evil' that possesses him.

But Jonah 'finds himself standing in God's presence' at last; and it happens at the very moment when 'he speaks of anger and death' (Zornberg, 2009, p. 103). Fully present to his lack in a way that was not possible for him in his earlier prayer from the fish's belly, he finally cries out. It is at that moment, when he speaks to himself of death, that he encounters God. As Zornberg says (p. 104), 'Jonah is claimed by God in the open wound of anger, grief, and death; it is this crying from a place of reality that transforms Jonah's pain into intimacy with God. None of the external realities have changed. 'The enigmas that enrage and sadden Jonah ... remain', to put it in Zornberg's words. Instead, 'God invites Jonah to bear them, even to deepen them, and to allow new perceptions to emerge unbidden. In a word, to stand and pray' (pp. 104–5).

Challenged by one of the respondents for her paper having taken the enigmatic character of the story of Jonah as its starting point, rather than to focus more on the surface text, Zornberg maintains (2008b, p. 366) that 'it is the characteristic of important literary narratives to be endlessly enigmatic'. Her premise, she adds, is precisely that the text in front of her 'is to be *read*, closely and alertly', that she does 'not "already know" its meaning' as she approaches it. Indeed, 'to already know its meaning is to close oneself to an essential encounter' (p. 368). The textual enigma, according to Zornberg, relates to human depth. 'Are we to see humans as having depth – as complex psychological organisms who generate layers of meaning which lie beneath the surface of their own understanding?'

Lear asks (p. 27). 'Or are we to take ourselves as transparent to ourselves?' For Zornberg (2008b, p. 368), 'Jonah becomes the focus of inquiry precisely because he is not transparent to himself.' Elaborating further on her approach, she states (p. 367): 'I assume that the expressiveness of the biblical text – or of any rich literary text – is largely found in its allusiveness and elusiveness ... texts ... invite and elude interpretation. To achieve a "last word" reading would be a mournful achievement.'

Zornberg's comment on the text's allusiveness makes it explicit that her reading is an intertextual one, which, as we saw, primarily engages with rabbinic texts and the inner-biblical links they had already made. Her approach is thus, as we said, midrashic, as she herself points out (p. 368): 'Literary interpretation – certainly of sacred texts – is unending. That is the highest compliment one can pay the text, acknowledging that its meaning is not exhaustible. Passionate pursuit is the spirit and method of such reading: the very word *midrash* suggests this.'[13]

For further reflection

1 What do you make of Zornberg's (and Aron's) comments in connection with Jonah and prayer – that is, that rather than 'standing up to' God and crying 'from the depths of pain and perplexity', Jonah's prayer is 'emotional plagiarism' that merely seeks to keep the chaos (*tehom*) at bay – and ends up covering an emptiness?

2 And what about Jonah enacting 'the human desire to know and to control the Other [both divine and human], to evade uncertainty and affirm mastery', and to seek to avoid the intrusiveness and excess of the other?

3 What do you think of the notions of Jonah fleeing into 'compulsive knowingness', and of too much knowledge becoming trivial knowledge that needs to be discarded? What might it mean to live 'openly with the fundamental question'?

4 What do you make of Zornberg's description of great literature as enigmatic, elusive and unending? And what about there being layers of meaning beneath the surface of our own understanding?

Reading Jonah through the lens of trauma

Two other psychological readings of the book of Jonah, though of a very different kind, have been suggested by Elizabeth Boase and Sarah Agnew on the one hand, and Juliana Claassens on the other. Boase and Agnew begin (p. 5) by drawing attention to the 'sound of silence' that haunts the text. Silence, they note, not only opens and closes the book; it pervades it. According to George Landes (1999, p. 274), there are no fewer than 'sixty-three places where the text is silent'. Another opening consideration is Boase and Agnew's conviction that the silences should be filled in more positively than is usually done. 'Too often ... readers read against Jonah and Jonah's community, filling the textual silences in ways that portray this prophetic figure and his community as anti-heroes – as object lessons on how not to behave' (Boase and Agnew, p. 6). In practice, this means that Jonah and his community are frequently portrayed as nationalistic, vengeful or egocentric.[14]

In contrast to this, Boase and Agnew seek to 'read with rather than against' Jonah and his community, understanding 'the silences through the lens of trauma and trauma theory', an issue that was briefly touched upon but not fully explored by Zornberg. Boase and Agnew suggest that 'Jonah's flight, anger, and his silence at the end of the book can be read sympathetically as reflective of a community whose memory and identity is shaped by its traumatic experiences', such as the destruction of Jerusalem, the exile, and life under Persian rule. Much could, of course, be said about trauma and trauma theory, but here it must suffice to note that 'trauma is a multi-disciplinary term used [for instance] in medical, psychiatric, psychological, sociological, literary, and historical disciplines' (Boase and Agnew, p. 8). Two other key observations are (1) that trauma 'refers to the impact of violence and suffering upon individuals and communities' and 'results in feelings of intense fear, helplessness, loss of control and threat of annihilation' (p. 9), and (2) that there has been increased awareness in recent years of the importance of trauma for the interpretation of biblical texts.[15]

Boase and Agnew maintain that silence in the book of Jonah expresses the incommunicability of trauma, the reality that people who have experienced trauma are, as Ruth Wajnryb (p. 84) puts it, constrained from 'using language to give voice to experience in a way that authentically or even adequately captures its horror'. While the authors of literature shaped by trauma may well recall the events that caused it, the difficulty lies in expressing the trauma in a way that would allow them to explain and make sense of it. Gaps and silences in the account may thus mirror gaps in the author's psyche, or they may be a textual performance of trauma. As far as textual interpretation is concerned, silences, therefore, may not so much be gaps in need of filling, as suggested by reader-response criticism, but expressions of the very reality of incommunicability itself. Boase and Agnew (p. 12) are concerned about readings of the gaps that interpret Jonah's attitude and behaviour – and by extension the attitude of the community to whom the book is addressed – as selfish, petulant, racist, xenophobic, petty or vindictive. Those readings, they suggest, 'effectively render further trauma to a community for whom meaning is already tenuous'. Indeed, they add (p. 14) that such judgmental and moralistic readings end up becoming 'imperialistic or anti-Jewish'. Over against this, they agree with Chesung Justin Ryu's conclusion (2009) that Jonah's original readership would have agreed with Jonah's initial flight and his subsequent anger at God sparing Nineveh, which they would have regarded as a 'miscarriage of justice' (Boase and Agnew, p. 15).

More specifically, they ask whether Jonah's flight might itself be a 'performance of trauma', given that it leads to a sense of isolation. Or might it be a manifestation of the traumatic fear or anxiety associated with the Assyrian enemy whose destructive, violent, oppressive behaviour Jonah wishes to avoid? Similarly, might Jonah's anger in 4.1–3 'give voice to a communal experience of a lack of narrative coherence and meaning' instigated by 'the ongoing wounding caused by life under empire'? Turning finally to Jonah's silence in response to God's concluding question (4.11), Boase and Agnew consider the traditional options of interpreting it as either acquiescence or resistance, or as a literary move of getting Jonah out of the way so the book's audience can answer the question for themselves. However, in line with their interpretation of the book through the lens of trauma, they are keen for us to consider 'the possibility that Jonah's inability to speak, his painful silence, evokes a memory of trauma, or might be representative of a collapse of meaning associated with trauma' (pp. 17–18). Indeed, the silence at the end of the book might also be another enactment of trauma. However we might understand it, Boase and Agnew ultimately challenge us (pp. 19, 20) to 'read Jonah's silence with compassion, as empathetic listeners bearing witness to the pain and inarticulateness of loss' rather than to condemn Jonah and his community and thus disempower and silence them further. They also maintain (p. 18) that some postcolonial readings, including some of those we explored earlier, 'listen for Jonah and Jonah's community more adequately by reading with, rather than against, Jonah'.

Another response to trauma has been explored by Claassens, who takes her cue from readings that focused on Jonah's comedic and humorous aspects, such as the ship in chapter 1 becoming a nervous wreck or the fasting cows in chapter 3 being clad in sackcloth and sitting on an ash heap. While acknowledging those facets, Claassens (p. 656) wonders whether there is anything to laugh about in a text that features a near-shipwreck with sailors fearing for their lives, a near-fatal drowning that leads to some harrowing descriptions of that person's encounter with death, and the planned destruction of Nineveh – a city with a population of 120,000 people – whose mere mention evokes traumatic memories. On the one hand, therefore, we have all those funny elements peppering the book of Jonah, while on the other hand there is, as Kenneth Craig maintained (p. 143), much that is 'too earnest for laughter'.

Claassens's solution to this incongruity is to apply the notion of 'tragic laughter' developed by Jacqueline Bussie in *The Laughter of the Oppressed*. This laughter, which arises in a context of trauma, according to Bussie (p. 4), 'interrupts the system and state of oppression, and creatively attests to hope, resistance, and protest in the face of the shattering of language and traditional frameworks of thought and belief'. Claassens, therefore, like Boase and Agnew, proposes to read Jonah as trauma literature but, unlike them, explores its response to 'the shattering of language' not in the text's silences but in its laughter. Tragic laughter, Claassens points out (p. 658), 'plays an important role in the formation of an alternative identity that stands over against that of the oppressors', which it does by interrupting the despair that oppression inflicts on its subjects. Tragic laughter is thus a means of resistance. As Freud had pointed out (1960, p. 103): 'By making our enemy small, inferior, despicable or comic, we achieve in a roundabout way the enjoyment of overcoming him – to which the third person … bears witness by his laughter.' Tragic laughter, therefore, is also a means of empowerment by fostering hope and enabling the survival of the human spirit.

David Downs, in an article entitled 'The specter of exile in the story of Jonah', maintains that memories of exile haunt the book and erupt in its language. One example of this is the use of the term 'hurl' (טול, *tul*) in chapter 1. In verse 4 God hurls a great wind at the sea (John Holbert (p. 79) comments that the preposition 'at' 'provides the vivid picture here of God … throwing a mighty wind at the sea'), whereupon the sailors hurl the cargo at (into)[16] the sea to make the ship more navigable (v. 5). Jonah tells them that it is really him that should be hurled at the sea (v. 12), which the sailors duly do in verse 15. In each of these cases, not only is the verb 'hurl' (טול, *tul*) used, but so is the prepositional object 'at the sea' (אֶל־הַיָּם, *'el-hayyam*). The sea in Hebrew thought is a force of chaos and conflict, and the term 'hurl' has close associations with exile: 'I will hurl you out of this land into a land that neither you nor your ancestors have known' (Jer. 16.13; see also Jer. 22.26, 28). According to Robert Carroll (1997, p. 65), hurling serves as a violent image that captures the 'aggression inherent in the savage acts which frequently accompanied deportation'. In his prayer, Jonah cries to God 'out of the belly of Sheol' (Jonah 2.2), which of course refers to the underworld, but in Isaiah 5.13–14 is also linked with the exile: 'my people go into exile without knowledge ... Sheol has enlarged its appetite and opened its mouth beyond measure.'

Claassens (p. 663) goes on to note how in the story of Jonah carnivalistic elements are used to help overcome fear. For instance, the fearsome Assyrians, the people of Nineveh, are portrayed in humorous terms, which even involves their 'repentant cows', as Mark Biddle puts it (locs 1326–9). All this serves to trivialize and ridicule but also to humanize the feared enemy – even the cruel Ninevites had animals. Appealing to American philosopher Martha Nussbaum's study of political emotions, Claassens concludes (p. 664) that 'comedy plays a vital role in communicating a sense of a shared human vulnerability that is common to all'. But how can these people who are associated with Israel's greatest suffering be the recipients of God's mercy? Once again, Bussie's observations on laughter fit rather well in this context. As she notes (pp. 178–9), 'where language fails us, laughter steps up and steps in to help us express the both/and, paradoxical character of our faith and our lives', to 'sustain the integrity of both the narrative of faith and the narrative of negativity and to hold both narratives in dialectical tension' (p. 155).

In fact, in presenting all these issues in the form of 'a comedy where everyone ultimately is rescued' (Whedbee, p. 216), the book of Jonah, according to Claassens (p. 666), 'provides a refreshing perspective, perhaps offering a type of counterworld' to the 'world of war and terror and carnage' that we find in many prophetic books. More specifically, it sharply contrasts with Nahum's 'revenge fantasies steeped in violence and bloodshed' (p. 669). Indeed, as William Whedbee has highlighted (locs 2430–1), apart from the Song of Songs, Jonah is the only book in the Old Testament where no one dies – with the exception, that is, of the *qiqayon*. Claassens concludes her investigation, noting (p. 670) that to see the book's comedic elements 'through the lens of tragic laughter helps us to appreciate just how important it may have been for Israel to hold on to humour in order to survive'. And she quotes Roy Eckardt who, in his study of comedy and tragedy in a post-Holocaust world, celebrated the fact that 'the underdogs, the fools, the clowns, the jesters, the children keep on dancing and singing and making jokes against every incongruity and against every mystery' (Eckardt, p. 412).

For further reflection

1 What do you make of Boase and Agnew's suggestion that Jonah's flight, anger and silence might be reflections of trauma in connection with the destruction of Jerusalem, the exile, and life under Persian rule? That silence might express the incommunicability of trauma?

2 And what about their concern that some readings – for example, those that portray Jonah and his community as selfish, racist or xenophobic (readings that have ended up becoming anti-Jewish) – might render further trauma to an already hurt community?

3 What, then, might it mean to read with compassion and empathy?

4 What do you make of the notion of 'tragic laughter' as something that enables resistance, protest and empowerment, affording hope in the formation of an alternative identity and enabling the survival of the human spirit? What about humorous elements not only trivializing and ridiculing but also humanizing the feared Other, as in the case of the Ninevites' cows? And what about the underdogs, fools and so on dancing, singing and joking in the face of incongruities and mystery?

5 Do you agree with Claassens that tragic laughter helps to explain the incongruities in Jonah, given that there are many comedic or humorous facets alongside others that may be too earnest for laughter?

6

Jonah's 'Otherkind': Ecological Readings

Exploring an ecological reading of the book of Jonah in connection with Arthur Boyd and Peter Porter's collection of poetry and art inspired by this biblical story, Anne Elvey adopts the term 'otherkind' as a reference to the non-human parts of creation. She traces that term back to James Nash, who suggests (p. 8) that 'The doctrine of creation, by a grace-filled and purposeful crafter, endows all life, human and otherkind, with a moral significance, and unites all life in a theocentric – and biological – bond, entailing human responsibilities to all our kin.' Eva van Urk agrees and indeed suggests (p. 208) that 'whether religious traditions can offer publicly inspiring and appreciative views of non-humans ... is of crucial importance in society and is an issue of public concern'.[1] She thus high-lights the importance of ecological biblical interpretation for Christian public discourse and engagement.

Ecological readings of Jonah are characterized not least by the desire to overcome the anthropocentrism that has beset almost all biblical interpretation and to pay attention to the roles played by non-human creatures, Nash's 'otherkind'. However, before we explore the fresh per-spectives on the book's interpretation made possible by this approach, it will be helpful to discuss the emergence and characteristics of ecological biblical interpretation more generally. The practice of ecological biblical criticism or ecological hermeneutics, of 'interpreting the biblical text in a manner consistent with contemporary ecological theory' (Hamon, p. 68), is still a relatively recent development that has now entered what might be described as its second phase.[2] We are therefore going to distinguish between an initial phase, characterized by some responses to a radical challenge that found Christianity to have been largely responsible for our contemporary ecological crisis, and the current phase, which is marked by attempts to formulate more carefully defined principles for ecological readings of the Bible. It may be helpful, however, to begin with some reflections on terminology. As I have noted elsewhere (Möller, 2020, pp. 18–19):

talk about the 'environment', while drawing attention to the habitat in which we live, tends to limit our world to little more than the stage on which the human drama unfolds. 'Nature', in turn, refers to the natural, physical or material world, the subject of the natural sciences. Although humanity is clearly part of nature, the term is most commonly understood as referring to the non-human part of the world. In addition to these, our tradition has bequeathed to us another term, 'creation' ... with its combined stress on the divine origin, the giftedness and the all-encompassing sphere of the created order, human and non-human, it remains the most helpful term for biblical and theological reflection.

Rephrasing the last sentence slightly, I would now say that 'creation' is *one of* the most helpful terms, as 'ecology' also commends itself due to its focus on 'the communities of living things in which we find our home (*oikos*)' (Horrell, 2010b, p. 1). Ernst Conradie notes (2010, p. 310) how the term *oikos* helpfully allows us to hold together key issues such as *eco*nomic justice, *eco*logical sustainability and *ecu*menical fellowship.

Initial responses to a radical challenge

Paula Gooder (p. 192) defines biblical ecological criticism as 'reading biblical texts in the light of the environmental and ecological challenges that face us in the twenty-first century'. As her definition indicates, ecological criticism is not so much a clearly defined methodological approach to the biblical texts as a specific perspective from which they are read. Many discussions of biblical ecological criticism take as one of their points of departure American historian Lynn White's (1907–87) trenchant criticism of the Christian tradition. In his 1967 article, 'The historical roots of our ecologic crisis', White charged Christianity with being responsible for introducing a dualism between humanity, uniquely created in God's image, and the rest of nature, and for allowing human-kind to exploit nature, all based on the understanding that Genesis 1.28 ('fill the earth and subdue it; and have dominion over ... every living thing') mandates human rule over the rest of creation. Suggesting that, 'especially in its Western form, Christianity is the most anthropocentric religion the world has ever seen' (White, p. 1205) and arguing that its understanding of creation led to a 'disenchantment of nature', White (p. 1206) maintains that 'Christianity bears a huge burden of guilt' for our ecological crisis. He furthermore believes (p. 1207) that 'we shall con-tinue to have a worsening ecological crisis until we reject the Christian axiom that nature has no reason for existence save to serve man'.

Early ecological readings have frequently sought to defend the Bible against the charges of anthropocentrism and of legitimating the exploitation of the natural world. Based on texts such as Genesis 1.26–28 and Psalm 8.6, it has been common to argue that what is envisaged here is human stewardship rather than dominion. After all, Genesis goes on to say that the first human being was 'to till [the garden of Eden] and keep it' (Gen. 2.15). Another point frequently made is that, with human beings having been created in God's image, 'dominion' should be understood not as a license to exploit but as a call for 'careful service for the earth' (Deane-Drummond, 2017, p. 23). Fleshing this out, Calvin DeWitt (pp. 65–7), in an article on 'Creation's environmental challenge to evangelical Christianity', formulates the following stewardship principles:

- To 'keep the creation as God keeps us'.
- 'To participate in the restoration and reconciliation of all things'.
- To provide for creation's Sabbath (see Exod. 20.8–11; 23.10–12; Lev. 25.3–7).
- To 'enjoy, but not destroy … God's good creation'.
- To 'first seek the kingdom, not self-interest'.
- To be content with the gifts creation bestows.
- To act on what we have understood to be right.

There are however several problems with this approach. The concept of stewardship does not feature in Genesis 1, nor is it a major biblical theme (Horrell, 2010b, p. 6). More importantly, as Conradie notes (2010, p. 305), it is 'too hierarchical, too managerial, too androcentric, aimed at those in positions of power, not visionary enough'. Rosemary Radford Ruether (p. 45) stresses the absurdity of the concept of human stewardship given 'the 4,599,600,000 years in which earth got along without humans at all'. Celia Deane-Drummond (2017, p. 25) worries that the stewardship approach does not address the question as to why we should care for creation, other than to say that it is God's command. In line with this, Conradie (2010, p. 306) expresses the concern that 'such a sense of responsibility [may not] be powerful enough to encourage people to address a challenge such as climate change'.

Coming back to Genesis 1.26–28, David Horrell (2010b, p. 6) questions whether the language used in those verses 'can so easily be softened and reclaimed'. As I have argued elsewhere (Möller, 2011), the language of subduing (כבש, kavash) and exercising dominion (רדה, radah) over creation is best understood against the ancient Near Eastern depiction of creation having occurred ex tumulto, of it having been an act of bringing order out of a chaos that is understood as a continuing reality in the world. To be sure, in striking contrast to other ancient Near Eastern texts, Genesis 1 does not depict an actual fight against the forces of chaos. Instead, God calmly transforms the 'formless void' by speaking an ordered world into existence and assigning the waters their limits. And yet there are 'textual hints that suggest that the notion of *creatio ex tumulto*, of creation out of chaos, features in the background as something that is taken for granted by the biblical writers' (Möller, 2011, p. 17). These textual hints include:

- The fact that neither the waters nor the darkness are identified as God's creation.
- That both need to be contained (Gen. 1.4, 6–7, 9–10; see Möller, 2011, pp. 18–19).
- That God commands humanity to subdue the earth and have dominion over it (Gen. 1.28) (pp. 20–3).
- The serpent questioning God's command (Gen. 3.1–5).

Given the problems inherent in the stewardship concept combined with the questions about its applicability to Genesis 1.26–28, it will come as no surprise that 'the emphasis has ... begun to shift away from human stewardship towards a more encompassing, reciprocal, unitive understanding of our relationship with the created world' (Möller, 2020, p. 19).

Another response to White's challenge was to re-read the biblical texts with the aim of demonstrating that they do provide resources for a positive attitude towards nature. Texts frequently identified in that context (see Horrell, 2008, pp. 192–3; 2010b, p. 5; and Conradie, 2010, p. 295) include those that speak of:

- The goodness of creation (Gen. 1.4, 10, 12, 18, 21, 25, 31).
- God's covenant with the whole earth (Gen. 9.9–17).
- The Sabbatical laws (Lev. 25).
- Creation's praise of God (Pss 19.1–4; 69.34; 96.11–12; 98.7–8; 103.22; 148.1–10; 150.6; Isa. 42.10; Rev. 5.13; see Deane-Drummond, 2017, p. 27).
- The decentring of humanity in Job 38.1—42.6.[3]
- A peaceable, non-violent new creation (Isa. 11.6–9; 65.25) or, as Deane-Drummond (2017, p. 28) puts it, 'a return to integrity and justice ... [a] vision of *Shalom* ... replete with accounts of ecological harmony'.
- Jesus' positive attitude to creation (Matt. 6.25–34; Luke 12.22–31).
- Creation's liberation and reconciliation in Christ (Rom. 8.19–23; Col. 1.15–20).
- The vision of a renewed heaven and earth (Rev. 21—22).

However, one concern with this approach is that its focus has been far too narrow. As Conradie (2010, pp. 295–6) says: 'The selection of favourite texts may unintentionally reinforce the perception that ecology is indeed a marginal concern in the Bible.' That, though, has not been the perception of Michael Maudlin and Marlene Baer, the editors of *The Green Bible*. Having highlighted in green any text understood to be relevant to concerns regarding the earth, Maudlin and Baer (p. I–15) comment:

> With over a thousand references to the earth and caring for creation in the Bible, the message is clear: all in God's creation – nature, animals, humanity – are inextricably linked to one another. As God cares for all of creation, so too we cannot love one dimension without caring for the others. We are called to care for all God has made.

However, as Horrell (2010b, p. 8) notes, there are significant problems with this approach as well in that it 'too easily gives the impression that ecological theology and ethics can simply be read from the pages of the Bible'.

Another area of concern for ecological readings has been to re-examine eschatological texts – such as Joel 2; 2 Peter 3.11–13; or Revelation 21—22 – that appear to envisage the future destruction of the earth. The focus here has been on the question of 'whether such eschatological views foster a view of the earth as merely temporary and soon-to-be destroyed habitation' (Horrell, 2010b, p. 3). Ernest Lucas among others has denied this with respect to 2 Peter 3, concluding instead (p. 97) that although that text 'is speaking of a radical transformation of the heaven and the earth, it is a renewal through transformation, not a total destruction of the old and its replacement by something quite different'.

For further reflection

1 What do you make of van Urk's claim that 'whether religious traditions can offer publicly inspiring and appreciative views of non-humans ... is of crucial importance in society and is an issue of public concern'?
2 What do you think of White's challenge that Christianity, 'the most anthropocentric religion the world has ever seen', is largely responsible for our ecological crisis?
3 And what about the stewardship concept? What might be its strengths and weaknesses?

Developing ecological-critical approaches to the Bible

While the initial responses noted above have been important in sparking an interest in an ecological interpretation of the Bible, they have been rather limited. This is evident, for instance, in their narrow focus on a comparatively small number of biblical texts; in a strong penchant for the stewardship model whose weaknesses we noted earlier; and in a defensive, apologetic approach to the biblical writings, which has tended to deny, obscure or downplay their anthropocentric stance (more on this below). In what follows, we are going to look at some more recent proposals for ecological biblical interpretation. As a starting point, it may be helpful to note with Kivatsi Kavusa (p. 231) that ecological interpretation requires 'interpreters to go beyond what has commonly been seen as the meaning of the biblical text in order to generate "new possibilities" of understanding biblical texts'.

An agrarian reading

An agrarian reading of the Bible has been developed by Ellen Davis, whose book *Scripture, Culture, and Agriculture* 'explores the agrarian mind-set of the biblical writers by bringing Israel's Scriptures into sustained conversation with the works of contemporary agrarian writers' (Davis, p. 1). Taking the important Old Testament theme of the land, Davis re-reads relevant texts in the light of the problems caused by 'the global dominance of corporation-controlled agriculture'. Her approach is a helpful contribution to ecological biblical interpretation in the way it points to some important ecotheological principles. Deane-Drummond (2017, pp. 20–1) sums these up as follows:

- To pay attention to the relationship between God, humanity and creation, rather than focusing exclusively on humanity.
- To consider non-human creatures as an integral part of creation.
- To pay more attention to the theology of creation found in the Old Testament wisdom literature.
- To re-read Jesus' ministry with an eye on how he relates to the natural world.
- To recover the true meaning of apocalyptic literature, which has sometimes been seen to reject the natural world.

Contemplative ecological biblical criticism

Why does ecological biblical criticism matter? Responses to this kind of question tend to be of a highly pragmatic nature. The more aware we become of the environmental dangers we are facing, the more we realize that urgent and radical action is needed. Given the influence of the Bible and its interpretation on the development of the Western world view and its approach to the natural world, it becomes imperative for Christians to re-read the biblical texts with ecological questions in mind. There is little doubt that pragmatic questions – not least about the very survival of our planet – are important, and yet the Old Testament and some modern voices, such as that of Trappist monk Thomas Merton, invite us to complement this with a more contemplative approach that opens up a way to a different, truer, healthier perspective on our world, one that is characterized by 'amazement, awe and growing love. It is a way that can lead to the recalibration of our hearts, minds and souls so we can learn to be with God's creation rather than merely use, exploit or even protect it for our own benefits' (Möller, 2020, p. 21).

A prolific poet, Merton (1953, p. 360) evocatively speaks of the 'huge chorus of living beings [that] rises up out of the world beneath [our] feet: life singing in the watercourses, throbbing in the creeks and the fields and the trees, choirs of millions and millions of jumping and flying and creeping things'. He delights in 'a small nation' of frogs 'chanting blissfully in praise of the spring rain' (1998, p. 68); the whistling of the quails, 'the voice of the present moment, the present festival' (1977, p. 21); or the 'gentle contemplative song of crickets' (1998, p. 176). In contrast to humanity's greed, endless consumption and the destruction that all of this occasions, Merton (1977, p. 80) envisages nature's far more humane counter-scenario, suggesting:

> The fields will laugh, the woods will be drunk with flowers of rebellion … Every plant that stands in the light of the sun is a saint and an outlaw. Every tree that brings forth blossoms without the command of man is powerful in the sight of God. Every star that man has not counted is a world of sanity and perfection. Every blade of grass is an angel singing in the shower of glory.

As I have noted elsewhere (Möller, 2020, p. 22): 'Being immersed in the natural world leads Merton to recognise the creatures' praise of God, praise that consists in simply being who they were created to be.' Being with nature also allowed Merton to recognize his close relationship with all God's creatures, both human and non-human, and 'how absolutely central' is the recognition 'that we are first of all part of nature' (2014, pp. 296–7). Merton thus teaches us the importance of learning to be present to our world which, he believed, 'leads to a deeper realization and understanding of the true nature of our world as God's precious, beautiful creation' as well as the essential unity of that creation (Möller, 2020, p. 23). Writing more than half a century later, Deane-Drummond (2017, p. 30) somewhat similarly suggests: 'Perhaps the greatest challenge in the development of eco-practice is setting aside a particular time for just being with the natural world and with God, in active rest understood as appreciation. Creation is not just "good," it is also declared holy.'

Merton, highly politically engaged and an outspoken critic of the burning issues of his time, shows himself to be thoroughly steeped in the language and imagery of the Old Testament, making it his own and allowing it to shape his attitude to God's creation. 'By the reading of scripture', he says (1953, pp. 215–16):

I am so renewed that all nature seems renewed around me and with me. The sky seems to be a purer, a cooler blue, the trees a deeper green, light is sharper on the outlines of the forest and the hills, and the whole world is charged with the glory of God and I find fire and music in the earth under my feet.

By their mere existence, and faithfully day upon day, the heavens proclaim God's glory, says Psalm 19. But do we even notice it? As Peter Craigie once pointed out (p. 181), 'to the sensitive, the heavenly praise of God's glory may be an overwhelming experience, whereas to the insensitive, sky is simply sky'. Commenting on the Hebrew term often translated 'declare' (the NRSV reads 'tell'), but which can also mean 'to chant', Samuel Terrien (pp. 209–10) suggests that the heavens 'not only "declare" the divine glory but also celebrate it in chanted melodies', thus making their joyful contribution to Merton's 'huge chorus of living beings'. However, this 'sacramental approach' to nature has been criticized by Conradie (2009, p. 204) as ineffective, naïve and romantic. He wonders:

whether a retrieval of the sacred will be powerful enough to resist industrialization. Throughout the centuries societies in which nature was regarded as sacred have nonetheless destroyed their natural habitation whenever economic incentives to do so emerged. A sacramental approach can also be somewhat naive and perhaps too romantic in calling for a return to a bygone era.

So where does that leave us? Contrary to what Conradie suggests, contemplative engagement with the biblical tradition is of course not about a naïve or romantic return to 'a bygone era' but rather about being 'transformed by the renewing of [our] minds' (Rom. 12.2). It is about allowing such texts as Psalm 98.7–9 or Isaiah 55.12 with their roaring seas, clapping floods and trees, singing mountains and hills to reorientate us, helping us to see a world that is continuously declaring its creator's praises. 'The Old Testament poets can help us to see our world ... in its richness and diversity', thus 'recalibrating our attitude to God's ... creation' (Möller, 2020, p. 26). As Douglas Christie notes (p. 29), it is our harmful 'habits of careless inattention that have put [our] ecosystem in jeopardy'. Indeed, he worries that 'in a world made desolate, the presence of the sacred and life itself will be lost to us. And with it will be lost our capacity for intimacy, delight, and wonder' (p. 26). Merton, the Old Testament poets and many other contemplatives help us to see that:

only a sustained practice of attention can help restore us to an awareness of who we are in relation to the larger whole that is rooted in authentic respect and reverence. Only such a renewed awareness can inform the kind of sustained action that will be required to realize lasting ecological restoration (Christie, p. 29).

Indeed, as Ruether has pointed out (p. 58):

Westernized consciousness must heal itself of its split-off divisions that have separated knowledge from wonder, reverence, and love before we can learn how to tell the cosmic story in a way that will rekindle an ethic and spirituality capable of calling us to the tasks of healing and sustaining the earth. We need scientist-poets who can retell the story ... in a way that can call us to wonder, to reverence for life, and to the vision of humanity living in community with all its sister and brother beings.

Therefore, as both Christie and Ruether insist, awareness of the deeper nature of God's creation, as expressed for instance by the Old Testament poets, is far from irrelevant to the contemporary ecological debate but can transform us and lead us to commit to sustained action and an ecologically sensitive and transformative lifestyle. It was precisely Merton's immersion in the biblical scriptures that awakened him and renewed his senses, calling him to wonder and reverence for life, enabling him to see 'the whole world [as] charged with the glory of God' (1953, pp. 215–16).

> **For further reflection**
>
> 1 What do you make of contemplative ecological biblical criticism? Does it have any relevance in the context of our contemporary ecological crisis?
> 2 Should that crisis receive more attention in our engagement with the biblical texts and in the preaching and teaching of the church?

The Earth Bible project

One of the pioneers and leading figures in ecological biblical criticism is Norman Habel, the founder of the Earth Bible project. As Horrell notes (2008, p. 193), Habel and the Earth Bible Team have produced 'the most methodologically developed approach to ecological criticism'. One of its characteristics is a profound scepticism regarding any attempt to see the Bible as consistently eco-friendly. Indeed, noting that many Christian traditions, especially in the West, have tended to devalue Earth, Habel (2000, p. 26) is concerned that this might also be true of the Bible itself. In contemporary thought, however, there is a new Earth consciousness, which 'invites us, a member of the Earth community, to return to the Bible, and in dialogue with the text, ascertain whether a similar kinship with Earth is reflected there' (Habel, 2000, p. 26). As the members of the Earth Bible Team point out, there are texts that 'may even celebrate Earth in a way that our contemporary anthropocentric eyes have not detected, or that we have regarded as the quaint language of ancient poetry' (Earth Bible Team, 2000, p. 40).

Commenting on the kinds of texts we considered above, in which creation sings God's praises, the Earth Bible Team (2000, p. 47) ask whether these reflect more than just poetry. Might they perhaps reflect 'an understanding of the common bond between humans and non-humans as worshippers before God'? Might they reflect an understanding of the Earth community as including 'entities with non-human voices and a capacity for worship'? Are the biblical storytellers, prophets and poets 'mediating the voice of Earth or members of the Earth community' (p. 48)? Noting primatologist Jane Goodall's observation that chimpanzees react to waterfalls with an expression of awe, Michael Gilmour asks (p. 88): 'Is it merely a poetic fancy for the psalmist to call on sea monsters, wild animals, cattle, creeping things, and flying birds to praise God (Ps 148.7, 10), or is it possible that in their own way they actually do just that?'

Gilmour goes on to conclude that 'within the theological-poetic language of the Bible it is certainly possible for non-humans to engage in forms of communion with their Maker'. Van Urk (p. 219) notes that 'animals may have their own independent relations to the Divine, alongside specific forms of human religiosity', while Peter Atkins, in an article on 'Praise by animals in the Hebrew Bible', similarly sees animals as distinct agents of praise, which assigns them 'a particular relationship with God and a level of commonality with humanity' (p. 512). In turn, Richard Bauckham (p. 151) points out that 'to recognize creation's praise is to abandon an instrumental view of nature'. Reflecting on Psalm 65.12–13 ('the pastures of the wilderness overflow, the hills gird themselves with joy, the meadows clothe themselves with flocks, the valleys deck themselves with grain, they shout and sing together for joy'), Howard Wallace (p. 63) suggests that:

> without the use of the metaphor the psalmist could not open our minds, let alone our ears, to hear Earth's voice. The metaphor points to a reality embodied within the physical world, one that our contemporary Western minds are not usually trained to comprehend. The psalmist helps us hear Earth's praise of God in the abundant fertility of the world around us.

Significantly, for the Earth Bible Team (2001, p. 26), these kinds of metaphors may be 'taking us back to the experience of ancient peoples who have a kinship with creation that Western thinking has abandoned' but that can still be found among many indigenous peoples today who regard the land as a living, spiritual and sacred subject. Biblical texts that speak of Earth's voice may thus be 'mediators of Earth's communication in a way that less sensitive Westerners may find hard to comprehend'.[4]

While these more sustained reflections already take the approach of the Earth Bible project beyond the contemplative reading of biblical texts by Merton and others, its most significant contribution may just lie in the unflinching recognition that other texts portray Earth as a mere 'property to be exploited, with God's blessing, in the interests of human beings' (Habel, 2000, p. 27). This then leads us to the realization that we must ask whether Earth and the non-human members of its community are 'suppressed, oppressed or celebrated' (p. 35). Hence, Habel and the Earth Bible Team call for critical engagement with the biblical texts, arguing that they need to be measured against the following ecojustice principles, as summarized by Habel (2008, p. 2) and here presented in italics (see Earth Bible Team, 2000, pp. 42–53; Eaton, 2000, pp. 64–9; and Deane-Drummond, 2017, pp. 32–4, for additional comments):

1 *Intrinsic worth: The universe, Earth and all its components have intrinsic worth/value.*

After all, 'they are vehicles to reflect the Creator's handiwork' (Earth Bible Team, 2000, p. 43). This principle is affirmed, for instance, in Genesis 1 and 1 Timothy 4.4–5, while texts such as Isaiah 66.2 appear to demean Earth, relegating it to an inferior position (Earth Bible Team, 2000, pp. 43–4). As for the principle itself, Heather Eaton (2000, p. 64) rightly points to an ambiguity pertaining to how one recognizes implicit value or acts upon that recognition.

2 *Interconnectedness: Earth is a community of interconnected living things that are mutually dependent on one another for life and survival.*

Quantum physics has drawn attention to the interconnected web of relationships that extends to every level of reality. Interconnectedness has therefore become a key principle for many environmental theorists and theologians (see Eaton, 2000, p. 65). However, texts such as Genesis 1.26–28 or Psalm 8 clearly envisage a hierarchical ordering, in which human beings, made only 'a little lower than God', exercise dominion over the rest of creation, which has been placed under their feet (see Carley). Given that emphasis, the Earth Bible Team (2000, p. 46) wonder whether there are other texts (such as Proverbs 8 or Romans 8 perhaps) that see humans as 'one with Earth, kin with the animals, and an integral part of an integrated Earth community'.

3 *Voice: Earth is a subject capable of raising its voice in celebration and against injustice.*

This builds on a growing sense, promoted by Deep Ecologists (see Devall and Sessions; and Drengson and Inoue)[5] or British scientist and environmentalist James Lovelock's Gaia hypothesis (Lovelock, 2000a, 2000b), that Earth is itself alive. Recognizing the application of the concept of voice to be an inherently anthropocentric move, the Earth Bible Team (2001, pp. 23, 24) point out that it is used as shorthand for the distinctive ways in which Earth and the Earth community might communicate; in other words, that it is their way of recognizing Earth as 'communicating as an equal'. The principle of Earth's voice is illustrated in Earth's blessing or praising God (as explored earlier), or in texts such as Jeremiah 12.4, 11 where desolate Earth mourns to God who responds in 16.18. According to Deane-Drummond (2017, p. 33), 'Jeremiah claims that moral order affects the order in creation.'

*4 **Purpose:** The universe, Earth and all its components are part of a dynamic cosmic design within which each piece has a place in the overall goal of that design.*

Deane-Drummond finds this principle illustrated in Romans 8.18–22, while the members of the Earth Bible Team (2000, p. 49) ask whether the 'grand "design" that confronts Job [is] anything like the pattern of eco-systems that we marvel at today'. Eaton (2000, p. 68) expresses Earth's purpose in the words of Catholic priest, cultural historian, world reli-gions scholar, and self-styled 'geologian' Thomas Berry (1914–2009), according to whom the universe is 'the primary sacred community, the primary revelation of the divine, the primary subject of incarnation, the primary unit of redemption, the primary referent in any discussion of reality or value'.

*5 **Mutual custodianship:** Earth is a balanced and diverse domain where responsible custodians can function as partners with, rather than rulers over, Earth to sustain its balance and a diverse Earth community.*

Eaton (2000, p. 68) argues that the shift from stewardship to custodianship addresses the unhelpful anthropocentrism of the former, instead draw-ing attention to human dependence upon the Earth. Deane-Drummond (2017, p. 33) notes that illustrations of this principle are difficult to find in the biblical texts, while the Earth Bible Team ask (2000, p. 51) whether Earth is ever considered sacred or a custodian in the biblical texts or whether these kinds of concepts might have been suppressed as part of the rejected Canaanite 'nature religion'. The concept of solidarity has been suggested as an alternative to custodianship (see Clifford, p. 185).

*6 **Resistance:** Earth and its components not only suffer from human injustices but actively resist them in the struggle for justice.*

The concerns of the Earth Bible Team are well summarized when they ask (2000, p. 52): 'Is Earth constructed by anthropocentric writers into a passive victim? Or are there Earth voices in the text resisting this con-struction of Earth as victim?' According to Deane-Drummond (2017, p. 33), for God to call upon wild animals to carry out a divine punish-ment (Jer. 12.9) hints 'at the eco-justice principle of *resistance*'. Does the groaning of creation in Romans 8.18–22 similarly reflect Earth's resist-ance? Should the land's vomiting out of its defilers (Lev. 18.24–30) be understood in that way (Earth Bible Team, 2000, p. 53)? Or is Eaton (2000, p. 69) correct to question the idea of Earth fighting back?

In practice, application of the ecojustice principles means that interpreters ask whether, or to what extent, biblical texts are consistent, or in conflict, with them, 'whether there is a concern for earth community in the text or whether earth is being treated unjustly' (Conradie, 2010, p. 307). Comparable to approaches such as feminist criticism, ecological criticism of the Bible as practised by the Earth Bible Team involves hermeneutical strategies of both suspicion and retrieval, with the issue of eco*justice* and the aim of recovering Earth's voice being paramount. As Habel (2008, p. 4) points out, anthropocentric bias, which relates to nature as an object, not only 'reinforces a sense of human superiority over nature, but has also contributed to a sense of distance, separation, and otherness'. Elsewhere, Habel had maintained (2000, p. 37) that it is important for us to acknowledge 'that as Western interpreters we are heirs to a long anthropocentric, patriarchal and androcentric approach to reading the text that has devalued Earth and that continues to influence the way we read the text'. It seems to me to be indisputable that:

> until relatively recently, our reading of the Bible, much as our engagement with the natural world, has been almost exclusively anthropocentric. We have reduced nature to an environment in which we happen to live or to resources that, at best, we must seek to 'use' more responsibly. Similarly, our reading of the biblical texts has focused on God's relationship with humanity, leading us to pay scant attention to the wider creation or the place of non-human creatures within creation (Möller, 2020, p. 18).

That said, of course, as the Earth Bible Team (2002, p. 1) aver, the biblical texts themselves also frequently 'reflect human interests at the expense of the non-human Earth community', which led former South African Archbishop Desmond Tutu (1931–2021) to ask (p. 7) whether the biblical text might 'de-value Earth by making the self-interest of humans its dominant concern'. To counter such tendencies, we must learn to recognize and listen to Earth as a subject with its own voice (see also Hamon, p. 67). As Habel (2000, pp. 33–4) puts it, 'rather than reflecting *about* the Earth as we analyse a text, we are seeking to reflect *with* Earth and see things from the perspective of Earth ... we stand with oppressed Earth in our dialogue with the text'. This for him leads to the following practical steps (2008, pp. 3–5): (1) *suspicion* of the text's anthropocentrism and/or our anthropocentric history of interpretation, (2) *identification* with any non-human characters and (3) *retrieval* of the Earth's own perspective or voice. Identification with Earth or the Earth community for Habel entails that we 'face the prior ecological reality of our kinship with

Earth', which 'raises our consciousness to the injustices against Earth as they are portrayed in the text, both at the hands of humans and God'. Retrieval, in turn, makes it necessary for us to be alert to the roles of Earth or members of the Earth community in the text rather than to ignore or suppress them. It means to value them and discern them as subjects 'with which we seek to relate empathetically', rather than as mere objects, textual topics, backdrops to human history, or 'lifeless entities upon which God and humans perform greater or lesser deeds' (Habel, 2000, pp. 29, 34, 37).

The approach developed by the Earth Bible Team is, as Horrell (2008, p. 193) recognized, 'the most methodologically developed approach to ecological criticism'. That said, Horrell is critical of the ecojustice principles, arguing (2010b, pp. 7–8) that in promoting these as the guiding norms authority no longer lies with the Bible or the Christian tradition. Noting that it is unclear to him 'how such readings might contribute to the reconfiguration *of the Christian tradition*', he sees it as essential that any ecological reading of the Bible must 'demonstrate that it offers an authentic rearticulation' of that tradition. Conradie (2006, p. 311; 2010, p. 308) describes the vision expressed in the six ecojustice principles as 'bold, audacious, uncompromising and attractive'. However, noting the lack of any references to either 'creation' or a 'Creator' as a result of the Earth Bible Team's desire to appeal to a wider, secular and interfaith readership, he similarly laments (2010, p. 309) that this makes the vision less persuasive 'within the traditions that have kept the reading of these texts alive'.

Horrell and Conradie are part of the 'Exeter Project', which seeks to offer ecological interpretation that is informed by traditional Christian theology while also reshaping it where necessary. Horrell, together with Cherryl Hunt and Christopher Southgate, two other contributors to the Exeter Project, argues that 'to be potentially persuasive as an attempt to reshape Christian ethics, an ecological reading of the Bible would need to demonstrate that it offers an authentic appropriation of the Christian tradition' (Horrell, Hunt and Southgate, p. 233). They therefore prefer what they call a 'revisionist hermeneutic' (pp. 233–8), which employs specific 'doctrinal/ethical lenses that can enable a positive, creative, yet also critical re-reading of the tradition' (p. 235).[6] Kavusa situates this revisionist approach between what he calls readings of recovery and readings of resistance. Revisionist readings, he suggests (pp. 244–5), 'do not aim to defend (recovery) or to reject (resistance) the classical Christian tradition, but to "re-claim" [and reshape] it historically in its ecological and cosmic fullness'. Like Horrell and Conradie, Kavusa is critical of the approach adopted by the Earth Bible project, noting that the interpretive authority here lies with the six ecojustice principles rather than the biblical texts (p. 249).

Deane-Drummond, by contrast, has come to different conclusions. Noting (2017, p. 31) that the ecojustice principles were 'arrived at in consultation with ecologists as well as biblical scholars', she suggests that the Earth Bible Team demonstrate 'a listening to the natural world that is in tune with the biblical wisdom tradition'. However, she adds that in addition to the principle of justice, she would also want to include 'ecologically relevant virtues such as faith, hope, and love, along with … wisdom, temperance, and humility as an aspect of what biblical traditions can affirm' (p. 34, with reference to her 2021 article 'The Bible and environmental ethics').

For further reflection

1 What do you make of the Earth Bible Team's claim that the Bible is largely anthropocentric and may therefore not be entirely eco-friendly? And what about Desmond Tutu's concern that the biblical text might contribute to the devaluing of Earth?

2 What do you think of the ecojustice principles of intrinsic worth, interconnectedness, voice, purpose, mutual custodianship and resistance? And what about the Earth Bible Team's emphasis on our kinship with Earth and the importance of us learning to reflect with Earth understood as a subject?

3 What do you make of Horrell and Conradie's criticism that the Earth Bible Team's approach does not allow us to formulate a specifically Christian approach to an ecological reading of the Bible? On the other hand, what do you think about the potential value of the ecojustice principles in the context of a wider, secular or interfaith debate?

4 Why does the Earth Bible Team insist on interpretive authority being given to their ecojustice principles? What might be the advantages, and the limitations, of such an approach?

Ecofeminist, 'ecobosadi' and 'ecolonial' perspectives

Ecofeminist perspectives on the proposals for ecological interpretation advanced by the Earth Bible project have been offered by Eaton (2000, p. 57), who suggests that 'ecofeminists desire to heal the wounds caused by the splits between nature and culture, mind and body, women and men, reason and emotion, spirit and matter, theory and action, and ultimately between humans and the Earth'. Eaton here highlights the various unhelpful dualisms that have been operative in traditional biblical interpretation (and the Western mindset more generally). Ruether, in connection with this, points out (p. 2) that ecofeminism 'explores how male domination of women and domination of nature are interconnected'. What these statements indicate is that for ecofeminists traditional interpretations of the biblical texts have not only been anthropocentric but also androcentric and patriarchal, and that these perspectives have effectively collaborated in denigrating women and Earth. As Ruether (p. 3) puts it: 'Domination of women has provided a key link, both socially and symbolically, to the domination of earth, hence the tendency in patriarchal cultures to link women with earth, matter, and nature, while identifying males with sky, intellect, and transcendent spirit.'

Eaton, for her part, points to a blind spot of traditional biblical interpretation. As she maintains (2000, p. 61), 'few [traditional] scholars address directly the ethical responsibility for, and the political consequences of, reading the Bible'. In contrast, 'ethical accountability of biblical interpretation is central to an ecofeminist perspective' (p. 62). In connection with this point, she notes that the six ecojustice principles proposed by the Earth Bible project must have priority over the biblical text, just as women's liberatory experiences must have priority over misogynist texts. 'If the Bible asserts that the earth is irrelevant, such a position will be refuted from the perspective of the [ecojustice] principles' (p. 63).

Another factor discussed by Ruether in connection with Christian attitudes to the earth are traditional views of mortality and evil. As she points out (Ruether, p. 139):

> The evaluation of mortal life as evil and the fruit of sin has lent itself to an earth-fleeing ethic and spirituality, which has undoubtedly contributed very centrally to the neglect of the earth, to the denial of our commonality with plants and animals, and to the despising of the work of sustaining the day-to-day processes of finite but renewable life.

And yet despite those problems, Ruether maintains (p. 206) that the Christian tradition encompasses some 'profoundly valuable themes for ecological spirituality and practice'. Indeed, in contrast to White's position noted earlier, she argues (p. 207) that the modern Western dualism of history and nature 'distorts the biblical perspective', adding (p. 210) that in Hebraic texts the 'social' and the 'natural' are 'knit together in one holistic experience'. For while 'the Hebraic view of relationship to God is undoubtedly highly androcentric, anthropocentric, and ethnocentric', it does envisage God as relating directly to nature (p. 208), a relationship that Ruether describes as 'animistically interpersonal' (p. 209).[7]

One of the valuable themes for ecological spirituality and practice identified by Ruether (p. 211) is the covenantal notion of the land as a gift of God. For her (p. 213), there is 'a model of redemptive eco-justice' here, not least in the sabbatical legislation pertaining to the land (see, for example, Exod. 23.10–12; Lev. 25.2–7), including the Jubilee (Lev. 25.8–55). And that covenantal arrangement depended on Israel treating the land with righteousness or else run the risk of being vomited out by the land if they defiled it (Lev. 18.28), which has become a particularly poignant concept in our own contemporary context. Ruether, in this connection, appeals to the notion of humanity having been created in God's image, which for her has 'profound ethical meaning' (p. 222). And she notes (pp. 21–2) that the Hebrew term for humankind assumes 'a deep kinship of humans [אָדָם, adam] and earth [אֲדָמָה, adamah]'. In analogy to the stewardship concept, which has been criticized as we saw for being too hierarchical and managerial, she variously portrays humanity's role in terms of 'enlightened guardianship' over, or a special relationship as caretakers for, the earth (pp. 222, 227). That said, however, Ruether also speaks of a 'community of interdependence', pointing out (pp. 227–8) that 'there must remain the larger sensibility, rooted in the encounter with nature as "thou," as fellow beings each with its own integrity'.

Writing as an 'Earth-conscious' African–South African woman and focusing on her Northern Sotho context, Madipoane Masenya (pp. 109–10) proposes an 'eco*bosadi*'[8] women's liberationist reading that does not define Africa and Africans from an outsider's perspective. An eco*bosadi* perspective discerns not only 'the androcentric elements in the text but also the class, race and Earth-demeaning elements', being conscious of how 'women and Earth … have been traditionally relegated to the realm of the inferior'. Masenya goes on to stress (p. 111) that anthropocentric readings have 'through the years served to cause harm to Earth, the non-male and the non-human members of the Earth community'. Interestingly, in connection with the Earth Bible project's focus on Earth's voice, Masenya notes that:

> as part of her context, an African–South African woman cannot exist apart from Earth. She is a woman who has through the years been taught to listen and hear Earth's voice(s). The principle of voice espoused by the Earth Bible is fundamental to her culture … The traditional Northern Sotho woman … has a bond with Earth and can actually hear Earth's voices more clearly than her male counterpart.

Masenya further explains (p. 112) how in her culture natural phenomena are frequently perceived as Earth's resistance to the violation of societal taboos. And she points out that an African–South African woman not only realizes that she cannot exist apart from Earth, but also understands that she 'participates in the struggle of Earth for justice'.

Tina Dykesteen Nilsen and Anna Rebecca Solevåg (pp. 666, 682) in turn argue for an 'ecolonial' approach – that is, an ecological approach informed by postcolonial insights. They believe (p. 672) that the three steps of suspicion, identification and retrieval outlined by the Earth Bible Team are 'too restrictive', and that the kind of ecological interpretation this has generated is too 'occupied with retrieving the "voice of Earth"', which they regard as a questionable concept (p. 673). However, they agree with the Earth Bible Team that ecological biblical hermeneutics should neither presuppose nor exclude conversation with Christian theology. Nilsen and Solevåg (p. 674) express a preference for an approach linked to the principles of the global, interdisciplinary and interreligious Earth Charter (https://earthcharter.org/), which address the areas of (1) respect and care for the community of life, (2) ecological integrity, (3) social and economic justice and (4) democracy, nonviolence and peace. Based on this, they believe (p. 675) that 'ecological hermeneutics should widen its horizon to look at the interconnections between exploitation of natural resources, poverty, imperialism/colonization, and gender inequality'.

For further reflection

1 What do you make of the link between the domination of women and the domination of nature as suggested by ecofeminist interpreters? And what about the ecofeminist desire to 'heal the wounds caused by the splits between nature and culture, mind and body, women and men, reason and emotion, spirit and matter, theory and action ... and ultimately between humans and the Earth'?

2 Is it important for us to take ethical responsibility for our reading of the Bible? What might that mean?

3 What do you make of Masenya's ecobosadi perspective? What does it add to Western ecofeminist thought? And what about Masenya's take on Earth's voice?

4 Lastly, what contribution does Nilsen and Solevåg's ecolonial approach make to our discussion?

Ecological readings of Jonah

As we think about ecological readings of Jonah, bearing in mind the general issues noted in our discussion so far, we begin with Conradie's observation that the book's picturesque nature owes much to its numerous references to the earth, its creatures, and natural forces, which are deeply involved in this remarkable story. He specifically lists the following (2005, pp. 225–6):

- Cosmology: heaven (1.9), dry land (1.9; 2.10), earth (2.6), mountains (2.6), the sun (4.8).
- Geography: Nineveh (1.1; 3.1–2; 4.11), Tarshish (1.3; 4.2), Joppa (1.3), the Jerusalem temple (2.4, 7).
- Forces of nature: the sea (1.4–5, 9), the storm at sea (1.4–5), calm at sea (1.15), the scorching desert wind (4.8), sun and shade (4.5, 8).
- Food (3.7–8), drinking water (3.7).
- Life cycles: three days and nights (1.17), living and dying (2.6; 4.3, 8–9), dawn and dusk (4.7, 10), being asleep and awake (1.5–6), eating and fasting (3.7–8), sprouting and withering (4.6–7).
- Plants: sea weeds (2.5), the *qiqayon* (4.6–7).
- Animals: the big fish (1.17; 2.1, 10), Nineveh's animals (3.7–8; 4.11), the worm (4.7), humans (Jonah, sailors, citizens, the king, his counsellors).

As Conradie notes (2005, p. 227), everything included here is 'intimately involved in God's acts of salvation and liberation that touch the whole earth community'. Kathryn Schifferdecker (p. 216) accordingly regards the role played by non-human creatures in the story of Jonah as remarkable, while Phyllis Trible (1996, pp. 482–3) suggests that ecology is 'a prominent theological theme throughout Jonah'. Ekaterina Kozlova (p. 1) goes even further when she claims that 'in Jonah characters of the "otherkind" are indispensable to God's economy'. Focusing on the animals, Yael Shemesh (p. 26) notes that they play an 'especially prominent role' as God's agents (the fish in 1.17; 2.10, the worm in 4.7), as an essential part of the repenting Ninevite community (3.7–8) and as objects of divine mercy (4.11). And yet non-human creatures have usually been regarded as little more than the backdrop against which Jonah's drama (or the drama between God and human beings) unfolds. Which, as Willie van Heerden (2014, p. 127) notes, 'is one way of objectifying nature, which contributes to a sense of distance, separation, and otherness'. So how might an ecological approach to the book address this? What are the key issues ecological interpretations would need to cover, and what insights might we expect to gain from them?

Alexander Abasili (pp. 238–9) focuses on the role of the book's non-human characters, seeking to ascertain their significance for ecojustice and noting that this emphasis 'recognizes in other creatures and natural systems the claim to be respected and valued and taken into account in societal arrangements' (Abasili is here quoting Gibson, p. 21). Yet, as we noted in our earlier discussion, alongside some potential ecological sensitivity and wisdom, biblical texts are frequently marked (and marred) by an anthropocentric perspective. So what have ecological interpretations of Jonah made of the text, and in what ways have they contributed to (a) its understanding and (b) its contribution to the contemporary ecological debate? Let us begin with some of the problems that have been noted before moving on to the ecological wisdom that has also been detected. While finding in the book of Jonah a 'dominant thrust ... of inclusiveness', Conradie (2005, p. 226) is worried about (1) the instrumentalization of non-human creatures, such as the fish, the *qiqayon* and the worm; (2) the book's only featured plant being scorched just to teach Jonah a lesson; and (3) the sea's function being reduced to that of a dangerous threat, with no acknowledgement of its life-giving role as 'the habitat from which our forms of life originated'. That said, Kozlova regards the sea's function as being elevated beyond a mere threat when she interprets its actions as performing a liturgical role in Jonah's cosmic burial. Conradie, while accepting that a short story such as Jonah cannot address everything, (4) also frets about God's mercy being limited to domesticated animals.

Shemesh (p. 9) notes that the fish serves as a *means* of punishment, trapping the prophet 'helplessly in its bowels for three days', and as a 'life raft' – Janet Gaines (p. 58) speaks of a 'benign sea taxi'. Like the worm (4.7), the fish also serves a 'didactic function' (Shemesh, p. 9), teaching both Jonah and the reader about God's sovereignty and compassion. As Rosa Ching Shao (p. 8) puts it: 'In every chapter, God uses people, creatures, inanimate objects, and events to teach Jonah important lessons about who God is, how God works, and God's purposes for humanity.' This instrumentalization of non-human creatures reflects an anthropocentric emphasis, according to which their role in the story is limited to that of serving human interests, such as Jonah's rescue and him and us being taught about God. A somewhat different perspective regards the non-human creatures as God's agents. Kozlova, for instance, (p. 1), notes one of the book's striking features as being its 'personification and agentivization of creation and inanimate objects', adding (p. 9) that it 'habitually personifies inanimate objects'. Examples of this include:

- The ship 'thinking' of breaking up (1.4).
- The sea 'going' and storming (1.11).
- The sea 'standing' (stopping) from its raging (1.15).
- God speaking to the fish (2.10).
- Nineveh's animals participating in penitentiary mourning rites (3.7–8).
- The plant being a 'son' of the night (4.10).[9]

This view is also alert to the fact that the fish (1.17), the *qiqayon* (4.6), the worm (4.7) and the sultry east wind (4.8) are each 'appointed' by God to perform their designated tasks – the Hebrew term מנה (*manah*), 'to appoint', being used in each case. Shemesh (p. 8) suggests that as God's agents the animals 'are totally subordinate to Him'. She adds (p. 12) that 'the use of a fish as the divine agent sharpens one of the story's messages: the Lord's absolute control of His world'. Widening her focus to include fauna, flora and the forces of nature (p. 13), Shemesh draws attention to the contrast between 'the animals (and all creation) and Jonah'. While the former are obedient to God, only Jonah tries to evade his mission. The same point has been made by van Heerden (2017, p. 474), who concludes that God 'uses animals, plants and storms to teach Jonah lessons about compassion, grace, and obedience'. The point about all creation's obedience vis-à-vis Jonah's disobedience to God leads Raymond Person to propose (p. 89) that the target of the book's satirical tone is not just ethnocentrism, as has frequently been concluded, but also anthropocentrism. And yet are not all these agents still employed for Jonah's benefit? This is certainly how Tova Forti (p. 373) interprets it when she concludes that the fish 'serves as an agent that affords Jonah the opportunity to recommit himself to his mission'.

Elvey (p. 80), in an ecological reading driven by a concern for contemporary climate change, specifically considers what she calls the 'agency of otherkind'. One of her starting points is Person's observation (p. 85) that the active, independent agency of other-than-human characters in Jonah tends to be overlooked. Yet while 'the Lord controls the winds, sea, and storm' (1.4), Person and Phoebe Stroede (p. 75) observe that 'once the Lord initiates it, the storm appears to take on a life of its own, at least as an active participant in the narrative'. The sea's agency, in turn, is affirmed in the sailors' question, 'What shall we do to you [Jonah], that the sea may quiet down for us?' (1.11). Person and Stroede (p. 75) therefore suggest that 'the Lord gave the sea a job to do and it is obediently following through with this task'. The narrator too affirms the sea's active agency in reporting that it 'ceased from its raging' (1.15). As again Person and Stroede point out, the text might well have said that 'the Lord calmed the sea', but in its actual wording it is the sea's agency that is highlighted. Person, in his study of the role of non-human characters in Jonah, argues (p. 85) that they 'should be understood as characters with their own individual integrity who respond obediently to the Lord and are valued as such by the Lord', and that their obedience is that of 'active, independent characters' (p. 87). They should therefore not be regarded as 'mere puppets of the Lord'. Shemesh (p. 25) agrees, noting that while an instrumentalist view of animals is not fully absent from Jonah, their lives nonetheless have an 'independent rationale'. Indeed, Person and Stroede (p. 74) believe that the story of Jonah 'undercuts our modern anthropocentric emphasis on the human and divine characters in the biblical text, asserting that other members of the Earth community are also active participants and co-creators'.

Becoming alert to the ways in which the story might undercut its traditional anthropocentric interpretation may be a step towards a new reading, one that pays more attention to the non-human characters on their own terms. Clearly, this would go some way to addressing the Earth Bible Team's ecojustice principles. It should also be noted in this context that Elvey (p. 83) sees the recognition of otherkind's 'interdependent co-agency' with divine and human agents as essential to our response to climate change. Looking at Jonah's psalm, she observes (p. 90) how the waters are depicted as independent 'oceanic agencies':

the flood surrounded me;
all your waves and your billows passed over me ...
the waters closed in over me;
the deep surrounded me ...
(Jonah 2.3, 5)

Elvey is concerned to challenge what she describes as illusionary construals of divine, human and otherkind agency, by which she means 'the illusion that divine agency is independent of the agencies of humans and most particularly of other-than-humans' (p. 90). As she goes on to affirm, 'divine and human actions are always enmeshed with and dependent on other-than-human agencies'. She therefore regards it as important that we reimagine our 'complex hybrid agencies', allowing the story of Jonah to challenge, much as anthropogenic climate change challenges, our 'hubristic illusions of human separateness and the behaviours stemming from these illusions' (p. 91). In contrast to some of the earlier readings considered above, Elvey thus questions the traditional notion of an independently operative divine sovereignty, arguing instead that the book of Jonah points us in the direction of what she calls 'interagency'. In line with this, Abasili (p. 243) notes that the fish is addressed by God (2.10), which he regards as indicating that there is a relationship between God and the fish. Person (p. 86) additionally notes that Nineveh's animals, the *qiqayon*, the worm and the wind also respond to divine commands, even if these are not explicitly mentioned.

In Boyd and Porter's *Jonah*, the prophet and the whale sign a contract. In this humorous, inventive retelling, the whale is depicted as an active agent that undertakes to deliver Jonah 'by means of vomiting, expelling or otherwise voiding the said Jonah on to a beach, promontory or any secluded part of the adjacent coast' (Boyd and Porter, p. 54). The prophet, in turn, is to honour 'all Whales, Leviathans, Sea Cows, Sea Lions, Sun Fish, Devil Rays, Mantas, Moby Dicks, Aquatic Dirigibles, Basking Sharks and every large denizen of the Deep whatsoever' (p. 56). Most significantly, Jonah agrees to 'actively foster the preservation of Whales and seek ordinances of governments and individuals that they will never engage in hunting Whales and kindred sea-dwelling species'. Not only does this interpretation highlight the agency of the fish – depicted (in line with popular imagination) by Boyd and Porter as a whale – it also shows how this change in perspective leads to the fish being appreciated as an equal partner, and the wider consequences this might have. For Trible (1996, pp. 482–3), the fish 'mediates between the deity and the human being', while Conradie (2005, p. 226) speaks of the fish as delivering 'God's astonishing mercy' by offering 'unexpected (if uncomfortable) safety and protection to Jonah in his deepest hour of need. This mercy is not manifested at a distance: it is one that enfolds Jonah like a mother's womb.' We therefore find here an example of what van Heerden (2014, p. 122) describes as: 'elements of the text that invite us, the readers, to imagine a life in partnership with the rest of nature – a partnership that may reduce a sense of distance, separation, and otherness, which would be an important step towards overcoming an anthropocentric bias'.

That said, Brent Strawn has offered some intriguing reflections on the significance of nature's vomiting in the book of Jonah, suggesting that partnership with humans may not always be straightforward for nature either. As he points out (p. 458), 'the book of Jonah does not happen without the natural world, and Jonah's mission to Nineveh does not happen without the natural world's vomiting'. It is of course Jonah's conduct that leads to the 'world's vomiting', as expressed vicariously by the fish (2.10). When Jonah later must learn a difficult lesson about God's mercy, that lesson, as Strawn points out, 'is made by means of a plant that has a very curious name that sounds an awful lot like "Jonah is certainly vomited"'. The name of the plant, as we have seen, is *qiqayon* whose components *qi* (קִ), *qa* (קָ) and *yon* (יוֹן) evoke the Hebrew phrase *qi'* (קִיא) *qa'* (קָא) *yonah* (יוֹנָה).[10] The third part is the Hebrew for Jonah, which is abbreviated to 'yon' in the plant's name, whereas the first two components combine into an emphatic verbal construction. The whole phrase can be translated as 'he/it has certainly vomited Jonah', which may be a circumlocution for 'Jonah has certainly been vomited'.[11] Strawn (pp. 458, 459) draws the conclusion that 'Jonah must learn some hard lesson – and evidently vomit is God's tool of choice' – and perhaps more importantly that 'human agency and activity affect the nonhuman subjects' in our text.

Moving on from the fish, we turn to the Ninevites' domestic animals, which play an intriguing role in 3.7–8. The Hebrew term בְּהֵמָה (*behemah*) can be used for four-footed animals in contrast to birds, fish and reptiles. Here, however, it refers more specifically to domestic animals, as is suggested by the additional references to cattle and sheep. These domestic animals are included in the king's edict that no one, neither human nor animal, is to 'taste anything' (v. 7). Indeed, the addition that they are not to graze or pasture (רעה, *ra'ah*; the NRSV translates this as 'feed') puts specific emphasis on the animals. In the next verse, we again find both humans and animals included in the demand that they all don sackcloth. Shemesh (p. 18) wonders whether the same is true for the stipulation that 'they shall cry mightily to God', concluding that, being deprived of food, the animals' inevitable lowing and bleating would be their way of doing just that.

Indeed, given the depiction of animals in other parts of the Old Testament, such as their praise of God in Psalm 148.10, 13, or their crying out to God in Job 38.41, Psalm 104.21, Psalm 147.9 and Joel 1.20, there is nothing too extraordinary in their crying to God in Jonah 3.8. Douglas Stuart (p. 493) in this context refers to the 'close interrelationship of humans and animals' in antiquity, noting that in Persian times and subsequent periods animals were sometimes included in mourning practices (see Herodotus 9.24; Plutarch, *Life of Alexander* §72; and Judith 4.10). Trible therefore suggests that 'the decree treats animals on a par with human beings'. Indeed, in contrast to those who regard the book's non-human characters as an element of its satirical tone, she asserts that 'the intent is not ridicule but respect, not parody but pathos. Nineveh cares for its animal population' (Trible, 1996, p. 483; also 1999, pp. 192–3). Person (pp. 88–9), while accepting that there is a satirical tone to the narrative, similarly cautions against limiting the animals' significance to playing a merely satirical role. Walter Moberly (pp. 156–7) admits the difficulty for modern readers is 'not to see animals in sackcloth as purely humorous' but suggests that 'the general high valuation of animals in relation to humans elsewhere in the OT ... could suggest a more positive and serious construal'.

Given the shared practice of fasting and mourning, Shemesh (pp. 19–20) highlights how the book of Jonah foregrounds 'the common destiny of human beings and animals', which connects with Ruether's point (p. 48) that 'a profound spirituality would arise if we would attempt to experience this kinship and make it present in our consciousness'. The book of Jonah, in other words, here affords us an opportunity to develop just such a spirituality. Ruether adds: 'Recognition of this profound kinship must bridge the arrogant barriers that humans have erected to wall themselves off, not only from other sentient animals, but also from simpler animals, plants, and the abiotic matrix of life in rocks and soils, air, and water.'

According to Forti (p. 371), the narrator relates to the animals 'as active protagonists in the realm of divine control over Creation', while James Limburg (p. 82) sees the passage as one of several biblical texts that speak of the 'solidarity between humans and animals'. Abasili (p. 247) in turn concludes that 'animals, among the Ninevites, are more like comrades than properties; they are appreciated as part of the Ninevite populace'. He adds that God, having seen the repentance of *all* Ninevites, including that of the animals, appropriately rescinds everyone's punishment. Abasili is thus drawing attention to the animals' instrumental role in Nineveh's appeal for God's mercy, an interpretation that is corroborated by the book's final words in 4.11. However, before we turn to those concluding words, we might just note that Jonah is said to have 'pitied' the *qiqayon* (4.10). Hebrew חוס (*khus*), only introduced at this point in the story, means 'pity', 'compassion', 'benevolence' or 'mercy'. Trible (1999, p. 197) suggests that in pitying the plant Jonah is acknowledging 'the integrity of the botanical creature', which is twice called a 'son of the night' (בֶּן־לַיְלָה, *bin-laylah*) by Yahweh (4.10).[12] God thereby, in Trible's words, 'accords it the status of human creatures, a status already accorded the animals of Nineveh'.

Not surprisingly, it is common for ecological interpreters to focus on the book's strategically placed final words, 'and also many animals', which as van Heerden (2017, p. 460) notes are 'an obvious starting point for retrieving ecological wisdom from the Jonah narrative'. Trible (1996, p. 483), considering 4.11 in the light of 3.7–8, comments that 'the deity acknowledges what the king knows. In issues of life and death, the animals of Nineveh matter alongside the people. On this strong ecological note, the book ends.'[13] Indeed, she finds in the book's ending a 'theology of pity' (1994, p. 223) in contrast to an earlier 'theology of repentance' (3.10) that 'embraces plant and animal, perhaps even a worm'. She also detects in 4.11 a significant development in that 'the divine use of nature [here] yields to respect for the integrity of creation' (1996, p. 525), adding that it is the animals that are 'Yahweh's last word'. For Shemesh

(p. 3), the book's ending indicates that God's mercy 'transcends human beings and includes animals as well'. Conradie (2005, p. 226) similarly highlights this vision of 'God's astonishing mercy that extends over the whole of creation'. Abasili (pp. 249–50) not only notes God's interest in Nineveh's non-human inhabitants but sees God's emphasis as being on 'the inherent value of every creature and the unity expected of all his creatures'. According to Person (p. 87), God's rhetorical question illustrates the worth of Nineveh's animals, suggesting that 'the Lord has compassion for them as created beings' and that God values them 'as active agents in the divine plan for creation'.

Such care for animals is not unique to the book of Jonah but is echoed, for instance, in the inclusion of animals in the Sabbath commandments (Exod. 20.10; 23.12; Deut. 5.14), in the demand that a mother bird not be taken alongside the eggs or fledglings (Deut. 22.6–7) or in the psalmist's declaration that God saves 'humans and animals alike' (Ps. 36.6). That said, however, these ecological readings stand in stark contrast to earlier anthropocentric interpretations that regarded the 'beasts' as unintelligent human beings (medieval French rabbi Rashi (1040–1105)) or as evildoers (Deuteronomy Rabbah).[14] They also differ from conclusions reached by influential figures such as Dominican philosopher and theologian Thomas Aquinas (1225–74), French philosopher René Descartes (1596–1650) or German philosopher Immanuel Kant (1724–1804), who saw animals as unworthy of moral consideration.[15] Of course, the point about God's care for the animals depends on our reading of Jonah's final verse. While it is usually rendered as a question ('should I not be concerned about …?'), the Hebrew text can also be read in a declarative sense as having God assert: 'I am not concerned about Nineveh' (Cooper, p. 158; Guillaume, p. 243) – and thus also not about the animals. On this reading, God merely *delayed* the Ninevites' punishment because of their repentance rather than granting them a final pardon. This would make good historical sense, as Nineveh was eventually destroyed, as its original readers would have known. And yet, as Ehud Ben Zvi (2009, p. 5) notes, later readers clearly understood Jonah 4.11 as a rhetorical question.[16]

Coming back to the animals' role in Jonah 4.11, for Shemesh (p. 25) the final verse shows not only that the lives of animals 'have an independent rationale', as they also do in Job 39—41, but that their fate is linked to that of us humans. After all, had Nineveh been wiped out, all its animals would have been destroyed with everything else. Indeed, noting the intertextual links with the judgement of Sodom and Gomorrah provided by the term 'to overthrow' (הפך, *hafakh*; Jonah 3.4; Gen. 19.25, 29; Deut. 29.22; Amos 4.11), T. A. Perry (p. 48) speaks of the 'language of utter extermination', which designates an all-inclusive punishment that would have devastated humans, animals, plants and the land on which Nineveh stood.

Shemesh (p. 25) suggests that 'this linkage imposes special responsibility on human beings, because their behavior affects the entire world' or cosmic order (cf. Abasili, p. 241). Van Urk (p. 215) accordingly suggests that this text 'lends itself to a recontextualization in the Anthropocene', noting that 'humans and animals are pictured together; they share the same fate', much as 'present-day humans and many animal species will suffer the consequences of the destructive ways of humanity'. According to Forti (p. 361) and Abasili (pp. 240–1), the same linkage between human behaviour and its effects on the non-human creation is already implied in the divine command that Jonah speak against Nineveh because of the city's evil (1.1). For Forti, this 'establishes human behavior and the maintaining of a universal social order of justice as a prerequisite for sustaining the cosmic order'.

Drawing some ecological conclusions about the implications for human behaviour and picking up Trible's language of 'pity', Strawn (p. 463) notes (1) that God's work in the book of Jonah involves 'pity on a plant, commands for a fish, the use of a worm, and concern for much cattle' and (2) that 'working for God for the sake of Ea(a)rth[17] is an exercise in godly compassion'. Abasili (pp. 251–2) offers more detailed conclusions when he says that the book of Jonah:

- 'suggests the beauty of all elements of creation working together';
- 'suggests the effectiveness of the creation family working together' (as illustrated by the averting of the catastrophe by means of 'the solidarity of [Nineveh's] humans and animals');
- 'calls us to treat creation as Yhwh treats it' (who treats all of creation with recognition and respect, demonstrating 'all-embracing care for every aspect of nature') (p. 253);
- 'teaches us that other aspects of nature are indispensable for the survival of humanity' (Jonah was rescued by a fish; the animals' repentance contributed to Nineveh's survival).

For further reflection

1 How would you describe the role of non-human creatures in the book of Jonah? Would you agree that they are 'indispensable to God's economy'? If so, how? Does the book instrumentalize non-human creatures? Or might they be seen as God's agents? What difference would that make?

2 What do you make of the suggestion that the book, in portraying the non-human creation as obedient compared to Jonah's disobedience, may be targeting anthropocentrism? Or does the book itself reflect an anthropocentric perspective? Or is it merely its subsequent interpretation that has been driven by anthropocentric concerns?

3 What, given the ecological issues we are facing, do you think of conclusions that the divine, human and non-human agencies in the book are interdependent, or that there is a partnership, solidarity and/or kinship between humanity and the rest of nature? Would you agree that the book can be read along these lines?

4 What about the book's ending – and God's mercy extending to the animals? How would you assess the significance of this?

5 Finally, what do you make of Abasili's conclusions quoted at the end of this section?

An Earth Bible Commentary on Jonah

Having surveyed various perspectives on reading Jonah ecologically, we now turn to Jione Havea's commentary in the Earth Bible Commentary series published by Bloomsbury, which offers the most extensive ecological reading to date. Mindful of our situation at the beginning of the twenty-first century, Havea sees an ecological approach as essential, maintaining (2020, loc. 255) that 'the analysis of Jonah, and of other biblical books, can no longer be undertaken as if one is blind to and ignorant of the ecological injustices that surround us'. In an earlier article, in which he reflected on 'islander worries', Havea (2018a, pp. 16–17) highlighted the issue of climate change, noting, for instance that Tuvalu and Kiribati, whose highest points are a mere four metres above sea level, are projected to be the first islands to disappear because of rising sea levels. However, this focus on climate change, Havea insists, should not obscure other ecological devastations, such as those of island space and livelihoods by the Japan–USA war or the testing of atomic bombs by France and the United States in island waters. All this leads him to quote Australian theologian Denis Edwards (1943–2019) who urges (p. 3): 'As the church itself is called to conversion to the side of the poor in the struggle of justice and to the side of women in their struggle for full equality, so the church itself is called to conversion to the side of suffering creation.'

Havea (2020, loc. 76) describes his work on Jonah as 'a commentary with land, sea, underworld and native (is)land orientations'. There is much of relevance to our earlier discussion of contextual approaches in his study, alongside some intriguing theological reflections on, for instance, the nature of Yahweh, none of which, however, we can consider here. Our emphasis rather must be on Havea's ecological focus. As he points out (locs 59–85), 'sea, wind, boat, fish, city, hinterland, sun, bush, worm and beasts – which are earth(ed) characters in the book of Jonah – ... have roles and voices in this narrative and they matter in this commentary', which focuses 'on the significance of earth(ed) subjects in and for the narrative'.

Havea adopts a hermeneutic of suspicion against anthropocentrism, which he combines with 'suspicion against dualistic views that see Earth as object for human interests ... against Earth-centred mindsets that ignore the powers of Earth to reject, consume and subjugate' (loc. 198). Havea's talk of the 'powers of Earth' is reminiscent of the Earth Bible Team's sixth ecojustice principle of resistance. It is interesting to note that he rejects (loc. 176) any 'drift towards romanticizing the agency and voices of Earth and of its creatures'. Earth, he suggests, engages in acts of rejection, consummation and subjugation, which is both an important addendum to our earlier consideration of creation's praise and a fruitful approach for engaging the issue of natural catastrophes. We already encountered a similar perspective in Masenya's essay, which also raised the possibility of seeing natural phenomena as Earth's resistance. Returning to the issue of anthropocentrism, Havea points out (loc. 198) that his reading aims to see 'the sea, boat, shrub, worm, wind, city and beasts for who they are rather than as "non-humans"'. Indeed, he notes (loc. 225) that:

> it is tricky to be anthropocentric with this story because the key character wants to die, to stop being human, and the favoured subject is a great city with many people and animals. A great fish rescued the main character in the sea (Jon. 1.17), and the repenting of beasts (Jon. 3.8–9) contributed to the sparing of the city and the people of Nineveh (Jon. 4.11). The Jonah narrative-and-novella, according to this overview, is far from being an anthropocentric construction.

Elsewhere (2018b, p. 44), Havea notes that to read 'on behalf of the sea/moana, one learns to relax the vigor of anthropocentrism in order to appreciate the gifts and forces of the sea/moana'. In his commentary (2020, loc. 232), he goes on to emphasize that Nineveh's beasts have voices, that they were not only ordered to 'cry mightily to God' (3.7–8) but were also heard by a relenting God. This leads him to conclude that a hermeneutic of suspicion must ask 'what prevents readers from hearing and identifying with beasts'. Lastly, before considering some examples from his interpretation of Jonah, we should note a couple of points about Havea's reading strategy. The first is that he distinguishes (locs 310–61, 1349, 3144) between a forward reading, which follows the flow of the narrative, requiring one to 'buy into the plotting of the narrator', and a backward reading, which 'flees from the presence of the biblical narrator' and their plotting. This reads beyond the narrative's limits 'into other stories and other narratives', including other biblical, Qur'anic and Pasifika stories as well as current concerns for the ecological conditions of the earth(ed) and the challenges of climate injustice.

The second point arises out of the first and leads Havea to posit (loc. 295) that 'there is room in this mode of biblical contextual interpretation for contesting the text', for freeing oneself from ancient mindsets (loc. 2988) and for engaging critically with how, for instance, God is portrayed. As he puts it (locs 201–25), 'a reading of the story of Jonah that does not critically engage with God and the narrator is not radical enough, especially given that Jonah initially (Jonah 1) refused to follow God's direction'. The aim for him (loc. 3038) is not just to hear the text's voice from the past but to confront it with 'the voices and cries in and from the present'. Havea acknowledges (loc. 3172) this as an example of what traditional scholarship calls eisegesis, a reading into the text that is 'a methodological sin in the eyes of the academy'. Yet he challenges us to consider whether exegesis is even possible without eisegesis.

But let us now look at a few examples from Havea's reading of Jonah. Beginning with the events on the sea (1.4–16), we note that, reading from the perspective of Earth, Havea begins by suggesting (loc. 569):

> The sea in itself was not the problem … The sea became a problem when Yhwh came casting and hurling his powers upon the sea. Things are not as expected. Against the expectation of the natives of the sea that a great storm is caused by the sea itself gathering its energy and brewing up a storm with fury, the narrative attributes the troubling of the sea to Yhwh.

Indeed, approaching the text from a Pasifika and Oceania context that draws attention to native people and cultures on the one hand, and the region's oceanic context on the other, Havea further notes (loc. 594) that those readers might be 'troubled with Yhwh using the energies of nature (e.g. wind) for personal vendetta, notwithstanding that Yhwh is believed to have made the earth and the sea'. He goes on to suggest (loc. 643) that 'Yhwh was not mindful of other subjects who were also affected by his troubling of the sea, including the sea itself.' Indeed, it is this 'disconnection and unreasonableness in the bullying acts of Yhwh' (loc. 569) that causes the boat to think about breaking up (Jonah 1.4). Havea, who prefers to speak of a 'boat', because 'ship' for Pasifika islanders connotes a specifically Western vessel (loc. 2807), then runs with the 'flares of novelty and remixing of reality' (loc. 2598) that the biblical narrative gives us when it envisages a thinking boat. It leads him to wonder 'how the boat might have thought of what happened in the biblical account'. Noting that a thinking boat would also have seen what happens in the water, he connects this (loc. 2672) with the devastating ecological impact of our pollution of the oceans, especially the plastic that ends up in the sea and is eaten by birds and sea creatures.

In Jonah the narrator ultimately abandons the boat at sea; it never reaches shore but is 'left drifting in the sea of the narrative towards the abyss of memory loss ... no scholarly community bothers to imagine its conditions or afterlife' (locs 2722, 2741). Again, connecting the narrative with the realities of contemporary life, Havea (loc. 2741) regards the abandoned boat 'as a reminder of refugees who are ignored or abandoned by scholarly and international communities'. His Pasifika reading, which considers rising water levels, climate refugees and boat people (as refugees arriving by boat are called in Australia), is a good example of social justice issues and ecological problems intersecting, as they so frequently do. In connection with the consideration of the plight of 'boat people' in our times, Havea offers some observations on the boat in the Jonah story functioning as a sanctuary. To pick up only one aspect of his discussion, he notes that the rituals of vows and sacrifices in 1.16 'affirm that worship involves more than words, and that sanctuary is a place where, to appropriate the words of De La Torre, "acts that demonstrate solidarity with the oppressed" are embodied' (loc. 2782, quoting De La Torre, 2019, p. 157). In his reading, both the fearful mariners and the fleeing prophet are oppressed by a bullying God, much as contemporary boat people are oppressed by the countries they are fleeing and by the international community which, with increasing hostility, is intent on shirking its responsibility to give them refuge.

Turning to Jonah 2, Havea (loc. 2292) laments that 'the belly of the fish as the context in which Jonah prayed does not impact how Jonah 2.1–10 is usually read'. Indeed, as he goes on to say, 'this is a fish story in which the fish does not really matter'. This leads him to offer a counter-reading in which the fish does matter. What he proposes to do (loc. 2516) is to '[dive] into the world of the narrative and [upset] the tendency to think of the fish (and other creatures of the sea) as mindless, unimportant and dispensable', to respect the fish and, taking advantage of the biblical narrative's fantasy world, read in 'solidarity with a noble creature of the sea' (loc. 2510). This last phrase reflects Havea's understanding of the fish being 'great' not simply in size but in stature. He further explains (loc. 2317):

> The reason and excuse for my interest in reading for the fish should be obvious – because i prefer to read for characters that are ignored and sidelined. And it makes a difference that i am a Pasifika native who loves and depends on what Tuvaluans call 'home of the fish' (*fale o ika*), referring to the saltwater sea.

As an example of Havea's respect for the fish, we might note his interest in the fish's reason for vomiting Jonah out as well as the fish's fate after having done so. On one level, the fish then dies what Havea (loc. 2366) describes as 'a literary death' in that the fish is never heard of in the story again. Reading from within his own Pasifika context, however, Havea adds that, according to 'native home-of-fish (*fale o ika*) knowledge ... a fish [actually] dies after it vomits. A fish that vomits is a dead fish. The landing (delivery) of Jonah onto dry land therefore marks the death of the fish.'

Commenting on Jonah 3.7–8, Havea notes and appropriates the alternative reading, according to which the animals/beasts are understood as 'a metaphor for people who are not accepted as civil subjects in the eyes of the king and the nobles ... non-subjects like slaves, stateless refugees ... or the Dalits in Hindu societies', who in this case 'have a role to play in the survival of the city' (loc. 1122). Having said that, however, Havea (loc. 1589) also considers the literal reading, drawing attention to the remarkable inclusion of the animals in the king's decree, which 'is different from the usual responses to beasts – fear, disgust or feeling sorry for beasts'. In similar vein, as he goes on to say (loc. 1196), God too 'is open to respond even to the words and actions of people and beasts that do not regularly worship God' (3.10).

Moving on to the book's ending, Havea, in his forward reading, notes (loc. 1366) that it employs what he describes as 'the beast metaphor' to highlight God's mercy, which is said to extend into the realm of animals. In his backward reading, he considers a range of Old Testament texts that allude to the beasts' vulnerability. Following extensive discussion, Havea makes a case for moving beyond the traditional reading of Jonah 4.11. While this reduces God's engagement with the beasts to God's mercy, he suggests (loc. 1509) that 'there are qualities in the beasts themselves that warrant their delivery', that 'there is beauty in the beasts' and (loc. 1589) that 'Yhwh was sorry for and in solidarity with the vulnerable beasts'. But this is not where it ends for, as Havea with many others before him maintains, God's words are not just addressed to Jonah but to all readers. As he puts it (loc. 1634), 'i imagine Yhwh at the end of the Jonah narrative asking readers, "Where's your compassion"' towards the city, the people and the beasts?

For further reflection

1 What do you make of Havea's way of conceptualizing Earth's resistance – that is, in terms of Earth engaging in acts of rejection, consummation and subjugation? Should we see natural catastrophes as examples of Earth's resistance?

2 And what do you think of Havea's hermeneutic of resistance, of fleeing from the presence and the plotting of the biblical narrator, of contesting the text and engaging critically with its portrayal of God?

3 What do you make of Havea's concept of confronting the biblical text with the 'voices and cries in and from the present'? And what about the ways in which he connects story elements, such as the abandoned boat, or the boat as sanctuary, with current realities such as the pollution of the seas, rising water levels, climate refugees and boat people?

4 What do you make of Havea's notion of a God who 'is open to respond even to the words and actions of people and beasts that do not regularly worship God'? And what about God sparing the animals because of their inherent qualities, because of their beauty?

Bibliography

Abasili, Alexander Izuchukwu, 'The role of non-human creatures in the book of Jonah: The implications for eco-justice', *Scandinavian Journal of the Old Testament*, 31/2 (2017), pp. 236–53.

Abrams, M. H., 1981, *A Glossary of Literary Terms*, 2nd edn, New York: Holt, Rinehart & Winston.

Achebe, Chinua, 1991, *Girls at War and Other Stories*, New York: Anchor.

Achebe, Chinua, 1994, *No Longer at Ease*, New York: Anchor.

Achebe, Chinua, 2001a, *Anthills of the Savannah*, London: Penguin.

Achebe, Chinua, 2001b, *Things Fall Apart*, London: Penguin.

Achebe, Chinua, 2003, *Home and Exile*, Edinburgh: Canongate.

Ackerman, James S., 1981, 'Satire and symbolism in the song of Jonah', in Halpern, Baruch, and Levenson, Jon D. (eds), *Traditions in Transformation: Turning Points in Biblical Faith*, Winona Lake: Eisenbrauns, pp. 213–46.

Ackerman, James S., 1989, 'Jonah', in Alter, Robert, and Kermode, Frank (eds), *The Literary Guide to the Bible*, London: Fontana, pp. 234–43.

Ahoga, Augustin Cossi, 2006, 'Jonah', in Adeyemo, Tokunboh et al. (eds), *Africa Bible Commentary*, Grand Rapids: Zondervan, pp. 2780–9.

Aichele, George et al., 1995, *The Postmodern Bible*, New Haven: Yale University Press.

Allen, Leslie C., 1976, *The Books of Joel, Obadiah, Jonah, and Micah*, Grand Rapids: Eerdmans.

Alter, Robert, 1981, *The Art of Biblical Narrative*, New York: Basic Books.

Andrag-Meyer, Franziska, and Mouton, Elna, 2005, 'African hermeneutics', in Jonker, Louis, and Lawrie, Douglas (eds), *Fishing for Jonah (Anew): Various Approaches to Biblical Interpretation*, Stellenbosch: SUN, pp. 207–19.

Anum, Eric, 2000, 'Comparative readings of the Bible in Africa: Some concerns', in West, Gerald O., and Dube, Musa W. (eds), *The Bible in Africa: Transactions, Trajectories and Trends*, Leiden: Brill, pp. 457–73.

Aristotle, 2013, *Poetics*, trans. by Anthony Kenny, Oxford: Oxford University Press.

Aron, Lewis, 'Jonah and applied psychoanalytic dialogue: Introduction', *Psychoanalytic Dialogues*, 18 (2008), pp. 300–6.

Asante, Molefi Kete, 1998, *The Afrocentric Idea*, rev. edn, Philadelphia: Temple University Press.

Ashcroft, Bill, Griffiths, Gareth, and Tiffin, Helen, 2002, *The Empire Writes Back: Theory and Practice in Post-Colonial Literatures*, 2nd edn, London: Routledge.

Ateek, Naim Stifan, 2008, *A Palestinian Christian Cry for Reconciliation*, Maryknoll: Orbis.

Atkins, Peter Joshua, 'Praise by animals in the Hebrew Bible', *Journal for the Study of the Old Testament*, 44/3 (2020), pp. 500–13.

Atwood, Margaret, 2003, *Negotiating with the Dead: A Writer on Writing*, London: Virago.

Bailey, Randall C. (ed.), 2003, *Yet with a Steady Beat: Contemporary U.S. Afrocentric Biblical Interpretation*, Atlanta: SBL.

Bailey, Randall C., Liew, Tat-siong Benny, and Segovia, Fernando F., 2009, 'Toward minority biblical criticism: Framework, contours, dynamics', in Bailey, Randall C., Liew, Tat-siong Benny, and Segovia, Fernando F. (eds), *They Were All Together in One Place? Toward Minority Biblical Criticism*, Atlanta: SBL, pp. 3–43.

Bakhtin, Mikhail, 1981, *The Dialogic Imagination: Four Essays*, ed. by Michael Holquist, trans. by Caryl Emerson and Michael Holmquist, Austin: University of Texas Press.

Bakhtin, Mikhail, 1984a, *Problems of Dostoevsky's Poetics*, ed. and trans. by Caryl Emerson, Minneapolis: University of Minnesota Press.

Bakhtin, Mikhail, 1984b, *Rabelais and His World*, trans. by Hélène Iswolsky, Bloomington: Indiana University Press.

Bal, Mieke, 1988, *Death and Dissymetry: The Politics of Coherence in the Book of Judges*, Chicago: University of Chicago Press.

Band, Arnold J., 'Swallowing Jonah: The eclipse of parody', *Prooftexts*, 10/2 (1990), pp. 177–95.

Bar-Efrat, Shimon, 1989, *Narrative Art in the Bible*, Sheffield: Almond.

Barr, James, 'Man and nature – the ecological controversy and the Old Testament', *Bulletin of the John Rylands Library*, 55/1 (1972), pp. 9–32.

Barton, John, 1996, *Reading the Old Testament: Method in Biblical Study*, 2nd edn, London: Darton, Longman & Todd.

Barton, John, 1998, 'Historical-critical approaches', in Barton, John (ed.), *The Cambridge Companion to Biblical Interpretation*, Cambridge: Cambridge University Press, pp. 9–20.

Bauckham, Richard, 2012, *Living with Other Creatures: Green Exegesis and Theology*, Milton Keynes: Paternoster.

Bauman, Zygmunt, 1998, 'Allosemitism: Premodern, modern, postmodern', in Cheyette, Bryan, and Marcus, Laura (eds), *Modernity, Culture and 'the Jew'*, Cambridge: Polity, pp. 143–56.

Becker, Ernest, 1973, *The Denial of Death*, New York: Free Press.

Becker, Eve-Marie, Dochhorn, Jan, and Holt, Else (eds), 2014, *Trauma and Traumatization in Individual and Collective Dimensions: Insights from Biblical Studies and Beyond*, Göttingen: Vandenhoeck & Ruprecht.

Bediako, Kwame, 1995, *Christianity in Africa: The Renewal of a Non-Western Religion*, Maryknoll: Orbis.

Ben Zvi, Ehud, 2003a, *Signs of Jonah: Reading and Rereading in Ancient Yehud*, Sheffield: Sheffield Academic Press.

Ben Zvi, Ehud, 2003b, 'What's new in Yehud? Some considerations', in Albertz, Rainer, and Becking, Bob (eds), *Yahwism after the Exile: Perspectives on Israelite Religion in the Persian Era*, Assen: Van Gorcum, pp. 32–48.

Ben Zvi, Ehud, 'Jonah 4:11 and the metaprophetic character of the book of Jonah', *Journal of Hebrew Scriptures*, 9/5 (2009), pp. 1–13.

Berger, Yitzhak, 2016, *Jonah in the Shadows of Eden*, Bloomington: Indiana University Press.

Berlin, Adele, 'A rejoinder to John A. Miles, Jr., with some observations on the nature of prophecy', *The Jewish Quarterly Review*, 66/4 (1976), pp. 227–35.

Berlin, Adele, 1994, *Poetics and Interpretation of Biblical Narrative*, Winona Lake: Eisenbrauns.

Bettelheim, Bruno, 1976, *The Uses of Enchantment: The Meaning and Importance of Fairy Tales*, New York: Alfred A. Knopf.

Bewer, Julius A., 1912, 'A commentary on Jonah', in Hinckley, G. Mitchell, Smith, John Merlin Powis, and Bewer, Julius A., *A Critical and Exegetical Commentary on Haggai, Zechariah, Malachi and Jonah*, Edinburgh: T & T Clark.

Biddle, Mark E., 2013, *A Time to Laugh: Humor in the Bible*, Macon: Smyth & Helwys.

Birch, Bruce C. et al., 1999, *A Theological Introduction to the Old Testament*, Nashville: Abingdon.

Blank, Sheldon H., '"Doest thou well to be angry?" A study in self-pity', *Hebrew Union College Annual*, 26 (1955), pp. 29–41.

Blower, David Benjamin, 2016, *Sympathy for Jonah: Reflections on Humiliation, Terror and the Politics of Enemy-Love*, Eugene: Resource Publications.

Boase, Elizabeth, and Agnew, Sarah, '"Whispered in the sound of silence": Traumatising the book of Jonah', *The Bible and Critical Theory*, 12/1 (2016), pp. 4–22.

Boase, Elizabeth, and Frechette, Christopher G. (eds), 2016, *Bible through the Lens of Trauma*, Atlanta: SBL.

Boer, Roland, and West, Gerald (eds), 2000, *A Vanishing Mediator? The Presence/Absence of the Bible in Postcolonialism*, Semeia, 88, Atlanta: SBL.

Bolin, Thomas M., 'Eternal delight and deliciousness: The book of Jonah after ten years', *Journal of Hebrew Scriptures*, 9/4 (2009), pp. 1–11.

Booth, Wayne C., 1983, *The Rhetoric of Fiction*, 2nd edn, London: Penguin.

Boyd, Arthur, and Porter, Peter, 1973, *Jonah*, London: Secker & Warburg.

Brenner, Athalya, 1993, 'Jonah's poem out of and within its context', in Davies, Philip R., and Clines, David J. A. (eds), *Among the Prophets: Language, Image and Structure in the Prophetic Writings*, Sheffield: JSOT, pp. 183–92.

Brettler, Marc Zvi, 1995, *The Creation of History in Ancient Israel*, London: Routledge.

Bridgeman, Valerie, 2010, 'Jonah', in Page, Hugh R., Jr et al. (eds), *The Africana Bible: Reading Israel's Scriptures from Africa and the African Diaspora*, Minneapolis: Fortress, locs 3489–577.

Briggs Myers, Isabel, and Myers, Peter B., 1995, *Gifts Differing: Understanding Personality Type*, Mountain View: CPP.

Burrows, Millar, 1970, 'The literary category of the book of Jonah', in Frank, H. T., and Reed, W. L. (eds), *Translating and Understanding the Old Testament*, Nashville: Abingdon, pp. 80–107.

Bussie, Jacqueline A., 2007, *The Laughter of the Oppressed: Ethical and Theological Resistance in Wiesel, Morrison, and Endo*, New York: T & T Clark.

Cannon, Katie Geneva, and Schüssler Fiorenza, Elisabeth (eds), 1989, *Interpretation for Liberation*, Semeia, 47, Atlanta: SBL.

Carley, Keith, 2000, 'Psalm 8: An apology for domination', in Habel, Norman C. (ed.), *Readings from the Perspective of Earth*, Sheffield: Sheffield Academic Press, pp. 111–24.

Carr, David M., 2014, *Holy Resilience: The Bible's Traumatic Origins*, New Haven: Yale University Press.

Carr, Dhyanchand, 1994, 'A biblical basis for Dalit theology', in Massey, James (ed.), *Indigenous People: Dalits: Dalit Issues in Today's Theological Debate*, Delhi: ISPCK, pp. 231–49.

Carroll, Robert P., 1990, 'Is humour also among the prophets', in Radday, Yehuda T., and Brenner, Athalya (eds), *On Humour and the Comic in the Hebrew Bible*, Sheffield: Almond, pp. 169–89.

Carroll, Robert P., 1997, 'Deportation and diasporic discourses in the prophetic literature', in Scott, James M. (ed.), *Exile: Old Testament, Jewish, and Christian Conceptions*, Leiden: Brill, pp. 63–85.

Chatman, Seymour, 1978, *Story and Discourse: Narrative Structure in Fiction and Film*, Ithaca: Cornell University Press.

Chen, Nan Jou, 2004, 'Jonah', in Patte, Daniel et al. (eds), *Global Bible Commentary*, Nashville: Abingdon (Logos Version).

Christie, Douglas E., 2013, *The Blue Sapphire of the Mind: Notes for a Contemplative Ecology*, Oxford: Oxford University Press.

Claassens, L. Juliana M., 'Rethinking humour in the book of Jonah: Tragic laughter as resistance in the context of trauma', *Old Testament Essays*, 28/3 (2015), pp. 655–73.

Clifford, Anne M., 1995, 'When being human becomes truly earthly: An ecofeminist proposal for solidarity', in Graff, Ann O'Hara (ed.), *In the Embrace of God: Feminist Approaches to Theological Anthropology*, Maryknoll: Orbis, pp. 173–89.

Clines, David J. A., and Exum, J. Cheryl, 'The new literary criticism', in Exum, J. Cheryl, and Clines, David J. A. (eds), *The New Literary Criticism and the Hebrew Bible*, Sheffield: JSOT, 1993, pp. 11–25.

Cohen, Jeffrey Jerome (ed.), 1996, *Monster Theory: Reading Culture*, Minneapolis: University of Minnesota Press.

Collins, John J., 2004, *Introduction to the Hebrew Bible*, Minneapolis: Fortress.

Conradie, Ernst M., 'Towards an ecological biblical hermeneutics: A review essay on the Earth Bible Project', *Scriptura*, 85 (2004), pp. 123–35.

Conradie, Ernst M., 2005, 'An ecological hermeneutics', in Jonker, Louis, and Lawrie, Douglas (eds), *Fishing for Jonah (Anew): Various Approaches to Biblical Interpretation*, Stellenbosch: SUN, pp. 219–27.

Conradie, Ernst M., 'The road towards an ecological biblical and theological hermeneutics', *Scriptura*, 93 (2006), pp. 305–14.

Conradie, Ernst M., 'Interpreting the Bible amidst ecological degradation', *Theology*, 112 (2009), pp. 199–207.

Conradie, Ernst M., 2010, 'What on earth is an ecological hermeneutics? Some broad parameters', in Horrell, David G. et al. (eds), *Ecological Hermeneutics: Biblical, Historical and Theological Perspectives*, London: T & T Clark, pp. 295–313.

Cook, Stephen Derek, 2019, '"Who knows?" Reading the Book of Jonah as a Satirical Challenge to Theodicy of the Exile', PhD thesis, University of Sydney.

Cooper, Alan, 1993, 'In praise of divine caprice: The significance of the book of Jonah', in Davies, Philip R., and Clines, David J. A. (eds), *Among the Prophets: Language, Image and Structure in the Prophetic Writings*, Sheffield: JSOT, pp. 144–63.

Copher, Charles B., 1991, 'The black presence in the Old Testament', in Felder, Cain Hope (ed.), *Stony the Road We Trod: African American Biblical Interpretation*, Minneapolis: Fortress, pp. 146–64.

Copher, Charles B., 1993, *Black Biblical Studies: Biblical and Theological Issues on the Black Presence in the Bible*, Chicago: Black Light Fellowship.

Corey, M. A., 1995, *Job, Jonah, and the Unconscious: A Psychological Interpretation of Evil and Spiritual Growth in the Old Testament*, Lanham: University Press of America.

Craig, Kenneth M., Jr, 1993, *A Poetics of Jonah: Art in the Service of Ideology*, Columbia: University of South Carolina Press.

Craigie, Peter C., 1983, *Psalms 1–50*, Waco: Word.

Crenshaw, James L., 1993, 'Jonah, the book of', in Metzger, Bruce M., and Coogan, Michael D. (eds), *The Oxford Companion to the Bible*, New York: Oxford University Press, pp. 380–1.

Crossan, John Dominic, 1988, *The Dark Interval: Towards a Theology of Story*, Salem: Polebridge.

Crouch, Walter B., 'To question an end, to end a question: Opening the closure of the book of Jonah', *Journal for the Study of the Old Testament*, 62 (1994), pp. 101–12.

Culler, Jonathan D., 1982, *On Deconstruction: Theory and Criticism after Structuralism*, Ithaca: Cornell University Press.

Culler, Jonathan D., 2002, *Structuralist Poetics: Structuralism, Linguistics and the Study of Literature*, London: Routledge.

Davidson, Steed Vernyl, 2018, 'Jonah', in Gossai, Hemchand (ed.), *Postcolonial Commentary and the Old Testament*, London: T & T Clark (Kindle version), locs 7877–8507.

Davies, Philip R., 2004, *Whose Bible Is It Anyway?* 2nd edn, London: T & T Clark International.

Davis, Ellen F., 2009, *Scripture, Culture, and Agriculture: An Agrarian Reading of the Bible*, Cambridge: Cambridge University Press.

Dawson, Terence, 2008, 'Literary criticism and analytical psychology', in Young-Eisendrath, Polly, and Dawson, Terence (eds), *The Cambridge Companion to Jung*, 2nd edn, Cambridge: Cambridge University Press, pp. 269–98.

Deane-Drummond, Celia, 2017, *A Primer in Ecotheology: Theology for a Fragile Earth*, Eugene: Cascade.

Deane-Drummond, Celia, 2021, 'The Bible and environmental ethics', in Marlow, Hilary, and Harris, Mark (eds), *The Oxford Handbook of Bible and Ecology*, Oxford: Oxford University Press.

De La Torre, Miguel A., 2007, *Liberating Jonah: Forming an Ethics of Reconciliation*, Maryknoll: Orbis.

De La Torre, Miguel A., 2019, 'Worship through sanctuary', in Burns, Stephen, and Cones, Bryan (eds), *Liturgy with a Difference: Beyond Inclusion in the Christian Assembly*, London: SCM Press, pp. 154–64.

Delitzsch, Franz, 1885, *A System of Biblical Psychology*, 2nd edn, trans. by Robert Ernest Wallis, Edinburgh: T & T Clark.

Devall, Bill, and Sessions, George, 1985, *Deep Ecology: Living as if Nature Mattered*, Layton: Gibbs Smith.

DeWitt, Calvin B., 2000, 'Creation's environmental challenge to evangelical Christianity', in Berry, R. J. (ed.), *The Care of Creation: Focusing Concern and Action*, Leicester: IVP, pp. 60–73.

Donaldson, Laura E., 'Postcolonialism and biblical reading: An introduction', *Semeia*, 75 (1996a), pp. 1–14.

Donaldson, Laura E. (ed.), 1996b, *Postcolonialism and Scriptural Reading*, Semeia, 75, Atlanta: SBL.

Downs, David, 'The specter of exile in the story of Jonah', *Horizons in Biblical Theology*, 31 (2009), pp. 27–44.

Drengson, Alan, and Inoue, Yuichi (eds), 1995, *The Deep Ecology Movement: An Introductory Anthology*, Berkeley: North Atlantic Books.

Dube, Musa W., 2000, *Postcolonial Feminist Interpretation of the Bible*, St Louis: Chalice.

Dube, Musa W., 2004, 'Postcolonial biblical interpretation', in Hayes, John H. (ed.), *Methods of Biblical Interpretation*, Nashville: Abingdon, pp. 361–6.

Earth Bible Team, The, 2000, 'Guiding ecojustice principles', in Habel, Norman C. (ed.), *Readings from the Perspective of Earth*, Sheffield: Sheffield Academic Press, pp. 38–53.

Earth Bible Team, The, 2001, 'The voice of Earth: More than metaphor?', in Habel, Norman C. (ed.), *The Earth Story in the Psalms and the Prophets*, Sheffield: Sheffield Academic Press, pp. 23–8.

Earth Bible Team, The, 2002, 'Ecojustice hermeneutics: Reflections and challenges', in Habel, Norman C., and Balabanski, Vicky (eds), *The Earth Story in the New Testament*, Sheffield: Sheffield Academic Press, pp. 1–14.

Eaton, Heather, 'Liaison or liability: Weaving spirituality into ecofeminist politics', *Atlantis*, 21/1 (1997), pp. 109–22.

Eaton, Heather, 2000, 'Ecofeminist contributions to an ecojustice hermeneutics', in Habel, Norman C. (ed.), *Readings from the Perspective of Earth*, Sheffield: Sheffield Academic Press, pp. 54–71.

Eckardt, Roy, 'Divine incongruity: Comedy and tragedy in a post-Holocaust world', *Theology Today*, 48/4 (1992), pp. 399–412.

Eco, Umberto, 1996, *The Island of the Day Before*, trans. by William Weaver, London: Minerva.

Eco, Umberto, 2001, *Foucault's Pendulum*, trans. by William Weaver, London: Vintage.

Eco, Umberto, 2004, *The Name of the Rose*, trans. by William Weaver, London: Vintage.

Edinger, Edward F., 2000, *Ego and Self: The Old Testament Prophets: From Isaiah to Malachi*, ed. by J. Gary Sparks, Toronto: Inner City Books.

Edwards, Denis, 2006, *Ecology at the Heart of Faith: The Change of Heart That Leads to a New Way of Living on Earth*, Maryknoll: Orbis.

Eisler, Michael Joseph, 'A man's unconscious phantasy of pregnancy in the guise of traumatic hysteria: A clinical contribution to anal erotism', *International Journal of Psycho-Analysis*, 2/3–4 (1921), pp. 255–86.

Elat, Moshe, 'Tarshish and the problem of Phoenician colonisation in the western Mediterranean', *Orientalia Lovaniensia Periodica*, 13 (1982), pp. 55–69.

Elliott, John H., 1993, *What Is Social-Scientific Criticism?*, Minneapolis: Fortress.

Ellmann, Lucy, 2019, *Ducks, Newburyport*, Norwich: Galley Beggar.

Elvey, Anne, 'Complex anachronism: Peter Porter's *Jonah*, otherkind, ancient and contemporary tempests, and the divine', *The Bible and Critical Theory*, 12/1 (2016), pp. 79–93.

Erickson, Amy, 2021, *Jonah: Introduction and Commentary*, Grand Rapids: Eerdmans.

Feinberg, Leonard, 1967, *Introduction to Satire*, Ames: Iowa State University Press.

Felder, Cain Hope (ed.), 1991, *Stony the Road We Trod: African American Biblical Interpretation*, Minneapolis: Fortress.

Felder, Cain Hope, 2004, 'Afrocentric biblical interpretation', in Hayes, John H. (ed.), *Methods of Biblical Interpretation*, Nashville: Abingdon, pp. 297–301.

Figiel, Sia, 1999, *Where We Once Belonged*, New York: Kaya.

Fingert, Hyman H., 'The psychoanalytic study of the minor prophet Jonah', *Psychoanalytic Review*, 41 (1954), pp. 55–65.

Fish, Stanley, 1980, *Is There a Text in This Class? The Authority of Interpretive Communities*, Cambridge: Harvard University Press.

Fishman, George, 'Commentary on paper by Aviva Gottlieb Zornberg', *Psychoanalytic Dialogues*, 18 (2008), pp. 307–16.

Fokkelman, Jan P., 1999, *Reading Biblical Narrative: An Introductory Guide*, trans. by Ineke Smit, Louisville: Westminster John Knox.

Forster, E. M., 1927, *Aspects of the Novel*, New York: Harcourt, Brace.

Forti, Tova, 'Of ships and seas, and fish and beasts: Viewing the concept of universal providence in the book of Jonah through the prism of Psalms', *Journal for the Study of the Old Testament*, 35/3 (2011), pp. 359–74.

Fowler, Robert M., 1991, *Let the Reader Understand: Reader-Response Criticism and the Gospel of Mark*, Minneapolis: Fortress.

Fowler, Robert M., 2008a, 'Reader-response criticism', in Gooder, Paula, *Searching for Meaning: An Introduction to Interpreting the New Testament*, London: SPCK, pp. 127–9.

Fowler, Robert M., 2008b, 'Reader-response criticism: Figuring Mark's reader', in Anderson, Janice Capel, and Moore, Stephen D. (eds), *Mark and Method: New Approaches in Biblical Studies*, 2nd edn, Minneapolis: Fortress, pp. 59–93.

Frankl, Victor, 1967, *Psychotherapy and Existentialism: Selected Papers on Logotherapy*, New York: Washington Square.

Freire, Paulo, 2000, *Pedagogy of the Oppressed*, 30th anniversary edn, trans. by Myra Bergman Ramos, New York: Continuum.

Freud, Sigmund, 1960, *Jokes and Their Relation to the Unconscious*, trans. by James Strachey, New York: W. W. Norton.

Freud, Sigmund, 2001, 'An evidential dream (1913)', in *The Standard Edition of the Complete Psychological Works of Sigmund Freud. Volume 12 (1911–1913): Case History of Schreber, Papers on Technique and Other Works*, trans. by James Strachey et al., London: Vintage, pp. 267–78.

Frolov, Serge, 'Returning the ticket: God and his prophet in the book of Jonah', *Journal for the Study of the Old Testament*, 24 (1999), pp. 85–105.

Fromm, Erich, 'The nature of dreams', *Scientific American*, 180 (1949), pp. 44–7.

Fromm, Erich, 1951, *The Forgotten Language: An Introduction to the Understanding of Dreams, Fairy Tales, and Myths*, New York: Rinehart.

Frye, Northrop, 2020, *Anatomy of Criticism: Four Essays*, Princeton: Princeton University Press.

Funk, Robert W., 1988, *The Poetics of Biblical Narrative*, Sonoma: Polebridge.

Gaines, Janet Howe, 2003, *Forgiveness in a Wounded World: Jonah's Dilemma*, Atlanta: SBL.

Gallagher, Susan VanZanten (ed.), 1994, *Postcolonial Literature and the Biblical Call for Justice*, Jackson: University Press of Mississippi.

Garbini, Giovanni, 1988, *History and Ideology in Ancient Israel*, trans. by John Bowden, New York: Crossroad.

Genette, Gérard, 1997, *Palimpsests: Literature in the Second Degree*, trans. by Channa Newman and Claude Doubinsky, Lincoln: University of Nebraska Press.

Gibson, William E., 2004, 'Eco-justice: What is it?' in Gibson, William E. (ed.), *Eco-Justice: The Unfinished Journey*, Albany: State University of New York Press, pp. 21–9.

Gillingham, Susan E., 1998, *One Bible, Many Voices: Different Approaches to Biblical Studies*, London: SPCK.

Gilmore, David D., 2003, *Monsters: Evil Beings, Mythical Beasts, and All Manner of Imaginary Terrors*, Philadelphia: University of Pennsylvania Press.

Gilmour, Michael J., 2014, *Eden's Other Residents: The Bible and Animals*, Eugene: Cascade.

Girard, René, 1986, *The Scapegoat*, trans. by Yvonne Freccero, Baltimore: Johns Hopkins University Press.

Goitein, S. D., 'Some observations on Jonah', *Journal of the Palestine Oriental Society*, 17 (1937), pp. 63–77.

Good, Edwin M., 1981, *Irony in the Old Testament*, 2nd edn, Sheffield: Almond.

Gooder, Paula, 2008, *Searching for Meaning: An Introduction to Interpreting the New Testament*, London: SPCK.

Gordon, Cyrus H., 1962, 'Tarshish', in Buttrick, George A. et al. (eds), *The Interpreter's Dictionary of the Bible*, New York: Abingdon, vol. 4, pp. 517–18.

Gottwald, Norman K., 1979, 'Sociological method in the study of ancient Israel', in Buss, Martin J. (ed.), *Encounter with the Text: Form and History in the Hebrew Bible*, Philadelphia: Fortress, pp. 69–81.

Gottwald, Norman K., 2003, 'African American biblical hermeneutics: Major themes and wider implications', in Bailey, Randall C. (ed.), *Yet with a Steady Beat: Contemporary U.S. Afrocentric Biblical Interpretation*, Atlanta: SBL, pp. 177–81.

Grayson, A. Kirk, 1976, *Assyrian Royal Inscriptions. Volume 2: From Tiglathpileser I to Ashur-nasir-apli II*, Wiesbaden: Otto Harrassowitz.

Green, Barbara, 2005, *Jonah's Journeys*, Collegeville: Michael Glazier.

Guillaume, Philippe, 'The end of Jonah is the beginning of wisdom', *Biblica*, 87 (2006), pp. 243–50.

Gunn, David M., 1999, 'Narrative criticism', in McKenzie, Steven L., and Haynes, Stephen R. (eds), *To Each Its Own Meaning: An Introduction to Biblical Criticisms and Their Application*, 2nd edn, Louisville: Westminster John Knox, pp. 201–29.

Gunn, David M., and Fewell, Danna Nolan, 1993, *Narrative in the Hebrew Bible*, Oxford: Oxford University Press.

Gutiérrez, Gustavo, 1988, *A Theology of Liberation: History, Politics, and Salvation*, 15th anniversary edn, trans. by Caridad Inda and John Eagleson, Maryknoll: Orbis.

Gutiérrez, Gustavo, 1991, *The God of Life*, trans. by Matthew J. O'Connell, London: SCM Press.

Habel, Norman C., 2000, 'Introducing the Earth Bible', in Habel, Norman C. (ed.), *Readings from the Perspective of Earth*, Sheffield: Sheffield Academic Press, pp. 25–37.

Habel, Norman C., 2003, 'The origins and challenges of an ecojustice hermeneutic', in Sandoval, Timothy J., and Mandolfo, Carleen (eds), *Relating to the Text: Interdisciplinary and Form-Critical Insights on the Bible*, New York: T & T Clark International, pp. 290–306.

Habel, Norman C., 2008, 'Introducing ecological hermeneutics', in Habel, Norman C., and Trudinger, Peter (eds), *Exploring Ecological Hermeneutics*, Atlanta: SBL, pp. 1–8.

Habel, Norman C., 2014, *Finding Wisdom in Nature: An Eco-Wisdom Reading of the Book of Job*, Sheffield: Sheffield Phoenix Press.

Halpern, Baruch, 1988, *The First Historians: The Hebrew Bible and History*, San Francisco: Harper & Row.

Halpern, Baruch, and Friedman, Richard Elliott, 'Composition and paronomasia in the book of Jonah', *Hebrew Annual Review*, 4 (1980), pp. 79–92.

Hamon, R. B., 'Teaching environmental activism and ecological hermeneutics', *Journal for Interdisciplinary Biblical Studies*, 2/1 (2020), pp. 66–80.

Hampl, Patricia, 1995, 'In the belly of the whale', in Büchmann, Christina, and Spiegel, Celina (eds), *Out of the Garden: Women Writers on the Bible*, New York: Ballantine, pp. 289–301.

Handy, Lowell K., 2007, *Jonah's World: Social Science and the Reading of Prophetic Story*, London: Equinox.

Hardt, Michael, and Negri, Antonio, 2000, *Empire*, Cambridge: Harvard University Press.

Hauser, Alan Jon, 'Jonah: In pursuit of the dove', *Journal of Biblical Literature*, 104/1 (1985), pp. 21–37.

Havea, Jione, 2012, 'First people, minority reading: Reading Jonah, from Oceania', in Boer, Roland, Carden, Michael, and Kelso, Julie (eds), *The One Who Reads May Run*, New York: Bloomsbury, pp. 176–85.

Havea, Jione, 'AdJusting Jonah', *International Review of Mission*, 102/1 (2013a), pp. 44–55.

Havea, Jione, 2013b, 'Jonah as a book of surprises and reversals', in Roncace, Mark, and Weaver, Joseph (eds), *Global Perspectives on the Bible*, Boston: Pearson, pp. 131–2.

Havea, Jione, 2014a, 'Engaging scriptures from Oceania', in Havea, Jione, Neville, David J., and Wainwright, Elaine M. (eds), *Bible, Borders, Belonging(s): Engaging Readings from Oceania*, Atlanta: SBL, pp. 3–19.

Havea, Jione, 2014b, 'Reading islandly', in Sugirtharajah, R. S. (ed.), *Voices from the Margin: Interpreting the Bible in the Third World*, 25th anniversary edn, Maryknoll: Orbis, pp. 77–92.

Havea, Jione, 'Sitting Jonah with Job: Resailing intertextuality', *The Bible and Critical Theory*, 12/1 (2016), pp. 94–108.

Havea, Jione, 2018a, 'Islander criticism: Waters, ways, worries', in Havea, Jione (ed.), *Sea of Readings: The Bible in the South Pacific*, Atlanta: SBL, pp. 1–20.

Havea, Jione, 2018b, 'Wet Bible: Stor(y)ing Jonah with Sia Figiel', in Havea, Jione (ed.), *Sea of Readings: The Bible in the South Pacific*, Atlanta: SBL, pp. 37–51.

Havea, Jione (ed.), 2018c, *Sea of Readings: The Bible in the South Pacific*, Atlanta: SBL.

Havea, Jione, 2020, *Jonah: An Earth Bible Commentary*, London: T & T Clark.

Havea, Jione, 2021a, *Losing Ground: Reading Ruth in the Pacific*, London: SCM Press.

Havea, Jione (ed.), 2021b, *Theologies from the Pacific*, Cham, Switzerland: Palgrave Macmillan.

Havea, Jione, Aymer, Margaret, and Davidson, Steed Vernyl (eds), 2015, *Islands, Islanders, and the Bible: RumInations*, Atlanta: SBL.

Havea, Jione, Neville, David J., and Wainwright, Elaine M. (eds), 2014, *Bible, Borders, Belonging(s): Engaging Readings from Oceania*, Atlanta: SBL.

Hendricks, Osayande Obery, 'Guerrilla exegesis: "Struggle" as a scholarly vocation. A postmodern approach to African-American biblical interpretation', *Semeia*, 72 (1995), pp. 73–90.

Herodotus, 2004, *The Histories*, trans. by G. C. Macaulay, ed. by Donald Lateiner, New York: Barnes & Noble.

Holbert, John C., '"Deliverance belongs to Yahweh!" Satire in the book of Jonah', *Journal for the Study of the Old Testament*, 21 (1981), pp. 59–81.

Holter, Knut, 2010, 'When biblical scholars talk about "global" biblical interpretation', in Holter, Knut, and Jonker, Louis C. (eds), *Global Hermeneutics? Reflections and Consequences*, Atlanta: SBL, pp. 85–93.

Holter, Knut, and Jonker, Louis C. (eds), 2010, *Global Hermeneutics? Reflections and Consequences*, Atlanta: SBL.

hooks, bell, 1990, *Yearning: Race, Gender, and Cultural Politics*, Boston: South End.

Hooper, John, 1550, 'An Oversighte and Deliberacioun upon the Holy Prophet Jonas: Made, and Uttered before the Kinges Majesty, and his Most Honorable Councell', in Carr, Samuel (ed.), *Early Writings of John Hooper, Lord Bishop of Gloucester and Worcester*, Cambridge: The Parker Society, 1843, pp. 435–558.

Horrell, David G., 2008, 'Ecological criticism', in Gooder, Paula, *Searching for Meaning: An Introduction to Interpreting the New Testament*, London: SPCK, pp. 192–4.

Horrell, David G., 2010a, *The Bible and the Environment: Towards a Critical Ecological Biblical Theology*, London: Routledge.

Horrell, David G., 2010b, 'Introduction', in Horrell, David G. et al. (eds), *Ecological Hermeneutics: Biblical, Historical and Theological Perspectives*, London: T & T Clark, pp. 1–12.

Horrell, David G., Hunt, Cherryl, and Southgate, Christopher, 'Appeals to the Bible in ecotheology and environmental ethics: A typology of hermeneutical stances', *Studies in Christian Ethics*, 21 (2008), pp. 219–38.

Hutter, Albert D., 1993, 'Poetry in psychoanalysis: Hopkins, Rossetti, Winnicott', in Rudnytsky, Peter L. (ed.), *Transitional Objects and Potential Spaces: Literary Uses of D. W. Winnicott*, New York: Columbia University Press, pp. 63–86.

Hyers, Conrad, 1987, *And God Created Laughter: The Bible as Divine Comedy*, Atlanta: John Knox.

Ingram, Virginia, 2012, 'Satire and cognitive dissonance in the book of Jonah, in the light of Ellens' laws of psychological hermeneutics', in Ellens, J. Harold (ed.), *Psychological Hermeneutics for Biblical Themes and Texts*, London: T & T Clark, pp. 140–55.

Isasi-Díaz, Ada María, 1996, *Mujerista Theology: A Theology for the Twenty-First Century*, Maryknoll: Orbis.

Iser, Wolfgang, 1978, *The Act of Reading: A Theory of Aesthetic Response*, Baltimore: Johns Hopkins University Press.

Jack, Alison M., 2012, *The Bible and Literature*, London: SCM Press.

Jaggi, Maya, 2001, 'Introduction', in Achebe, Chinua, *Anthills of the Savannah*, London: Penguin, pp. vii–xiv.

Jenks, Gregory C., 2014, 'The sign of Jonah: Reading Jonah on the boundaries and from the boundaries', in Havea, Jione, Neville, David J., and Wainwright,

Elaine M. (eds), *Bible, Borders, Belonging(s): Engaging Readings from Oceania*, Atlanta: SBL, pp. 223–38.

Jenson, Philip, 1999, *Reading Jonah*, Cambridge: Grove Books.

Jobling, David, 2004, 'Structuralism and deconstruction', in Hayes, John H. (ed.), *Methods of Biblical Interpretation*, Nashville: Abingdon, pp. 201–8.

Joerstad, Mari, 2019, *The Hebrew Bible and Environmental Ethics: Humans, Non-humans, and the Living Landscape*, Cambridge: Cambridge University Press.

Jonker, Louis, 2005, 'Narrative approaches', in Jonker, Louis, and Lawrie, Douglas (eds), *Fishing for Jonah (Anew): Various Approaches to Biblical Interpretation*, Stellenbosch: SUN, pp. 95–108.

Jonker, Louis, 2010, 'The global context and its consequences for Old Testament Interpretation', in Holter, Knut, and Jonker, Louis (eds), *Global Hermeneutics? Reflections and Consequences*, Atlanta: SBL, pp. 47–56.

Jonker, Louis, and Arendse, Roger, 2005, 'Cultural-anthropological approaches', in Jonker, Louis, and Lawrie, Douglas (eds), *Fishing for Jonah (Anew): Various Approaches to Biblical Interpretation*, Stellenbosch: SUN, pp. 47–58.

Jung, C. G., 2017, *Psychological Types*, trans. by H. G. Baines, rev. by R. F. C. Hull, London: Routledge Classics.

Juvan, Marko, 2008, *History and Poetics of Intertextuality*, trans. by Timothy Pogačar, West Lafayette: Purdue University Press.

Kassel, Maria, 2012, 'Jonah: The Jonah experience – for women too?', trans. by Nancy Lukens, in Schottroff, Luise, and Wacker, Marie-Theres (eds), *Feminist Biblical Interpretation: A Compendium of Critical Commentary on the Books of the Bible and Related Literature*, trans. by Lisa E. Dahill et al., Grand Rapids: Eerdmans, pp. 411–20.

Kavusa, Kivatsi J., 'Ecological hermeneutics and the interpretation of biblical texts yesterday, today and onwards: Critical reflection and assessment', *Old Testament Essays*, 32/1 (2019), pp. 229–55.

Kille, D. Andrew, 2001, *Psychological Biblical Criticism*, Minneapolis: Fortress.

Kille, D. Andrew, 2012, 'Analytical psychology and biblical interpretation: *Jung and the Bible* (Rollins, 1983)', in Ellens, J. Harold (ed.), *Psychological Hermeneutics for Biblical Themes and Texts*, London: T & T Clark, pp. 7–20.

Kim, Hyun Chul Paul, 'Jonah read intertextually', *Journal of Biblical Literature*, 126/3 (2007), pp. 497–528.

King, Martin Luther, Jr, 2010, *Strength to Love*, Minneapolis: Fortress.

Koenig, Sara M., 2011, *Isn't This Bathsheba? A Study in Characterization*, Eugene: Pickwick.

Kozlova, Ekaterina E., 'Jonah 2: A death liturgy for the doomed prophet', *Journal of Hebrew Scriptures*, 20/5 (2020), pp. 1–21.

Kuan, Jeffrey Kah-Jin, 2004, 'Asian biblical interpretation', in Hayes, John H. (ed.), *Methods of Biblical Interpretation*, Nashville: Abingdon, pp. 303–11.

Kugel, James L., 1986, 'Two introductions to midrash', in Hartman, Geoffrey H., and Budick, Sanford (eds), *Midrash and Literature*, New York: Yale University Press, pp. 77–103.

Kunz-Lübcke, Andreas, 'Jonah, Robinsons and unlimited gods: Re-reading Jonah as a sea adventure story', *The Bible and Critical Theory*, 12/1 (2016), pp. 62–78.

Kwok Pui-Lan, 'Discovering the Bible in the non-biblical world', *Semeia*, 47 (1989), pp. 25–42.

Kwok Pui-Lan, 1995, *Discovering the Bible in the Non-Biblical World*, Maryknoll: Orbis.

LaCocque, André, and Lacocque, Pierre-Emmanuel, 1990, *Jonah: A Psycho-Religious Approach to the Prophet*, Columbia: University of South Carolina Press. (An earlier version was published in 1981 as *The Jonah Complex*.)

Landes, George M., 'The "three days and three nights" motif in Jonah 2.1', *Journal of Biblical Literature*, 86 (1967), pp. 446–50.

Landes, George M., 1999, 'Textual "information gaps" and "dissonances" in the book of Jonah', in Chazan, Robert, Hallo, William W., and Schiffman, Lawrence (eds), *Ki Baruch Hu: Ancient Near Eastern, Biblical, and Judaic Studies in Honor of Baruch A. Levine*, Winona Lake: Eisenbrauns, pp. 273–93.

Landy, Francis, 1990, 'Humour as a tool for biblical exegesis', in Radday, Yehuda T., and Brenner, Athalya (eds), *On Humour and the Comic in the Hebrew Bible*, Sheffield: Almond, pp. 99–115.

Laplanche, Jean, and Pontalis, Jean-Bertrand, 2018, *The Language of Psychoanalysis*, Abingdon: Routledge.

Lasine, Stuart, 'Jonah's complexes and our own: Psychology and the interpretation of the book of Jonah', *Journal for the Study of the Old Testament*, 41/2 (2016), pp. 237–60.

Lasine, Stuart, 2020, *Jonah and the Human Condition: Life and Death in Yahweh's World*, London: T & T Clark.

Lawrence, Marion, 'Ships, monsters and Jonah', *American Journal of Archaeology*, 66/3 (1962), pp. 289–96.

Lawrie, Douglas, 2005a, 'The hermeneutics of suspicion: The hidden worlds of ideology and the unconscious. Introduction', in Jonker, Louis, and Lawrie, Douglas (eds), *Fishing for Jonah (Anew): Various Approaches to Biblical Interpretation*, Stellenbosch: SUN, pp. 167–71.

Lawrie, Douglas, 2005b, 'Psychoanalytical approaches', in Jonker, Louis, and Lawrie, Douglas (eds), *Fishing for Jonah (Anew): Various Approaches to Biblical Interpretation*, Stellenbosch: SUN, pp. 171–89.

Lawrie, Douglas, 2005c, 'The role of the reader', in Jonker, Louis, and Lawrie, Douglas (eds), *Fishing for Jonah (Anew): Various Approaches to Biblical Interpretation*, Stellenbosch: SUN, pp. 112–28.

Lear, Jonathan, 1998, *Open Minded: Working out the Logic of the Soul*, Cambridge: Harvard University Press.

Levine, Etan, 'Jonah as a philosophical book', *Zeitschrift für die alttestamentliche Wissenschaft*, 96 (1984), pp. 235–45.

Lewis, Chaim, 'Jonah – a parable for our time', *Judaism*, 21/2 (1972), pp. 159–63.

Licht, Jacob, 1986, *Storytelling in the Bible*, 2nd edn, Jerusalem: Magness.

Lifshitz, Ze'ev Haim, 1994, *The Paradox of Human Existence: A Commentary on the Book of Jonah*, Northvale: Jason Aronson.

Limburg, James, 1993, *Jonah: A Commentary*, London: SCM Press.

Lindsay, Rebecca, 2012, '(Re)Viewing Nineveh: Reading Jonah's Marginal Empire with Postcolonial Imaginations', Bachelor of Theology thesis, School of Theology, Charles Sturt University.

Lindsay, Rebecca, 'Overthrowing Nineveh: Revisiting the city with postcolonial imagination', *The Bible and Critical Theory*, 12/1 (2016), pp. 49–61.

Lovelock, James, 2000a, *The Ages of Gaia: A Biography of Our Living Earth*, 2nd edn, Oxford: Oxford University Press.

Lovelock, James, 2000b, *Gaia: A New Look at Life on Earth*, 2nd edn, Oxford: Oxford University Press.

Lucas, Ernest, 'The New Testament teaching on the environment', *Transformation*, 16/3 (1999), pp. 93–9.

McKenzie, Steven L., and Haynes, Stephen R. (eds), 1999, *To Each Its Own Meaning: An Introduction to Biblical Criticisms and Their Application*, 2nd edn, Louisville: Westminster John Knox.

McKibben, Bill, 2010, *Eaarth: Making a Life on a Tough New Planet*, New York: Henry Holt.

McKnight, Edgar V., 1988, *Postmodern Use of the Bible: The Emergence of Reader-Oriented Criticism*, Nashville: Abingdon.

McKnight, Edgar V., 1999, 'Reader-response criticism', in McKenzie, Steven L., and Haynes, Stephen R. (eds), *To Each Its Own Meaning: An Introduction to Biblical Criticisms and Their Application*, 2nd edn, Louisville: Westminster John Knox, pp. 230–52.

McKnight, Edgar V., 2004, 'Reader-response criticism', in Hayes, John H. (ed.), *Methods of Biblical Interpretation*, Nashville: Abingdon, pp. 179–83.

McLaren, Peter, 2000, 'Whiteness is … the struggle for postcolonial hybridity', in Kincheloe, Joe L. et al. (eds), *White Reign: Deploying Whiteness in America*, New York: St Martin's Griffin, pp. 63–75.

McNinch, Timothy C., '"Who knows?" A Bakhtinian reading of carnivalesque motifs in Jonah', *Vetus Testamentum* (published online ahead of print, 2021), pp. 1–17.

Magonet, Jonathan, 1983, *Form and Meaning: Studies in Literary Techniques in the Book of Jonah*, 2nd edn, Sheffield: Almond.

Magonet, Jonathan, 1992, 'Jonah', in Freedman, David Noel (ed.), *The Anchor Bible Dictionary*, New York: Doubleday, vol. 3, pp. 936–42.

Malina, Bruce J., 2008, 'Social science criticism', in Gooder, Paula, *Searching for Meaning: An Introduction to Interpreting the New Testament*, London: SPCK, pp. 13–15.

Maluleke, Tinyiko Samuel, 2000, 'The Bible among African Christians: A missiological perspective', in Okure, Teresa (ed.), *To Cast Fire upon the Earth: Bible and Mission Collaborating in Today's Multicultural Global Context*, Pietermaritzburg: Cluster, pp. 87–112.

Marcus, David, 1995, *From Balaam to Jonah: Anti-Prophetic Satire in the Hebrew Bible*, Atlanta: Scholars.

Martin, Dale B., 1999, 'Social-scientific criticism', in McKenzie, Steven L., and Haynes, Stephen R. (eds), *To Each Its Own Meaning: An Introduction to Biblical Criticisms and Their Application*, Louisville: Westminster John Knox, pp. 125–41.

Martin, Ellen, 'Raiding Jonah: Reading through object relations theory', *Essays in Literature*, 20/1 (1993), pp. 70–83.

Masenya, Madipoane, 2001, 'An eco*bosadi* reading of Psalm 127:3–5', in Habel, Norman C. (ed.), *The Earth Story in the Psalms and the Prophets*, Sheffield: Sheffield Academic Press, pp. 109–22.

Maslow, Abraham H., 'Neurosis as a failure of personal growth', *Humanitas*, 3 (1967), pp. 153–69.

Maslow, Abraham H., 1993, *The Farther Reaches of Human Nature*, London: Penguin.

Mather, Judson, 'The comic art of the book of Jonah', *Soundings*, 65/3 (1982), pp. 280–91.

Maudlin, Michael G., and Baer, Marlene (eds), 2008, *The Green Bible*, New York: HarperCollins.

Mbembe, Achille, 'Necropolitics', trans. by Libby Meintjes, *Public Culture*, 15/1 (2003), pp. 11–40.

Mburu, Elizabeth, 2019, *African Hermeneutics*, Carlisle: HippoBooks.

Mele, Alfred R., 2004, 'Motivated irrationality', in Mele, Alfred R., and Rawling, Piers (eds), *The Oxford Handbook of Rationality*, Oxford: Oxford University Press, pp. 240–56.

Melville, Herman, 2002, *Moby-Dick or The Whale*, Ware: Wordsworth Editions.

Merton, Thomas, 1953, *The Sign of Jonas*, New York: Harcourt, Brace.

Merton, Thomas, 1955, *No Man Is an Island*, San Diego: Harcourt.

Merton, Thomas, 1977, *Raids on the Unspeakable*, Tunbridge Wells: Burns & Oates.

Merton, Thomas, 1998, *The Other Side of the Mountain: The End of the Journey*, ed. by Patrick Hart, New York: HarperOne.

Merton, Thomas, 2014, *Conjectures of a Guilty Bystander*, New York: Image.

Miles, John R., 1990, 'Laughing at the Bible: Jonah as parody', in Radday, Yehuda T., and Brenner, Athalya (eds), *On Humour and the Comic in the Hebrew Bible*, Sheffield: Almond, pp. 203–15.

Moberly, R. W. L., 'Preaching for a response? Jonah's message to the Ninevites reconsidered', *Vetus Testamentum*, 53/2 (2003), pp. 156–68.

Möller, Karl, 2011, 'Images of God and creation in Genesis 1–2', in Grant, Jamie A., Lo, Alison, and Wenham, Gordon J. (eds), *A God of Faithfulness*, New York: T & T Clark, pp. 3–29.

Möller, Karl, 'A precious gift: Caring for our common home', *The Merton Journal*, 27/2 (2020), pp. 18–28.

Moon, Cyris H. S., 1985, *A Korean Minjung Theology: An Old Testament Perspective*, Maryknoll: Orbis.

Moore, Stephen D., and Segovia, Fernando F. (eds), 2005, *Postcolonial Biblical Criticism: Interdisciplinary Intersections*, London: T & T Clark International.

More, Joseph, 'The prophet Jonah: The story of an intrapsychic process', *American Imago*, 27/1 (1970), pp. 3–11.

Mosala, Itumeleng J., 1989, *Biblical Hermeneutics and Black Theology in South Africa*, Grand Rapids: Eerdmans.

Muilenburg, James, 1972, 'Poetry', in Roth, Cecil (ed.), *Encyclopedia Judaica*, Jerusalem: Keter, vol. 13, pp. 670–81.

Muldoon, Catherine L., 2010, *In Defense of Divine Justice: An Intertextual Approach to the Book of Jonah*, Washington: Catholic Biblical Association of America.

Murray, Paul, 2002, *A Journey with Jonah: The Spirituality of Bewilderment*, Blackrock, Co. Dublin: Columba.

Nash, James A., 'Toward the ecological reformation of Christianity', *Interpretation*, 50/1 (1996), pp. 5–15.

Neusner, Jacob, and Avery-Peck, Alan J., 2004, *The Routledge Dictionary of Judaism*, New York: Routledge.

Niditch, Susan, 1993, *War in the Hebrew Bible: A Study in the Ethics of Violence*, Oxford: Oxford University Press.

Nilsen, Tina Dykesteen, and Solevåg, Anna Rebecca, 'Expanding ecological hermeneutics: The case for ecolonialism', *Journal of Biblical Literature*, 135/4 (2016), pp. 665–83.

Nirmal, A. P., 1988, 'A dialogue with Dalit literature', in Prabhakar, M. E. (ed.), *Towards a Dalit Theology*, Delhi: ISPCK, pp. 64–82.

Nussbaum, Martha C., 2013, *Political Emotions: Why Love Matters for Justice*, Cambridge: Harvard University Press.

O'Day, Gail R., 2004, 'Intertextuality', in Hayes, John H. (ed.), *Methods of Biblical Interpretation*, Nashville: Abingdon, pp. 155–7.

Olley, John W., '"The god of heaven": A look at attitudes to other religions in the Old Testament', *Colloquium*, 27 (1995), pp. 76–94.

Orwell, George, 2022, 'Inside the whale', *The Orwell Foundation*, https://www.orwellfoundation.com/the-orwell-foundation/orwell/essays-and-other-works/inside-the-whale/ (accessed 11 March 2022). Originally published in *Inside the Whale and Other Essays*, London: Victor Gollancz, 1940.

Paine, Thomas, 1882, *The Age of Reason: The Theological Works of Thomas Paine. Volume 2*, Chicago: Belford, Clarke.

Park, Jongsoo, 2004, 'The spiritual journey of Jonah: From the perspective of C. G. Jung's analytical psychology', in Kaltner, John, and Stulman, Louis (eds), *Inspired Speech: Prophecy in the Ancient Near East*, London: T & T Clark, pp. 276–85.

Parker, Eve, 2022, *Trust in Theological Education: Deconstructing 'Trustworthiness' for a Pedagogy of Liberation*, London: SCM Press.

Perry, T. A., 2006, *Jonah's Arguments with God: The Honeymoon Is Over!*, Peabody: Hendrickson.

Person, Raymond F., Jr, 2008, 'The role of nonhuman characters in Jonah', in Habel, Norman C., and Trudinger, Peter (eds), *Exploring Ecological Hermeneutics*, Atlanta: SBL, pp. 85–90.

Person, Raymond F., Jr, and Stroede, Phoebe, 2011, 'The story of Jonah as retold by the sea', in Habel, Norman C., and Trudinger, Peter (eds), *Water: A Matter of Life and Death*, Hindmarsh: ATF, pp. 73–80.

Pippin, Tina, 2003, 'On the blurring of boundaries', in Bailey, R. C. (ed.), *Yet with a Steady Beat: Contemporary U.S. Afrocentric Biblical Interpretation*, Atlanta: SBL, pp. 169–76.

Plumwood, Val, 1993, *Feminism and the Mastery of Nature*, London: Routledge.

Plutarch, 1973, 'The life of Alexander', in *The Age of Alexander: Nine Greek Lives*, trans. by Ian Scott-Kilvert, Harmondsworth: Penguin.

Pollard, Arthur, 1970, *Satire*, London: Methuen.

Powell, Mark Allan, 1990, *What Is Narrative Criticism?*, Minneapolis: Fortress.

Powell, Mark Allan, 2004, 'Narrative criticism', in Hayes, John H. (ed.), *Methods of Biblical Interpretation*, Nashville: Abingdon, pp. 169–72.

Radday, Yehuda T., 1990, 'On missing the humour in the Bible: An introduction', in Radday, Yehuda T., and Brenner, Athalya (eds), *On Humour and the Comic in the Hebrew Bible*, Sheffield: Almond, pp. 21–38.

Rashkow, Ilona N., 2000, *Taboo or not Taboo: Sexuality and Family in the Hebrew Bible*, Minneapolis: Fortress.

Rashkow, Ilona N., 2012, 'Psychology and the Hebrew Bible, read through the lenses of Freud and Lacan', in Ellens, J. Harold (ed.), *Psychological Hermeneutics for Biblical Themes and Texts*, London: T & T Clark, pp. 236–56.

Rees, Anthony, 'Getting up and going down: Towards a spatial poetics of Jonah', *The Bible and Critical Theory*, 12/1 (2016), pp. 40–8.

Rieger, Joerg, 2007, *Christ and Empire: From Paul to Postcolonial Times*, Minneapolis: Fortress.

Riffaterre, Michael, 1978, *Semiotics of Poetry*, Bloomington: Indiana University Press.

Riley, Stephen Patrick, 'When the empire does not strike back: Reading Jonah in light of empire', *Wesleyan Theological Journal*, 47/1 (2012), pp. 116–26.

Robinson, Bernard P., 'Jonah's qiqayon plant', *Zeitschrift für die alttestamentliche Wissenschaft*, 97 (1985), pp. 390–403.

Rollins, Wayne G., 1999, *Soul and Psyche: The Bible in Psychological Perspective*, Minneapolis: Fortress.

Rollins, Wayne G., 2004, 'Psychology and biblical studies', in Hayes, John H. (ed.), *Methods of Biblical Interpretation*, Nashville: Abingdon, pp. 399–405.

Ruether, Rosemary Radford, 1992, *Gaia and God: An Ecofeminist Theology of Earth Healing*, New York: HarperOne.

Ryu, Chesung Justin, 'Silence as resistance: A postcolonial reading of the silence of Jonah in Jonah 4.1–11', *Journal for the Study of the Old Testament*, 34/2 (2009), pp. 195–218.

Salberg, Jill, 'Jonah's crisis: Commentary on paper by Aviva Gottlieb Zornberg', *Psychoanalytic Dialogues*, 18 (2008), pp. 317–28.

Sanneh, Lamin, 2009, *Translating the Message: The Missionary Impact on Culture*, 2nd edn, Maryknoll: Orbis.

Sasson, Jack M., 1990, *Jonah: A New Translation with Introduction, Commentary, and Interpretation*, New Haven: Yale University Press.

Schifferdecker, Kathryn M., '"And also many animals": Biblical resources for preaching about creation', *Word and World*, 27/2 (2007), pp. 210–23.

Schweitzer, Albert, 1948, *The Psychiatric Study of Jesus: Exposition and Criticism*, trans. by Charles R. Joy, Boston: Beacon.

Seibert, Eric A., 2012, *The Violence of Scripture: Overcoming the Old Testament's Troubling Legacy*, Minneapolis: Fortress.

Seitz, Jonathan, 2013, 'Jonah as missionary', in Roncace, Mark, and Weaver, Joseph (eds), *Global Perspectives on the Bible*, Boston: Pearson, pp. 126–7.

Shao, Rosa Ching, 2019, *Jonah: A Pastoral and Contextual Commentary*, Carlisle: Langham Global Library.

Shemesh, Yael, '"And many beasts" (Jonah 4:11): The function and status of animals in the book of Jonah', *Journal of Hebrew Scriptures*, 10/6 (2010), pp. 1–26.

Sherwood, Yvonne, 'Cross-currents in the book of Jonah: Some Jewish and cultural midrashim on a traditional text', *Biblical Interpretation*, 6/1 (1998), pp. 49–79.

Sherwood, Yvonne, 2000, *A Biblical Text and Its Afterlives: The Survival of Jonah in Western Culture*, Cambridge: Cambridge University Press.

Shulman, Dennis G., 'Jonah: His story, our story; his struggle, our struggle: Commentary on paper by Aviva Gottlieb Zornberg', *Psychoanalytic Dialogues*, 18 (2008), pp. 329–64.

Simon, Uriel, 1999, *Jonah*, Philadelphia: Jewish Publication Society.

Ska, Jean Louis, 1990, *'Our Fathers Have Told Us': Introduction to the Analysis of Hebrew Narratives*, Rome: Editrice Pontificio Istituto Biblico.

Slicer, Deborah, 'Is there an ecofeminist–Deep Ecology debate?', *Environmental Ethics*, 17 (1995), pp. 151–69.

Song, Choan-Seng, 'From Israel to Asia: A theological leap', *Theology*, 79 (1976), pp. 90–6.

Staffell, Simon, 'The mappe and the Bible: Nation, empire and the collective memory of Jonah', *Biblical Interpretation*, 16/5 (2008), pp. 476–500.

Steinberg, Naomi, 2004, 'Social-scientific criticism', in Hayes, John H. (ed.), *Methods of Biblical Interpretation*, Nashville: Abingdon, pp. 275–9.

Sternberg, Meir, 1987, *The Poetics of Biblical Narrative: Ideological Literature and the Drama of Reading*, Bloomington: Indiana University Press.

Strawn, Brent A., 'On vomiting: Leviticus, Jonah, Ea(a)rth', *Catholic Biblical Quarterly*, 74 (2012), pp. 445–64.

Stuart, Douglas, 1987, *Hosea–Jonah*, Waco: Word.

Sugirtharajah, R. S., 1998a, *Asian Biblical Hermeneutics and Postcolonialism: Contesting the Interpretations*, Maryknoll: Orbis.

Sugirtharajah, R. S. (ed.), 1998b, *The Postcolonial Bible*, Sheffield: Sheffield Academic Press.

Sugirtharajah, R. S., 2002, *Postcolonial Criticism and Biblical Interpretation*, Oxford: Oxford University Press.

Sugirtharajah, R. S., 2005, *The Bible and Empire: Postcolonial Explorations*, Cambridge: Cambridge University Press.

Sugirtharajah, R. S. (ed.), 2006, *The Postcolonial Biblical Reader*, Oxford: Blackwell.

Sugirtharajah, R. S., 2012, *Exploring Postcolonial Biblical Criticism: History, Method, Practice*, Oxford: Wiley-Blackwell.

Sugirtharajah, R. S. (ed.), 2016, *Voices from the Margin: Interpreting the Bible in the Third World*, 25th anniversary edn, Maryknoll: Orbis.

Summerfield, Henry, Ryken, Leland, and Eldredge, Laurence, 1992, 'Jonah', in Jeffrey, David Lyle (ed.), *A Dictionary of Biblical Tradition in English Literature*, Grand Rapids: Eerdmans, pp. 409–11.

Terrien, Samuel, 2003, *The Psalms: Strophic Structure and Theological Commentary*, Grand Rapids: Eerdmans.

Thomas, Huw, 2021, *In the Way of the Story: Reading Biblical Narrative*, Eugene: Wipf & Stock.

Tiemeyer, Lena-Sofia, 'A new look at the biological sex/grammatical gender of Jonah's fish', *Vetus Testamentum*, 67 (2017), pp. 307–23.

Tiemeyer, Lena-Sofia, 2019, 'Jonah, the eternal fugitive: Exploring the intertextuality of Jonah's flight in the Bible and its later reception', in Høgenhaven, Jesper, Poulsen, Frederik, and Power, Cian (eds), *Images of Exile in the Prophetic Literature*, Tübingen: Mohr Siebeck, pp. 255–68.

Tiemeyer, Lena-Sofia, 2022, *Jonah through the Centuries*, Chichester: Wiley Blackwell.

Timmer, Daniel, 'The intertextual Israelite Jonah *face à l'empire*: The post-colonial significance of the book's cotexts and purported neo-Assyrian context', *Journal of Hebrew Scriptures*, 9/9 (2009), pp. 2–22.

Todorov, Tzvetan, 1981, *Introduction to Poetics*, trans. by Richard Howard, Minneapolis: University of Minnesota Press.

Trible, Phyllis, 1994, *Rhetorical Criticism: Context, Method, and the Book of Jonah*, Minneapolis: Fortress.

Trible, Phyllis, 1996, 'The book of Jonah: Introduction, commentary, and reflections', in Keck, Leander E. et al. (eds), *The New Interpreter's Bible. Volume 7: Introduction to the Apocalyptic Literature, Daniel, The Twelve Prophets*, Nashville: Abingdon, pp. 461–529.

Trible, Phyllis, 1999, 'A tempest in a text: Ecological soundings in the book of Jonah', in Cook, Stephen L., and Winter, S. C. (eds), *On the Way to Nineveh*, Atlanta: Scholars, pp. 187–200.

Trudinger, Paul, 'Jonah: A post-exilic verbal cartoon?', *The Downside Review*, 107 (April 1989), pp. 142–3.

Tutu, Desmond, 2000, 'Foreword', in Habel, Norman C. (ed.), *Readings from the Perspective of Earth*, Sheffield: Sheffield Academic Press, pp. 7–8.

Ukpong, Justin S., 2002, 'Reading the Bible in a global village: Issues and challenges in African reading', in Ukpong, Justin S. et al. (eds), *Reading the Bible in the Global Village: Cape Town*, Atlanta: SBL, 2002, pp. 9–40.

Vaka'uta, Nāsili, 2013, 'A Tongan island reading of Jonah as oriented toward the ocean', in Roncace, Mark, and Weaver, Joseph (eds), *Global Perspectives on the Bible*, Boston: Pearson, pp. 128–9.

Van Aarde, Andries G., 'Progress in psychological biblical criticism', *Pastoral Psychology*, 64 (2015), pp. 481–92.

Van Duzer, Chet, 2013, *Sea Monsters on Medieval and Renaissance Maps*, London: The British Library.

Van Heerden, Schalk Willem, 'Shades of green – or grey? Towards an ecological interpretation of Jonah 4:6–11', *Old Testament Essays*, 30/2 (2017), pp. 459–77.

Van Heerden, Willie, 'Humour and the interpretation of the book of Jonah', *Old Testament Essays*, 5/3 (1992), pp. 389–401.

Van Heerden, Willie, 'Psychological interpretations of the book of Jonah', *Old Testament Essays*, 16/3 (2003), pp. 717–29.

Van Heerden, Willie, 'Ecological interpretations of the Jonah narrative – have they succeeded in overcoming anthropocentrism?', *Journal for Semitics*, 23/1 (2014), pp. 114–34.

Van Seters, John, 1983, *In Search of History: Historiography in the Ancient World and the Origins of Biblical History*, New Haven: Yale University Press.

Van Urk, Eva, 'Public theology and the Anthropocene: Exploring human–animal relations', *International Journal of Public Theology*, 14 (2020), pp. 206–23.

Von Rad, Gerhard, 1991, *Holy War in Ancient Israel*, trans. by Marva J. Dawn, Grand Rapids: Eerdmans.

Wajnryb, Ruth, 2001, *The Silence: How Tragedy Shapes Talk*, Crows Nest: Allen & Unwin.

Walker, Alice, 2006, 'Coming Apart' (1979), in Phillips, Layli (ed.), *The Womanist Reader*, London: Routledge, pp. 3–11.

Walker, Alyssa, 'Jonah's genocidal and suicidal attitude – and God's rebuke', *Kairos: Evangelical Journal of Theology*, 9/1 (2015), pp. 7–29.

Walker, Steven C., 2013, *Illuminating Humor of the Bible*, Eugene: Cascade.

Wallace, Howard N., 2001, '*Jubilate Deo omnis terra*: God and Earth in Psalm 65', in Habel, Norman C. (ed.), *The Earth Story in the Psalms and the Prophets*, Sheffield: Sheffield Academic Press, pp. 51–64.

Warrior, Robert Allen, 2016, 'A Native American perspective: Canaanites, cowboys, and Indians', in Sugirtharajah, R. S. (ed.), *Voices from the Margin: Interpreting the Bible in the Third World*, 25th anniversary edn, Maryknoll: Orbis, pp. 283–90.

West, Gerald O., 'Juxtaposing "many cattle" in biblical narrative (Jonah 4:11), imperial narrative, neo-indigenous narrative', *Old Testament Essays*, 27/2 (2014), pp. 722–51.

Whedbee, J. William, 2002, *The Bible and the Comic Vision*, Minneapolis: Fortress.

White, Lynn, Jr, 'The historical roots of our ecologic crisis', *Science*, 155 (1967), pp. 1203–7.

Whitelam, Keith W., 1998, 'The social world of the Bible', in Barton, John (ed.), *The Cambridge Companion to Biblical Interpretation*, Cambridge: Cambridge University Press, pp. 35–49.

Wilson, Christopher P., 1979, *Jokes: Form, Content, Use and Function*, London: Academic Press.

Wilt, Timothy L., 1993, 'Jonah: A battle of shifting alliances', in Davies, Philip R., and Clines, David J. A. (eds), *Among the Prophets: Language, Image and Structure in the Prophetic Writings*, Sheffield: JSOT, pp. 164–82.

Wimbush, Vincent L., 'Historical/cultural criticism as liberation: A proposal for an African American biblical hermeneutic', *Semeia*, 47 (1989), pp. 43–55.

Wimbush, Vincent L. (ed.), 2000, *African Americans and the Bible: Sacred Texts and Social Textures*, New York: Continuum.

Wink, Walter, 2010, *The Bible in Human Transformation: Toward a New Paradigm for Biblical Study*, Minneapolis: Fortress.

Winnicott, D. W., 'The location of cultural experience', *International Journal of Psycho-Analysis*, 48 (1967), pp. 368–72.

Winnicott, D. W., 2018, *The Maturational Processes and the Facilitating Environment*, Abingdon: Routledge.

Wolff, Hans Walter, 1986, *Obadiah and Jonah: A Commentary*, trans. by Margaret Kohl, Minneapolis: Augsburg.

Zornberg, Avivah Gottlieb, 'Jonah: A fantasy of flight', *Psychoanalytic Dialogues*, 18 (2008a), pp. 271–99.

Zornberg, Avivah Gottlieb, 'Reading the biblical text, conscious and unconscious meaning, diagnosing Jonah: Reply to commentaries', *Psychoanalytic Dialogues*, 18 (2008b), pp. 365–70.

Zornberg, Avivah Gottlieb, 2009, *The Murmuring Deep: Reflections on the Biblical Unconscious*, New York: Schocken.

Notes

Chapter 1: Jonah's Readers: Perspectives on Interpretation

1 For those who are interested, some of the most helpful commentaries on Jonah are Sasson; Limburg; Simon; and Erickson.

2 Midrash (מִדְרָשׁ), the process of traditional Jewish (rabbinic) biblical interpretation (and a collection of texts), often focuses on what has been left unsaid, seeking to fill in the gaps in texts. Sherwood (2000, p. 114) describes midrash as a 'generative space', noting (p. 112) that 'any grammatical quirk, inconsistency, or lacuna' in the text becomes 'the excuse for another narrative'. According to Kugel (p. 80), midrash often employs a bit of a joking approach, seeking, for instance, to expose the 'dissonance between the religion of the rabbis and the Book from which it is supposed to be derived'.

Chapter 2: Jonah's World: Historical and Social-Science Perspectives

1 On these, see Barton (1996, chs 2 to 4); Gillingham (ch. 6); McKenzie and Haynes (chs 2 to 5); and Gooder (chs 1 to 5).

2 For introductions to social-scientific criticism, see, for instance, Elliott; Whitelam; Martin (1999); Steinberg; Jonker and Arendse; and Malina.

3 During the time of the Babylonian exile, the former kingdom of Judah became Yehud, a province of the Neo-Babylonian Empire.

4 Judith and Tobit are part of the Old Testament Apocrypha.

5 There are numerous studies on violence and the depiction of a violent/warrior God in the Old Testament. A classic is von Rad's *Holy War in Ancient Israel*. Niditch's *War in the Hebrew Bible: A Study in the Ethics of Violence* raises the question of whether there is a biblical war ideology that is critical of war itself, while Seibert's *The Violence of Scripture* has a strong focus on 'nonviolent reading strategies'. For an investigation of holy war terminology in Jonah 1, see Wilt.

6 Tiemeyer (2017) sees the anomaly as an obscure lengthened nominal form that may occur at the end of a Hebrew clause and does not indicate a change in gender, while Sherwood (2000, p. 116) surmises that it may be a scribal error.

7 For further illustrations and commentary, see Van Duzer; and Lawrence. To view the paintings by van Heemskerk and Lastman, go to https://commons.wikimedia.org/wiki/File:Jonah_Cast_on_Shore_by_The_Fish_1566_print_by_Maarten_van_Heemskerck,_S.I_55699,_Prints_Department,_Royal_Library_of_Belgium.jpg; and https://commons.wikimedia.org/wiki/File:Pieter_Lastman_-_Jonah_and_the_Whale_-_Google_Art_Project.jpg.

Chapter 3: Jonah's Art and Reception: The Poetics of a Biblical Narrative

1 Additional introductions to narrative criticism, besides the ones listed in the previous paragraph, include Gunn; Powell (1990, 2004); Jonker (2005, with a special focus on Jonah); Jack; and Thomas.
2 On these, see, for example, Chatman (pp. 147–51); Powell (1990, pp. 19–21); and Jonker (2005, pp. 98–100).
3 The diagram, albeit in a simpler form that excluded the inner two boxes depicting the text's message, goes back to Chatman (p. 151).
4 On characterization, see, for example, Powell (1990, pp. 51–67); and Jonker (2005, p. 97).
5 This exemplifies Craig's strongly text-centred focus. As reader-response critics insist, readers come to the text with preconceived ideas about both God and Jonah – and a host of other things (see the illuminating discussion in Sherwood (2000, ch. 1)) – and read the text in the light of those ideas *and* the textual data.
6 See Craig (p. 180) for a list of the quotes and allusions.
7 The question of the precise identity of this plant continues to be disputed, with most interpreters settling on either the castor oil plant or the bottle gourd (Strawn, p. 455). Jenks (pp. 235–6), commenting on Jerome's rendering of the word as 'cucumber', notes that this novel translation led to riots among the Christian crowds at Carthage. For an in-depth study, see Robinson. LaCocque and Lacocque (pp. 156–8) stress the similarity between Hebrew קִיקָיוֹן (*qiqayon*) and Greek κυκεών (*kukeon*), a beverage made from a barley concoction and used in the Eleusinian Mysteries in connection with initiation ceremonies. They understand the function of the *qiqayon* in ironic terms: 'the tree that was supposed to be, for the prophet, a breakthrough toward the sacred, dies in one night'.
8 One common suggestion is to identify Tarshish with Cádiz in southwest Spain (already proclaimed to be the 'opinion of learned men' by Father Mapple in his famous sermon in *Moby Dick*, published in 1851), the ancient Phoenician trading port of Tartessos (see, for example, Elat, pp. 66–7). However, as Handy notes (pp. 27, 144), there are numerous proposals, stretching 'from the subcontinent of India to the Atlantic coasts of either Europe or Africa and pretty much everywhere in between', and the bibliography of studies concerned with the issue is vast. For Handy's own discussion, see pp. 27–31.
9 The Mishnah, completed c. AD 200, collects what was known as the 'oral law'. Neusner and Avery-Peck describe it as a 'philosophical law code' (p. 93). See their article for further information.
10 One of the characteristics of the new heaven and earth is precisely that 'the sea was no more' (Rev. 21.1).
11 Van Heerden (1992, p. 390), based on Wilson's work *Jokes: Form, Content, Use and Function*, distinguishes between relief, conflict and incongruity theories of humour and applies the last of these to his study of the book of Jonah. He distinguishes between irony and humour (p. 391), both of which he finds in Jonah, arguing that 'the humorist focuses on humanness in a more sympathetic way' and that 'humour, in contrast to irony, is characterised by warmth, kindness, and reconciliation'.

12 This is Hyers's reading (p. 106), who believes the 120,000 people 'who do not know their right hand from their left' are infants, which to him suggests a total population of one million. Ateek (p. 70) similarly speaks of '120,000 innocent children'.

13 They have been gleaned from the works of Good; Holbert; Mather; Hauser; Hyers; Band; Carroll (1990); Miles; van Heerden (1992); Crenshaw; Marcus; Jenson; Murray; Whedbee; Biddle; Walker (2013); and Lindsay (2016). As the descriptions are composites from all these sources, no quotation marks have been applied.

14 It is found in 1.2, 4 (twice), 10, 12, 16, 17; 3.2, 3, 5, 7; 4.1, 6, 11.

15 Intertextual studies of Jonah include Magonet (1983, ch. 4); Kim; Muldoon; Berger; Havea (2016); and Tiemeyer (2019), who trace intertextual echoes well beyond the ones noted here.

16 On monsterization and monster theory, see Cohen.

17 Havea (2020, loc. 395) explains: 'I use the lowercase with my first person "i" out of respect to the other persons – "you," "she," "he," "it," "them" and "others" – without whom my "i" loses its subjectivity. I do not see the point in capitalizing my first person, for i exist because of and in relation to other persons and subjects.'

18 Introductions to reader-response criticism have been provided, for instance, by McKnight (1988, 1999, 2004); Fowler (1991, 2008a, 2008b); Aichele et al.; Barton (1996, ch. 13); and Lawrie (2005c).

Chapter 4: Jonah's Challenge: Contextual, Liberationist and Postcolonial Interpretation

1 For a book series offering a 'platform for biblical critics and authors particularly from Africa, Asia, Latin America, the Caribbean, the Pacific, and Eastern Europe', see the International Voices in Biblical Studies section on the Society of Biblical Literature website at: https://www.sbl-site.org/publications/Books_IVBS.aspx. There is as yet no volume on Jonah, but for some valuable general reflections see, especially, *Global Hermeneutics?* by Holter and Jonker.

2 See, for instance, Copher's works on the black presence in the Old Testament.

3 *The Empire Writes Back* was also the title of the 1989 book by Ashcroft, Griffiths and Tiffin, which was one of the first major theoretical accounts of postcolonial texts, theory and culture.

4 To view this painting by Thomas Jones Barker, go to https://commons.wikimedia.org/wiki/File:The_Secret_of_England%27s_Greatness%27_(Queen_Victoria_presenting_a_Bible_in_the_Audience_Chamber_at_Windsor)_by_Thomas_Jones_Barker.jpg.

5 On Hendricks's notion of 'guerrilla exegesis', see below under 'Postcolonial biblical interpretation'.

6 For further discussion of Afrocentric and African American biblical interpretation, see the works by Cannon and Schüssler Fiorenza; Felder (1991); Wimbush (2000); Bailey; and Mburu.

7 For some brief reflections, also from within a Taiwanese context, on Jonah as 'the archetype of bad mission', see Seitz.

8 Relevant volumes include Havea, Neville and Wainwright; Havea, Aymer and Davidson; and Havea (2018c; 2021a; and 2021b).

9 The term 'Dalit', meaning 'broken' or 'scattered', refers to the oppressed peoples of India, especially the 'untouchables'. On Dalit theology, see Nirmal; and Carr (1994).

10 Coined by Isasi-Díaz, the term *mujerista* refers to a Hispanic form of liberationist theology.

11 Womanism, in contrast to feminism, pays attention to the history and everyday experiences of women of colour, especially black women. The term was coined by Alice Walker in her 1979 short story 'Coming Apart' (see Walker, 2006).

12 On theological education and a pedagogy of liberation, see Parker (2022).

13 On the festival of booths or Sukkot, the plural of *sukkah*, see Leviticus 23.43.

14 As we saw earlier, it is Jonah's connection with Jeroboam II (2 Kings 14.23–27) that suggests an eighth-century setting.

15 One of the leading experts on postcolonial interpretation is R. S. Sugirtharajah. See his works listed in the Bibliography, but see also Gallagher; Donaldson (1996b); Boer and West; Dube (2000); and Moore and Segovia.

16 To view John Speed's map, go to: https://commons.wikimedia.org/wiki/File:The_National_Library_of_Israel_-_Canaan_as_it_was_possessed_both_in_Abraham_and_Israels_dayes_with_with_the_stations_and_bordering_nations.jpg.

17 Similar comparisons of the Ninevites or Assyrians with the Nazis have been suggested by Crouch (p. 113), according to whom 'the closest thing … to the atrocities of Nineveh is Hitler's Germany'; and Frolov (p. 102), who notes that if instead of the Ninevites 'we had, for example, former Nazis or Khmer Rouge, the prophet would hardly look funny or bloodthirsty'.

Chapter 5: Jonah's Depth: Psychological Biblical Criticism

1 For a much fuller discussion of the history of psychological readings of the Bible, see the works of Rollins (1999, chs 1 to 3; 2004) and Kille (2001).

2 This aspect of Carl Jung's work, developed in *Psychological Types*, was adopted by Isabel Briggs Myers and Katherine Cook Briggs to create the Myers-Briggs Type Indicator, a tool for identifying 16 personality types.

3 In psychoanalytic theory, the *id*, *ego* and *superego* describe distinct agents in a person's mental life, with the *id* representing uncoordinated instinctual desires, the *superego* playing a critical, moralizing role, and the *ego* mediating between the two.

4 For a summary and review of the readings by Corey and Edinger, see van Heerden (2003, pp. 719–24).

5 Gaines (p. 73), in connection with the notion of birth, points to Jonah's evocation of 'the belly of Sheol' (2.2), featuring Hebrew בֶּטֶן (*beten*), which could also be translated as 'the *womb* of Sheol'.

6 One would expect the reference to be to the Northern Kingdom and to read 'Samaria' or 'Israel'.

7 The Talmud is the central text of Rabbinic Judaism. There are two versions, the Babylonian Talmud (*Bavli*) and the earlier Jerusalem Talmud (*Yerushalmi*).

They contain the teachings of the rabbis, dating from the period before Christ to the fifth century AD.

8 Based on the work of Melanie Klein, object relations theory disagrees with Freud's belief that humans are motivated by their sexual and aggressive drives, maintaining instead that the primary motivation is the need for contact with others and to form relationships.

9 This is a work of Jewish exegesis and retellings of biblical stories written in the eighth or ninth century.

10 This is another work of Jewish exegesis, in this case focused on the book of Exodus. It is also known as Mekilta de Rabbi Ishmael.

11 Sukkah is one of the tractates of the Talmud. 'J' indicates that the reference is to the Jerusalem Talmud rather than the Babylonian version. Midrash Tehillim is a midrash on the Psalms. On Pirke de Rabbi Eliezer, see note 9 above. Yalkut Shimoni is an 'aggadic' compilation on the books of the Hebrew Bible. 'Aggadah' refers to 'tales' or 'lore' – that is, to narratives based on, or responding to, biblical texts (see Neusner and Avery-Peck, p. 4).

12 Zornberg is here quoting Lear (p. 54).

13 Green (pp. 125–6) notes that midrash shows 'a text ever-relevant', allowing 'fresh experience to find a footing in tradition' and seeking to 'show how texts can be seen to be in endless dialogue'. She goes on to explore 'Jewish midrashic readings of Jonah' (pp. 126–30).

14 See Lasine (2016, p. 240; 2020, pp. 121–2) for impressively comprehensive lists of the charges that have been laid at Jonah's door by a host of readers.

15 See, for instance, Becker, Dochhorn and Holt; Boase and Frechette; and Carr (2014).

16 It is common for biblical translations to render אֶל ('el) differently, depending on the object with which it occurs. The NRSV, for instance, has God hurling the great wind 'upon' the sea, while the sailors throw the cargo 'into' it. I am here following Holbert (pp. 65, 68–9), who consistently translates it as 'at'. Note also that the NRSV translates טוּל (tul) 'hurl' in the case of God hurling the great wind (1.4) and 'throw' when the sailors deposit Jonah in the sea (1.5, 12, 15).

Chapter 6: Jonah's 'Otherkind': Ecological Readings

1 For a recent discussion of the Old Testament and environmental ethics that includes consideration of non-humans, see Joerstad (2019).

2 Introductions to and programmatic essays on ecological readings of the Bible include Barr; Conradie (2004, 2005, 2006, 2009, 2010); Deane-Drummond (2017, ch. 2); the Earth Bible Team (2000, 2002); Eaton (2000); Habel (2000, 2003, 2008); Horrell (2008, 2010a, 2010b); Horrell, Hunt and Southgate; and Kavusa.

Biblical commentaries devoted to ecological interpretation can be found in the Earth Bible Commentary series, published by Sheffield Phoenix Press, with volumes on Genesis 1—11, Numbers, Deuteronomy, Job, Matthew, Luke and Romans; and An Earth Bible Commentary series, published by Bloomsbury, with volumes on Ruth, Psalms, Ecclesiastes, Jonah, John, Acts, Ephesians, Colossians and Hebrews. Both series are edited by Habel.

In addition to these, the Earth Bible series published by Sheffield Academic Press, and again edited by Habel, features five volumes of essays. The first introduces the project and features a range of readings of biblical texts from the perspective of Earth, while the other four cover the Earth story in Genesis, wisdom traditions, the Psalms and the prophets, and the New Testament.

3 For an 'eco-wisdom' reading of Job, see Habel (2014).

4 It is interesting to note in this context that, as Havea (2014a, p. 10) has pointed out, ecological hermeneutics 'has been shaped to a significant extent by contributors from Oceania'.

5 For ecofeminist criticisms of the Deep Ecology movement, see Plumwood; Slicer; and Eaton (1997).

6 Conradie (2006, 2009, 2010) has argued for the importance of 'doctrinal keys' or 'doctrinal constructs' for the development of ecological interpretation grounded in the Christian tradition.

7 As Ruether (p. 299) points out, animism is not about the deification of nature but the 'recognition of personlike life in nature'.

8 *Bosadi*, as Masenya explains, means 'womanhood' or a woman's private parts.

9 The phrases in inverted commas ('thinking', 'going', 'standing' and 'son') are literal translations from the Hebrew. For further explanation, see the relevant sections in Sasson (1990).

10 On this wordplay, see also Halpern and Friedman (1980, pp. 85–6); and Band (p. 189).

11 It could also be translated 'Jonah has certainly vomited', taking Jonah to be the subject of the phrase. However, the reading adopted here assumes that the plant's name is meant to evoke the fish's earlier vomiting of Jonah.

12 The Hebrew, adopting an unusual phrase that is unique to Jonah, literally says 'which [referring to the *qiqayon*] became a son of the night and perished a son of the night' (שֶׁבִּן־לַיְלָה הָיָה וּבִן־לַיְלָה אָבָד, *shebbin-laylah hayah uvin-laylah 'avad*). As Sasson comments (p. 313), 'The gap between life and death is measured by an interval separating one evening from another'. The NRSV reads 'it came into being in a night and perished in a night'.

13 A markedly different reading has been suggested by Bolin (pp. 9–11), according to whom Yahweh's reference to the animals reflects the deity's anticipated feasting on the Ninevites' forthcoming animal sacrifices. However, while animal sacrifices are implied in the use of זבח (*zavakh*; 'to sacrifice') in 1.16 and 2.9, no such sacrifices are mentioned in either 3.7–8 or 4.11.

14 This is an aggadah or homiletic commentary on Deuteronomy.

15 See Shemesh, pp. 3–4 and van Urk, pp. 210–13, for some brief discussion.

16 Ben Zvi explores the textual signals that encourage an interrogative reading, while also surveying the arguments for a declarative one. Based on Handy's belief (p. 15) that the book's authors were serving both the Jerusalem temple cult and the Persian administration, van Heerden (2017, p. 468) relates the declarative or assertive reading, which underlines Yahweh's power, to the Persian imperial context, while connecting the interrogative reading with its emphasis on the divine mercy with the Jerusalem temple.

17 The spelling 'ea(a)rth' is a conflation of the standard term 'earth' and McKibben's spelling 'eaarth' in his book of that title. Having been forever transformed by anthropogenic clima(c)tic changes, the old planet earth, McKibben suggests, no longer exists. The newly coined name 'eaarth' is designed to refer to the new, fundamentally changed reality that has emerged in its stead.

Index of Biblical References

Old Testament

New Testament

Index of Other Ancient Texts

Jewish Works

Ancient Greek Works

Index of Names and Subjects

126, 130, 157–61, 165, 167, 169–70
gender of 18, 111, 121, 191n6, 196n11
as monster 18–19, 115, 123
vomiting Jonah up on land 31, 35, 41, 47, 49–51, 65, 94, 161, 170
Fish, Stanley 56, 58
Fishman, George 125–6, 128–9
Floyd, George 74
Fokkelman, Jan P. 21
Forster, E. M. 28
Forti, Tova 159, 163, 165
Fowler, Robert M. 27, 193n18
Francis of Assisi 42
Frankl, Viktor Emil 119
Frechette, Christopher G. 195n15
Freire, Paulo 80
Freud, Sigmund 102, 104, 106, 108, 111–12, 119, 135, 195n8
Friedman, Richard Elliott 196n10
Frolov, Serge 46, 194n17
Fromm, Erich 110, 120
Frye, Northrop 47
Funk, Robert W. 21

Gaines, Janet Howe 38, 45, 117–19, 122–4, 158, 194n5
Gallagher, Susan VanZanten 194n15
Garbini, Giovanni 19
Genette, Gérard 44
Gibson, William E. 158
Gillingham, Susan E. 191n1
Gilmore, David D. 18
Gilmour, Michael J. 147–8
Girard, René 80, 82
God (Yahweh) 4, 12–15, 17, 19–20, 23–4, 26, 29–30, 32–3, 35–6, 43, 47, 49, 66, 69–70, 73, 79–80, 83, 93, 97,

111, 114–16, 124, 126, 131, 141–2, 150, 155, 158–60, 163, 196n13, 196n16
feared, obeyed by all creatures (apart from Jonah) 13, 30, 40–2, 51, 88–9, 159, 161
image, portrayal of 15, 17, 26, 47–8, 67, 76, 78–9, 84, 97, 112, 117–18, 124, 130, 160, 168, 171, 192n5
mercy, compassion, love of 1, 12, 26, 30–3, 42, 53, 57, 65, 69–70, 79, 81, 88, 97–101, 122, 129, 136, 157, 163–7, 170, 196n16
(un-)ethical behaviour and violence of 20, 26, 40, 46, 76, 88–9, 91–5, 124, 152, 168–9, 191n5
'Go down' (ירד, yarad) 34–5, 51, 126
Gods, worship of 31, 65–6
Goitein, Shelomo D. 45
Good, Edwin M. 44–5, 47, 193n13
Goodall, Jane Morris 147
Gooder, Paula 10, 139, 191n1
Gordon, Cyrus H. 34
Gottwald, Norman K. 10, 75
'Great' (גָּדֹול, gadol) 32, 35–6, 42–3, 50–1, 88, 91, 95, 113, 123, 128, 130–1, 135, 167–8, 170
Green, Barbara 4, 74, 195n13
Griffiths, Gareth 193n3
Grimm, Brothers 123
Guerrilla exegesis 64, 85–7, 193n5
Guillaume, Philippe 164
Gunn, David M. 21–2, 120, 192n1
Gutiérrez, Gustavo 77, 81

Wordsworth, William 7
'Worm', the (תּוֹלֵעָה) 1, 19, 28–9,
   33, 43–4, 49, 66, 116, 124,
   131, 157–9, 161, 163, 165, 167

Yehud 12, 17, 20, 191n3

Zornberg, Avivah Gottlieb 110,
   125–33, 195n12